100

Recipes from America's Best Smokehouses, Pits, Shacks, Rib Joints, Roadhouses, and Restaurants

ARDIE A. DAVIS, PhB AND **CHEF PAUL KIRK, CWC, PhB, BSAS**

AMERICA'S BEST

BBQ

IN SEARCH OF THE BEST BBQ!

SLAB SPECIAL $10.00

BOB'S RIB SHACK AHEAD

Andrews McMeel
Publishing, LLC

Kansas City

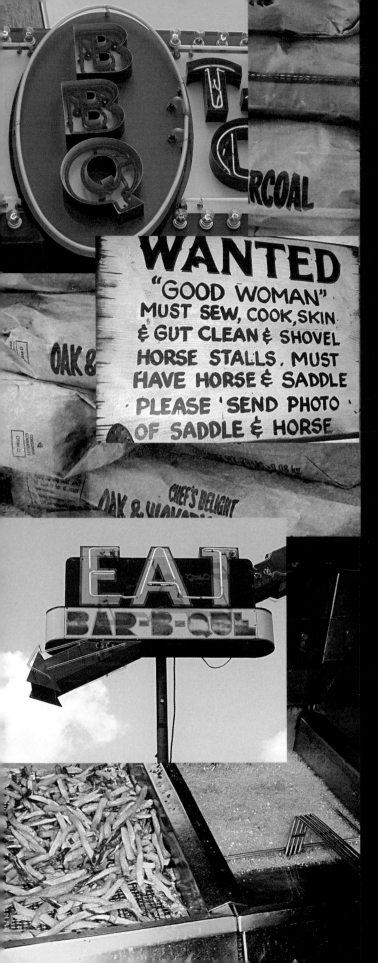

10 11 12 13 WKT 10 9 8 7 6 5 4

Library of Congress Cataloging-in-Publication Data

Davis, Ardie A.
  America's best BBQ : 100 recipes from America's best
smokehouses, pits, shacks, rib joints, roadhouses, and
restaurants / Ardie A. Davis & Paul Kirk. — 1st ed.
     p. cm.
  ISBN-13: 978-0-7407-7811-7
  ISBN-10: 0-7407-7811-0
  1. Barbecue cookery—United States. I. Kirk, Paul, 1941– II.
Title.
  TX840.B3D343 2009
  641.7'6—dc22

                         2008047428

www.andrewsmcmeel.com

America's Best BBQ

For Gretchen.
Ardie

For Jessica.
Paul

Contents

ACKNOWLEDGMENTS

We've done research for this book for a collective total of more than a hundred years, although when we each got hooked by barbecue, we didn't have this book in mind. Thanks to our agent, Dennis Hayes, we got an offer from Kirsty Melville at Andrews McMeel that we couldn't turn down. Two years later we had a book!

We owe a debt of gratitude to our wives, children, and extended family for tolerating the time we spent researching and writing to complete this project. Extra doses of tolerance and understanding were required from our wives. Thus you'll see their names on the dedication page.

In all human endeavors we stand on the shoulders of those who have gone before us. This is especially true in the culinary realm. Therefore we offer a tip of the hat and a sincere thanks to the millions of cooks, known and unknown, who have advanced today's culinary arts, especially barbecue, from humankind's primal beginnings.

Thanks to barbecue friends Steve Holbrook, Vince Staten, John Raven, Johnny White, Tony Stone, Don McLemore, Chris Lilly, David Klose, Bill and Barbara Milroy, Guy Simpson, Carolyn Wells, Judith Fertig, Karen Adler, Rich Davis, John Willingham, Rick Browne, Bruce Bjorkman, Lolis Eric Elie, Roland Carrier, Paula Peck, Bob Lyon, Chef Louis Szathmary, and many others. Gary Wells, Al Lawson, Cousin Homer, Jim Quessenberry, and Giancarlo Gianelli and other late pitmaster friends, we will always miss you. May you rest in peace.

Special thanks to Dennis Hayes, our friend, our barbecue buddy, and now our agent. Dennis had the idea for this book more than a decade ago. This book is due in large part to his vision and persistence and his passion for good eats, barbecue in particular.

Finally, it has been fun and a pleasure to work with the Book Division team at Andrews McMeel. Kirsty Melville, head of the Book Division, Lane Butler, our editor, our hats are off to you, Tim Lynch, Diane Marsh, Blake Stevens, John Carroll, and the marketing team!

INTRODUCTION

A mix of cars and trucks is parked here. Cadillacs, rusty pickups, fancy SUVs, vans, flashy new pickups, sports cars, limos, sedans—they are all here for one reason: the barbecue. Out back there's hickory, oak, pecan, apple, or mesquite, scrambled like it's ready for business. Forget neatness. This is a working woodpile.

Customers are lined up outside the door at 11:15 in the morning. Inside, the people are happy. The joint is already crowded. Be patient. You'll get a seat. Smell the barbecue while diners dig in with gusto. Soon you'll be chowing down on America's best barbecue—slathered meats, crunchy fries, corn bread, coleslaw, beans, and other delectable eats. It's worth the wait.

This book honors American barbecue and the people who make it. Here you'll find more than 100 recipes for out-of-this-world appetizers, tender and smoky meats cooked low and slow, sweet and spicy sauces and rubs, homemade sides, and even a few decadent downhome desserts—if you've saved room. And because food tastes better when you know the people and stories behind the recipes, we'll introduce you to some famous and not-so-famous pitmasters and barbecue personalities, living and dead. Some come from long lines of proud pitmasters, some have been at the craft most of their lives, and others are up-and-coming barbecuers. All view barbecue as an art and a craft. It's not a job, it's a profession, and they take great care to ensure that each day's barbecue is even better than the last.

The next best thing to being at one of the best barbecue joints in America is to get it direct—if they will ship it to you. Many of the places in this book sell their sauces, rubs, and other products by phone and online. We list the address, phone number, and Web site when available so that you can buy direct from the source and try it for yourself.

Another great way to enjoy America's best barbecue is to cook it yourself. The usual drill when writers visit a barbecue joint is to take some photos, sample some dishes, then publish a knockoff recipe from the menu. Whenever possible, our recipes and techniques come straight from the source. A frequent reply when we asked for a recipe was, "If I tell you, I'll have to shoot you" or "Sorry. Our recipes are trade secrets. We don't give them out." We expected to hear that, and often enough we did—especially when we were strangers to the owner. Then "No" turned to "Okay," or "Sure, I'll give you our recipe," after we got better acquainted. "Yes" was instant from most pitmasters who know us. We're honored to know quite a few, and many are friends. Many of the recipes that were given to us have never been published before. When original top-secret recipes were denied us, and we thought you would like something similar, we came up with our own version, thanks to Paul's talents as a championship pitmaster and a certified working chef.

We bring a lot of baggage to this book. We've been involved in the business, sport, and art of barbecue for more than fifty years each. We have many friends in barbecue. Paul also does a lot of consulting and is involved in sev-

eral restaurants. It's a daunting task to select a hundred places out of more than eight thousand. It's a little subjective, maybe not altogether fair. Occasionally we're influenced by the mystique or personal good memories of a place or both. Our choices reflect our prior knowledge of barbecue joints across the nation and recommendations from trusted friends, family, colleagues, and fans who heard about the book and told us about places we should try. We also checked books, articles, and online sources for tips.

Many barbecue books rate joints with numbers; others rate with stars, rib bones, or other symbols. The bottom line is that all ratings are subjective, including ours, and that could serve up a little controversy. Our top 100 are not ranked from 1, best, to 100, less good than the other 99. Each joint in this book is, in our view, one of the best in America. They are all on the same playing field, with varying strengths and weaknesses. That aside, we have each named our Top Ten joints at the back of the book, the ones we feel are the best in America. If your favorite barbecue joint isn't in here, maybe we haven't tried it, or maybe we tried it and didn't like it. You will agree with us sometimes, and sometimes you won't. *We* don't even always agree with each other about a particular place. We get over it, and so will you!

The menu is similar across America's barbecue joints, with regional variations. The standard meats are pork ribs, beef brisket, pork shoulder, sausage, chicken, and turkey. A few places serve duck, and we wish more would. Some southern joints offer pork only. In parts of Kentucky the featured meat is lamb or mutton. You can get *cabrito* (goat) at many Texas barbecue joints. We've included a good mix of main dishes, and while most of the recipes come from Kansas City and the so-called barbecue belt from North Carolina to Texas, we've loosened the belt a notch or two to include a few recipes from places like Vermont, New Mexico, Washington, New York, and California. People everywhere love and appreciate good barbecue.

At most barbecue joints, you can expect starters, sandwiches, dinners, sides, and dessert. Some serve breakfast, but, to our regret, we haven't found one that serves barbecue for breakfast. Meat is the heart of barbecue, and many joints these days treat starters, sides, and desserts as afterthoughts, serving labor-saving dishes from off-premise suppliers. Real made-from-scratch American barbecue starters, sides, and desserts are still out there, however. We just don't find as many as we used to. But the ones you'll find in the chapters in this book are the real deal and therefore examples of the best you'll find out there.

More than just your standard ribs, beans, and coleslaw (though plenty of those are included, too), *America's Best BBQ* also includes recipes for burgoo, gumbo, Rocky Mountain oysters, barbecue brisket nachos, smoked catfish, barbecued baloney, bison ribs, barbecue spaghetti, pig salad, fried peach pie, barbecue sundae, and many more recipes that will drive barbecue fans hog wild.

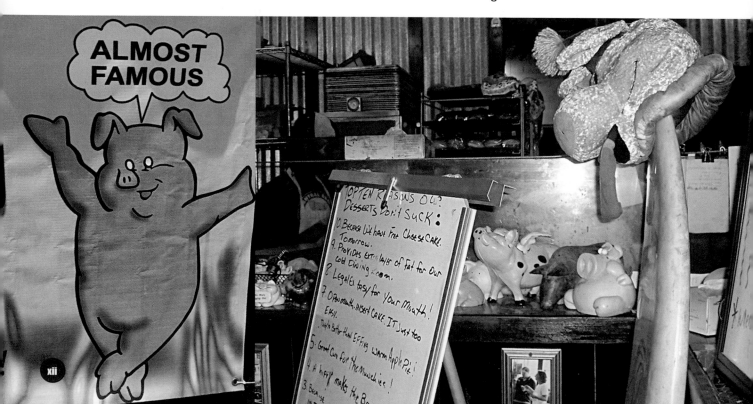

Picking the Best

We're picky about some things and lenient on others. We used two main standards in selecting the best barbecue joints. First, barbecue joints should specialize in barbecue, not just a barbecue item or two as part of a larger menu of nonbarbecue foods. (Admittedly, though, we occasionally fudge on this if we really like the joint!) Second, we're OK with gas or electric assist, but the cooking fuel should be wood or charcoal. Our only exception is eastern North Carolina whole-hog cooking. Increasing numbers of barbecue joints there have switched from wood to gas. Since little if any smoke penetrates a whole hog during cooking with wood or charcoal, we're OK with that. It's the quality of the hog, the cooking procedure, the sauce, and the presentation that make one whole hog different from another.

We judge **starters** on appeal and taste. Many barbecue joints don't offer starters, finding that their customers fill up just fine on meat and sides. Those that do serve starters know that they have to be pretty tempting to make folks risk filling up before they even reach the main event. From Brunswick stew to fried cheese grits, and more, the starters in this book meet that standard.

We judge **main dishes** on appearance, tenderness, and taste. Whether served on paper, plastic, Styrofoam, or fine china, the meat itself has to have eye appeal, with good color and texture. Tenderness is key. You should be able to cut good barbecue meat with a plastic knife and fork. We love House Park Barbecue's slogan, "Need no teef to eat my beef," and Stevenson's Bar-B-Que proclaims their meat is, "Tender as a mother's love." That's just how it should be. The best barbecue joints serve moist, flavorful meat that isn't overpowered by seasonings. Seasonings should only complement the meat flavor. All of the restaurants in every chapter of this book excel at the meat and bones of barbecue—literally.

We judge **sides** on appearance and taste. They should look good and complement the meat without overshadowing it. As with starters, a good side makes you want to save a little room, and here you'll find some standout recipes for such classic favorites as beans, slaw, and potato salad, as well as some unique sides we've discovered in our barbecue travels, such as the Vanized Potato and some jalapeño hushpuppies.

We judge **desserts** on appearance and taste. Things like just how decadent and fattening they are never come into play. We don't know the connection between bananas and barbecue, but a good many joints serve banana desserts, and we've included a few here—banana pudding, banana cream pie, bananas Foster. You'll also find the fried pies so ubiquitous in the South, cobbler and crisp, homemade ice cream, and more. A good dessert makes us say, "I shouldn't have eaten that, but I'm sure glad I did," and you won't regret overdoing it with any one of the desserts in this book.

Value is part of the overall equation for any restaurant—good quality, good portions, and a good price. Everything on the menu needn't be great. Some places excel in cooking one meat and fall short on others, but overall, the restaurants in this book are equals. Portions aren't usually a problem at barbecue joints, but the best places make you want to fill up on a little bit of everything—and then go back for more. Price is also a small factor, but since barbecue places usually aren't fancy, you usually get a good deal for your meal. Most places even offer daily specials.

Service is important, too. Contrary to what people who have never waited tables may think, it is not an easy job that anyone could do. We've both waited tables, so we know. Building rapport with a wide variety of customers and orchestrating the complete dining experience requires smart work and hard work. A good server can even tell us about the pit, the smoke, and the cooking procedures. Tipping isn't necessary at many barbecue joints because they serve on an order/pickup basis, but when you have competent servers, it's nice to reward them with a generous gratuity. They earn it.

Ambience is intangible, and most joints with ambience aren't fancy. They should be welcoming and comfortable. The place should feel special and make you glad you're there and want to come back. As our barbecue buddy Eldert Walker always says at his restaurant, "Come for the food. Leave with the experience." We've tried to capture as much ambience as possible in the pages of this book, with stories about the restaurants and owners, sidebars on barbecue culture and trivia, and hundreds of full-color photos that we've collected through decades of travel to restaurants and contests.

A barbecue joint's longevity or fame is of less importance to us. We've been to famous old places that are past their heyday and living on a reputation no longer deserved. Of the few chains that appear here, there is no guarantee that the quality we found at the restaurant listed will be exactly the same at other locations in the chain. New or old, chain or not, what matters most is the quality of the food, the service, and the ambience.

Most of the recipes in this book are scaled down for home-size entertaining, though several will serve a crowd. After all, barbecue is best when shared. And when you're putting that much time and care into your cooking, it should—and will—be appreciated by as many people as possible. There's nothing like a backyard cookout, some cold drinks, and some hot, smoky barbecue to bring families, friends, and neighbors together around the table.

If you're new to barbecue, there's a section called Barbecue Basics at the back of the book. It will give you the lowdown on barbecue and tell you what you need to know to select, maintain, and use gas and charcoal grills. A few of the recipes call for precooked meat, so we've included some basic meat cooking instructions, too. There are also a lot of tips and tricks we've picked up over the years, so seasoned barbecuers may want to take a look. There's even some information on meat cuts and meat doneness to ensure safe and proper cooking.

When you use the recipes here, remember that barbecue is about making it your own. One cook and another, following the same recipe, will not come up with two dishes that taste exactly the same. The professionals who contributed the recipes to this book use professional-grade equipment, and the results might not be exactly the same on a home grill, but you'll still end up with some fantastic barbecue, and the tips, techniques, and tricks from these renowned pitmasters can crank up your barbecue to new heights of greatness.

We've been fortunate to live lives steeped in barbecue—its history, lore, culture, traditions, and methods. Some of our recipes may trigger good memories of places you've been. Some may introduce you to places you'll want to visit. If you can't get to the places yourself, this can be your armchair tour of the best swine dining establishments in America, and we hope you have as much fun reading it as we've had putting it all together. So pull up a chair, grab a Wet-Nap, and dive in.

Starters

Starters, or appetizers, should jump-start your appetite. Some will fill you up before you get to the main course and dessert. We like both kinds—starters that jump-start and starters that fill.

As a rule, many places don't put starters on the menu. Many equate sides with starters, and some offer smaller portions of certain sides as a starter, such as a cup of gumbo or Brunswick stew. We've found a few unusual starters, such as Atomic Buffalo Poppers, RMOs (Rocky Mountain Oysters), fried pickles, and deep-fried bacon. The best starters have eye appeal—they look delicious and shout, "You're going to love this!"—complement the rest and set you up for the foods that follow, and have come-back appeal that makes you want more.

We have a feast of starters for you in this chapter. As Woody Guthrie used to say, "Take it easy, but take it!"

Onion Strings

RUB (Righteous Urban Barbecue)

208 W. 23rd St.
New York, NY 10011
212-524-4300
http://www.rubbbq.net

Since Paul developed the menu and recipes and trained the kitchen staff, and his name and caricature is all over the joint, the decision to put Righteous Urban Barbecue (RUB) here was Ardie's, and he picked this place on its own merits. RUB is an oasis of real barbecue in a city with a mix of real and fake barbecue. Ardie has eaten at several joints in New York City that serve oven-roasted meats slathered with barbecue sauce and call it barbecue. He imagines a cook in these kitchens singing, "Wood is just a four-letter word," to the tune of the Bob Dylan classic. Give us real hardwood smoke in our barbecue—not liquid smoke. RUB isn't the only real barbecue in town, and some other New York City favorites are in here as well, but RUB is Ardie's favorite thus far.

RUB barbecue is cooked to perfection. It looks real and tastes real because it is real. Ardie ordered onion strings as an appetizer, and they were so delicious he had to push the plate away to avoid filling up before his pulled pork sandwich arrived. Thin, lightly battered, deep-fried, and sprinkled with Paul's award-winning rub, a mouthful of these crispy straws will put a smile on your face and will definitely jump-start your appetite.

ONION STRINGS

Serves 6 to 8

1 large yellow onion

1 quart whole milk

8 cups (2 pounds) all-purpose flour

1 tablespoon salt

1 tablespoon finely ground black pepper

Lard or canola oil, for deep-frying

Barbecue rub

Slice the onions crosswise as thin as you can, about 1/16 inch thick. If you have a mechanical meat slicer, set it on 2 or 3, depending on your machine. Separate the onion slices, place in a bowl or other container, pour the milk over the strings, and toss gently to cover. If the milk does not cover the onions, add water. Cover the onion mixture and refrigerate for at least 3 hours or overnight.

Put the lard or oil in your deep-fryer and preheat to 350°F (or in a deep pot and measure the oil temperature with a deep-frying thermometer). Combine the flour, salt, and pepper in a large bowl and blend well. Remove a handful of onions from the milk marinade, shaking off any excess. Place the onions in the flour mixture, scatter some of the flour on top of the strings, and toss to coat thoroughly. Shake off any excess flour. Deep-fry the strings until golden brown, 3 to 5 minutes, separating the strings with metal tongs. Drain on paper towels and sprinkle with your favorite rub to taste. Repeat with the rest of the onion strings and serve hot.

Onion Rings

Leonard's Pit Barbecue

5465 Fox Plaza Dr.
Memphis, TN 38115
901-360-1963
http://www.leonardsbarbecue.com

eonard's is a Memphis barbecue icon. It bears the name of the founder, Leonard Heuberger, who opened the place in 1922. His 5-cent barbecue pulled pork sandwiches, sauced with vinegar, tomato, and spices, then topped with coleslaw, became a Memphis standard. Leonard's sandwich with onion rings on the side has been popular ever since. So popular, indeed, that Leonard's moved to larger quarters and became the largest drive-in restaurant anywhere. According to the many stories you can hear at Leonard's, Elvis ate there from his teen years onward, often partying with friends until daybreak.

Dan Brown owns today's Leonard's. He has worked there since his teen years and learned the business, recipes, cooking procedures, and traditions directly from Mr. Heuberger. Our recipe for the home cook tastes similar to what you'll get at Leonard's, but don't miss the genuine item on your next trip to Memphis.

ONION RINGS

Serves 6 to 8

1½ cups all-purpose flour

¼ cup cornmeal

¼ cup onion powder

1 teaspoon sugar

2 teaspoons salt

1½ to 1¾ cups milk, or more as needed

1 large egg

Canola oil, for deep-frying

4 large onions, sliced into ½-inch rings

Put the flour, cornmeal, onion powder, sugar, and salt in a large bowl. Add 1½ cups milk, the egg, and ½ cup water. Whisk until only slightly lumpy. It should have the consistency of pancake batter. If it's too thick, add ¼ cup milk or more to thin it down.

Put the oil in your deep-fryer and preheat to 365°–375°F (or in a deep pot and measure the oil temperature with a deep-frying thermometer). Dip the onion rings in the batter. Fry 3 or 4 coated rings at a time, turning the rings when they float to the top. Continue turning the rings until they are golden brown, 3 to 5 minutes. Remove the rings from the grease and drain on paper towels. Serve immediately.

ARDIE'S BARBECUE POSTCARDS

Postcards thrive today, contrary to predictions that e-mail, text messaging, and cell phone–transmitted photos, videos, and conversations would put the postcard industry out of business. Anywhere you travel you'll find postcards featuring local scenery to send home to friends and relatives. You're home before the card arrives, but the recipients know you thought about them while you were away.

Postcards were in their heyday in the early 1900s. Travel by auto was the norm. Most of the 608 million postcards mailed in 1908 hit the designated mailbox well before the sender returned home. Today there's a huge network of postcard collectors, a.k.a. *deltiologists.* Some collect, trade, or sell cards on many subjects or locales. Others focus on a few or one category. Ardie collects barbecue postcards. His friend Ken Wilson in Dripping Springs, Texas, got him hooked, bless Ken's soul. Ken has thousands of postcards. He is active in the nationwide network of postcard collectors who meet in person and online to swap or sell cards.

Barbecue postcards are hard to find. Ardie has scanned hundreds of boxes of cards in flea markets and antique stores to no avail. Ken found most of Ardie's cards at postcard collector shows. Some are older, and some are from contemporary barbecue joints. Postcards are an important part of modern barbecue history. They belong in a Barbecue Hall of Fame or Museum, if a real one ever gets legs. All are treasures. Here are a few of Ardie's favorites:

Grand Opening, April 17, Koppen's
Roadside Bar-B-Que (1948)

Oklahoma Joe's, Albuquerque

The 9th Wonder of the World, Curtis' All American Bar-B-Q Chicken and Ribs, Putney, VT

Hog Heaven, San Francisco—"Cornered by a Boar"

Eat Free
Barbecued Buffalo
and Dance to the Music of
Al Menke's Orchestra
at
Gaylord, Sunday, Oct. 9

Eat Free Barbecued Buffalo and Dance to the Music of
Al Menke's Orchestra at Gaylord, Sunday, October 9

Barbecue at Will Rogers's Ranch, Santa Monica

Brisket Nachos

Tom's Ribs

North Central San Antonio
121 N. Loop 1604 West at Stone Oak
San Antonio, TX 78232
210-404-RIBS (7427)
http://www.tomsribs.com/home.html

We've found great nachos at barbecue joints across America. Tom's are delicious! Imagine noshing on tostada chips topped with chopped barbecued brisket, warm chile con queso, shredded cheddar and Jack cheeses, and Tom's fresh salsa. Here's our version to make at home. It is a great party platter or plate.

BRISKET NACHOS

Serves 4 to 6

3 ounces tricolored tortilla chips

¼ pound chopped barbecued brisket (page 208)

½ cup queso sauce

½ cup cooked or drained canned pinto beans

½ cup shredded cheddar cheese

½ cup shredded Monterey Jack cheese

½ cup homemade salsa or your favorite restaurant or store-bought salsa

Preheat the oven to 400°F. Place the chips on an ovenproof serving plate, then top with half of the brisket, queso sauce, and pinto beans. Repeat with another layer of each, then top with both cheeses and the salsa. Bake for 2 to 3 minutes, or until the cheese is melted. Serve warm.

Deviled Eggs

Miss Myra's Pit BBQ

3278 Cahaba Heights Rd.
Cahaba Heights, AL 35243
205-967-6004

Paul loves deviled eggs, and when he heard about Miss Myra's Pit BBQ Deviled Eggs, his mouth watered. While he was initially disappointed to learn that the deviled eggs, like menu items at most restaurants, are named for the restaurant, not the cooking method, he really enjoyed them, finding them a little different from most.

Miss Myra's does serve real pit hickory-smoked barbecue, cooked in a custom-built brick pit at the restaurant, which was opened in 1984 by Myra Grissom and her late husband. Today it is still a family-run operation. Myra's daughter, Rennae Wheat, and husband, Buck Wheat, along with Rennae and Buck's daughter, Myra, and an aunt, Helen Gilbert, keep the busy restaurant going. Myra Grissom still comes to work but has cut back on her work hours.

Although barbecued pork butt is the best-seller, the ribs, beef, and chicken with the famous Alabama white sauce (mayo, vinegar, and spices) hold their own with customers. Miss Myra's is a joint where you definitely want to save room for dessert. Try each of the six different pies, plus two pound cakes and banana pudding, at each visit; then pick a regular favorite. Be careful if you start with pound cake, though. It's so good you may never get past it, but we strongly suggest you give the others a chance. Very good eats!

DEVILED EGGS

Makes 1 dozen

6 large eggs

3 tablespoons mayonnaise

1 tablespoon sweet pickle relish

1 teaspoon Worcestershire sauce

1 teaspoon distilled white vinegar

Salt and black pepper

Paprika, for garnish

Pimiento-stuffed green olives, for garnish

Put the eggs in a saucepan and cover with cold water. Bring the water to a boil and immediately remove the pan from the heat. Cover and let the eggs stand in hot water for 10 to 12 minutes. Remove from the hot water and run under cold water to cool. Peel the eggs and cut in half lengthwise.

Carefully remove the yolks from the eggs and put them into a medium bowl. Scoop out and discard a little bit of the white to make a more generous cup for filling. Mash the egg yolks, mayonnaise, relish, Worcestershire sauce, and vinegar to make a smooth mixture. Season the mixture with salt and pepper to taste.

Spoon the mixture into the egg whites or pipe with a pastry bag for a more elegant look. Garnish with a sprinkle of paprika and top some of the eggs with a slice of pimiento-stuffed green olive. Chill and serve.

Brunswick Stew

Johnny Harris Restaurant & Barbecue Sauce Company

1651 E. Victory Dr.
Savannah, GA 31404
912-354-7810
http://www.johnnyharris.com

Phil Donaldson, second-generation owner of Johnny Harris Restaurant & Barbecue Sauce Company, is one of the last true southern gentlemen. It is no surprise that the entire Johnny Harris restaurant exudes Phil's signature southern hospitality.

The restaurant has been a Savannah landmark and favorite eats place since the 1920s. You can get its history online or on-site, but what's best to do is get some Johnny Harris barbecue. We like the ribs, pulled pork, chicken, and all the sides at Johnny Harris.

We've been fans since we first tasted Johnny Harris Original sauce almost three decades ago. The sauce's full-bodied, intense flavor comes from the French-style reduction process, by which the sauce is simmered until it has about a third less volume than it started out with. This makes a rich, hearty complement to the barbecue. A small portion is all you need.

Johnny Harris sauce also stars in the restaurant's Brunswick Stew. There is none better. Don't even think about substituting another sauce. Phil says this is "the main ingredient," so get the original Johnny Harris. If you're not in Savannah, order it online. Hats off and applause to Phil Donaldson for sharing this recipe!

BRUNSWICK STEW

Serves 10 to 12

1 pound smoked pork, cooked and diced

1 pound smoked chicken, diced

½ teaspoon black pepper

½ teaspoon hot red pepper flakes

1 teaspoon hot sauce, or to taste

2 tablespoons minced onion

1½ cups ketchup

3 cups diced, peeled, cooked potatoes

3 (15- to 16-ounce) cans niblet corn

½ cup prepared yellow mustard

2 tablespoons salt

½ cup white vinegar

Johnny Harris Original barbecue sauce, to taste

Put all the ingredients in a slow cooker set to medium-low or in a Dutch oven over medium-low heat. Cover and simmer until hot and bubbly, about 2 hours. Taste and add more salt and/or hot sauce as desired.

Burgoo

Moonlite Bar-B-Q Inn

2840 W. Parrish Ave.
Owensboro, KY 42301
800-322-8989 or 270-684-8143
http://www.moonlite.com

In the seventeenth century burgoo was a mush served to sailors during ocean voyages. You wouldn't want to eat it unless you were starving. Today's burgoo is not mush. It tastes so good you can never get enough. Some of the best burgoo in the world is served every day in Owensboro, Kentucky. This recipe makes 3 gallons, which Paul says is "just enough for a big lunch. But I have been told that I am a big eater." It also freezes well. Although Moonlite's recipe has been widely circulated, a book about America's best barbecue wouldn't be complete without this burgoo. Hats off to the Bosley family for keeping this icon of American barbecue going strong!

BURGOO

Makes 3 gallons

4 pounds mutton

1 (3-pound) chicken

¾ pound green cabbage, minced

¾ pound onion, minced

5 pounds potatoes, peeled and diced

2 (17-ounce) cans niblet corn, or 2 cups fresh corn kernels

¾ cup ketchup

3 (10¾-ounce) cans tomato puree

Juice of 1 lemon

¾ cup white vinegar

½ cup Worcestershire sauce

2½ tablespoons salt, or to taste

2 tablespoons black pepper

1 teaspoon cayenne, or more to taste

Put the mutton in a large pot with enough water to cover and bring to a boil over medium-high heat. Reduce the heat to low and simmer for 2 to 3 hours, stirring occasionally. Discard the broth and the bones and finely chop the meat. Set aside.

Boil the chicken in 2 gallons of water in a large kettle over medium heat until tender. Remove the chicken and set aside to cool. Add the cabbage, onion, potatoes, corn, ketchup, and 1 gallon of water to the chicken broth. Bring to a boil.

Meanwhile, chop the chicken meat. Discard the bones and skin. When the potatoes are tender, after 20 or 30 minutes, add the chopped chicken, mutton, tomato puree, lemon juice, vinegar, Worcestershire sauce, salt, black pepper, and cayenne. Simmer over low heat for 2 hours or longer, stirring occasionally as it thickens. Serve with saltine crackers or corn bread if desired.

WHAT TO DRINK WITH BARBECUE

Beverages are essential to the barbecue experience. When the barbecue is world class, just about any beverage will do. Matching the right beverage with the right barbecue can, however—to borrow an expression from Mark Twain—make the difference between a lightning bug and a bolt of lightning.

In the majority of barbecue joints your beverage options are water, iced tea, soda, and beer. Many these days also offer wine. Iced tea has been called "the house wine of the South." Expect iced tea in southern barbecue joints—sometimes sweet, sometimes not, and sometimes you get a choice. The rule is, drink what doesn't distract from the barbecue. If it enhances the barbecue, so much the better!

Hot Pickles

Luling City Market
Real Texas Bar-B-Que

4726 Richmond Ave.
Houston, TX 77027
877-526-2271 or 713-871-1903
http://www.lulingcitymarket.com

 uling's Is one of Ardie's all-time favorite sauces. Its post oak–smoked brisket sandwiches are superb, and the mustard base sauce is addictive, one of the best we've ever tasted. You can order Luling's famous hot pickles online or try our version of Fire and Ice Pickles. They have quite a bite! They are great in tuna salad, deviled eggs, or anywhere else you would use chopped pickles.

HOT PICKLES

Makes 1 gallon

1 gallon sliced hamburger dills

11¼ cups (5 pounds) white cane sugar

1 (2-ounce) bottle Tabasco or other hot sauce

Drain the pickle slices in a very large colander for about 5 minutes. Meanwhile, mix the sugar and Tabasco in a large bowl. Place a layer of pickles back into the pickle jar and follow it with a layer of the sugar mixture. Continue layering pickles and sugar mixture, using a large spoon to push each layer down. When finished, shake the jar or turn it up and down a few times. Set on counter. Turn next day. Repeat for several days until the pickles become transparent. The pickles are ready to eat after a few days. The pickles can be eaten the next day, but the longer they marinate in the juice, the better they are. You can store them on the counter or in the refrigerator. When stored in the refrigerator, they get extra-crunchy.

Note: Sugar is now sold in 4-pound bags, so you'll need a little more than a standard-size bag for this recipe.

11

Buffalo-Style Chicken Wings

Brooks' House of Bar-B-Q

5560 Hwy. 7
Oneonta, NY 13820
800-498-2445 or 607-432-1782
http://www.brooksbbq.com

When it comes to barbecued chicken, the Brooks family of Oneonta, New York, stands above the crowd. They started with a poultry business in 1941. Their barbecued chicken business has thrived since the mid-1950s. The barbecue started with catering, then a small concession stand, followed by an 80-seat restaurant. So many customers hungry for barbecue flocked to the restaurant that in 1965 Brooks' House of Bar-B-Q established a permanent home with a 300-seat restaurant on the former Ralph Holcomb Farm. Brooks sports a 38-foot-long pit, billed as the "largest indoor charcoal pit in the East." On weekdays Brooks hosts an average of 600 customers a day. On weekends the customer average cranks up to 1,100. Chicken and pork spareribs comprise Brooks' barbecue fare. Oven-roasted turkey and beef are served with Brooks' famous barbecue sauce.

Brooks' is in step with the unique upstate New York tradition of serving marinated grilled boneless skinless chunks of chicken in a roll. Similar fare in Italy is called *spiedini,* but in New York the term is *spiedies.* Brooks' spiedies are second to none. Brooks' excellent spiedie sauce, barbecue sauces, and rubs are available online or via a phone call to the restaurant. Try them on all of your grilled or barbecued chicken.

Brooks' has come a long way since family patriarch Griffin Brooks and his wife and food management expert, Frances, started their poultry farm in 1941. Brooks' ownership passed on to son John and daughter-in-law Joan in 1975, and since 2005 John and Joan's son Ryan and daughter-in-law Beth have carried the Brooks' torch into the third generation.

After you try Ryan's recipe for chicken wings, you may switch your preference from Buffalo chicken wings to Oneonta chicken wings! Try mixing Brooks' Original Bar-B-Q Sauce with the Medium Chicken Wing Sauce. Straight Brooks' Original Bar-B-Q Sauce is great, too!

BUFFALO-STYLE CHICKEN WINGS

Serves 4

Brooks' Grillin' Rub

2 pounds chicken wings, wings and drums separated and tips removed

1 cup Brooks' Mild, Medium, or Hot Chicken Wing Sauce

Blue cheese dip or dressing, for serving

Celery and carrot sticks, for serving

Preheat a grill to high and then turn back to medium when ready to start grilling.

Shake Brooks' Grillin' Rub on the raw chicken wings. Place the wings on the grill and turn frequently until done, 25 to 30 minutes. Remove from the grill and let rest for 5 minutes. Place the cooked wings in a bowl, cover with the wing sauce, and shake to coat the wings. Serve with blue cheese dip or dressing and celery and carrot.

Gumbo

BB's Lawnside Bar-B-Q

1205 E. 85th St.
Kansas City, MO 64131
816-8BB-RIBS (822-7427)
http://www.bbslawnsidebbq.com

indsay Shannon, proprietor, with his wife, Jo, calls BB's a "road-house juke joint." True to Lindsay's description, the building looks like a roadhouse. From streetside there is a large parking lot, no lawn. Inside there's a full-service bar on one end and dining tables with blues band space on the other. The walls and ceilings sport blues, barbecue, and swine signs, posters, pictures, and other memorabilia. There is living history here as well, with live blues and great barbecue. Blues entertainers such as Shine Top Jr. Boogie Piano, Lee McBee & the Confessors, and the Scotty Boy Daniels Band appear often, as does a roadhouse full of other blues talent.

Lindsay, a blues and barbecue expert, pegs the 1930s as the start of the barbecue and blues tradition in Kansas City. Thanks to BB's and several other Kansas City venues, the tradition thrives today. Lindsay even takes time off from the restaurant every Sunday night to host a blues show on a local radio station.

BB's head pitmaster, Mike Nickel, knows his way around the barbecue pit as well as Lindsay knows "where bar-b-q meets the blues." Barbe-cue is in Mike's blood. When he isn't cooking at BB's, he's competing in barbecue cooking con-tests. At BB's, Mike has the honor of cooking with

one of the most unusual and historic barbecue pits in the nation. In fact, the pit may be unique; we know of no other custom-built pit made from granite stones salvaged from the old Kansas City crosswalks, when the streets were paved with gravel. It's no stretch of the imagination to say that Big Joe Turner, Charlie Parker, Count Basie, Ma Rainey, and other blues greats walked on those very stones! The thick granite stones hold heat well, enhancing BB's slow and low barbecue method of cooking. The pit still works well after more than fifty years of smoking.

There is something magical about picking up a hickory-smoked rib cooked in a historic pit and savoring each bite as you listen to the blues. Here's how Lindsay puts it: "When the blues music floats off the bandstand, it wafts across your plate of barbecue, imparting a flavor you can only get in Kansas City at BB's."

BB's also makes great gumbo. Try a cup as a starter or get a bowl and make it your main course. Here's the recipe, straight out of BB's recipe and operations manual—the "Bible."

GUMBO

Makes 8 to 10 quarts

1 pound (4 sticks) butter

4 large onions

4 large green bell peppers

1 celery stalk, any leaves removed

Salt and black pepper

Garlic powder

5 store-bought smoked sausages (1½ pounds), thinly sliced

2 smoked ham ends, or about 1 pound sliced smoked ham

2 smoked turkey ends, or about 1 pound sliced smoked turkey

3¾ (28-ounce) cans Hunt's crushed tomatoes

2 (49-ounce) cans Swanson's chicken broth

2 (3½- to 4½-pound) whole chickens, cooked

1 (16-ounce) package frozen okra

1 tablespoon red mild ground pepper

1 (6-ounce) bottle Louisiana hot sauce

Put the butter in a large skillet or stockpot with ½ cup water and heat over medium-high heat. Chop the onions, green peppers, and celery and add them to the pot. Sauté the vegetables until they soften, 7 to 8 minutes; then sprinkle lightly with salt, pepper, and garlic powder and stir. Transfer to a 10-quart pot.

Cut up the sausages, ham, and turkey and add to the vegetables. Then add the crushed tomatoes and chicken broth, stirring to mix well. Bring to a boil over high heat for about 15 minutes. Once the crushed tomatoes and broth mix throughout the veggies and meats, reduce the heat to low and simmer for about 15 minutes.

Meanwhile, remove the skins from the cooked chickens, pull the chicken meat off the bones in small to medium chunks, and add them to the pot. Then add the okra, red pepper, and hot sauce. Simmer for 15 minutes more. Do not let it boil. Serve.

Volcanic Goat Cheese

Gordon's on the Green (formerly Gordy's Steak & BBQ Smokehouse)

13500 Interurban Ave. South
Tukwila, WA 98168
206-267-7427
http://www.gordonsonthegreen.com

This recipe from the former Gordy's Steak & BBQ Smokehouse is worth passing along. Paul enjoyed it as an appetizer when Pacific Northwest barbecue icon Bob Lyon introduced him to some of the best barbecue in the Pacific Northwest. Before feasting on excellent barbecue brisket, ribs, and pulled pork, they enjoyed this appetizer. Gordon's uses Demitri's Bloody Mary Seasoning, but you can use any brand.

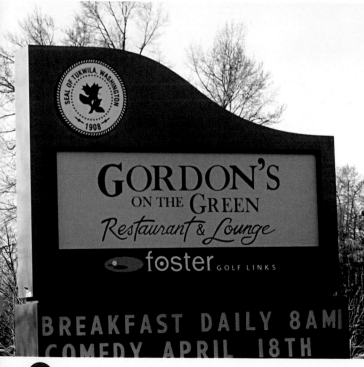

VOLCANIC GOAT CHEESE

Serves 4

3 Roma tomatoes, cut in half and seeded

1 tablespoon balsamic vinegar

2 teaspoons Montreal Steak Seasoning, finely ground

2½ cups tomato juice

½ cup Bloody Mary mix

1 cup barbecue sauce

1 tablespoon granulated garlic

1 tablespoon granulated onion

1 to 2 tablespoons chipotle chiles in adobo sauce

¾ pound goat cheese

Fresh chives, for garnish

Low-calorie garlic crostini, for serving

Preheat your smoker to 250°F. Place the tomatoes on a sheet pan and sprinkle with the balsamic vinegar and seasoning. Smoke for 40 to 60 minutes, or until soft to the touch. Cool down and save the juices.

Remove the tomato skins and process the tomatoes, the reserved juices, tomato juice, Bloody Mary mix, barbecue sauce, garlic, onion, and chiles in a food processor.

Warm 2½ ounces of the sauce in each of 4 rarebit dishes or ramekins and place 3 (1-ounce) slices of goat cheese in the sauce. Place under the hot broiler just to warm the top of the cheese. Garnish with chives cut about 1 inch long. Serve with the crostini.

FINDING GOOD BARBECUE
WHEN YOU'RE NEW IN TOWN

Finding good barbecue is easy when you know whom to ask and what to ask. If there's any to be found in the town or city you find yourself in as a stranger, ask the right questions to the right people and you'll soon be munching on the best barbecue in town. The right people to ask are:

Taxi drivers

Police officers

Firefighters

After asking the obvious, find out what the recommended place is known for. It may be good at some things but not others.

Once you've arrived at a joint, we recommend you put it to the test our friend Vince Staten told us about. You want a yes answer to each question.

- Is the owner's name on it?
- Is there a cluttered working woodpile out back?
- Is barbecue the specialty of the house?
- Are the premises clean enough to make you feel comfortable, but not so squeaky clean that it looks like more time is spent with Windex, brooms, and mops than with fire, meat, and sauce?
- Is there a mix of clunkers and shiny new vehicles in the parking lot?
- Is there a mix of blue collars, jeans, T-shirts, skirts, and suits at the tables?
- Are there any flies?

Or you could ask your doctor if this joint is right for you.

"Checkpoint Chicky" Wings

The BBQ Shack

1613 E. Peoria St.
Paola, KS 66071
913-294-5908
http://www.thebbqshack.com

ick Schoenberger is known in barbecue circles as "Shake." He is a competition barbecuer who made a successful transition from contestant to full-time pitmaster and restaurant proprietor. After winning a truckload of awards at barbecue contests, Rick started catering under the name Double Barrel BBQ Co. When his wife took calls for him back then, he was usually working on a catering job, so she'd tell the caller, "He's out in the shack."

After successful runs at catering, cooking at the local American Legion and VFW posts, and marketing his sauce and rub under the BBQ Shack name, Shake opened the restaurant in 2006. Two years later business was so brisk that he moved to the current location, with more seating and easier access. Guy Fieri paid a visit and aired it with positive raves on his Food Network *Diners, Drive-Ins and Dives* show.

The BBQ Shack has racked up impressive sales records in a small Kansas town that is a short commute from heavyweight barbecue competition in Kansas City. We have yet to catch Shake reading or quoting Shakespeare, but he has had that nickname since sixth grade, so he is surely no stranger to the works of the Bard!

The BBQ Shack will feel like Hog Heaven to Andy Griffith and *Mayberry RFD* fans. Andy, Barney, Goober, Aunt Bee, and other characters from the two popular shows would feel at home and honored at the BBQ Shack, where there is enough *Mayberry* memorabilia to call the Shack a *Mayberry* shrine. Most menu items are named after a *Mayberry* character or place. "Checkpoint Chicky" is the scene of Sheriff Barney Fife's speed trap. When Andy argued with Barney about his strict enforcement of the speed limit, Barney's classic reply was, "Now Andy, if you let them take 30, they'll take 35. If you let them take 35, they'll take 40," and so on. Same goes for Shake's wings. It's a good idea to make more than you think your guests will take. You can make the all-purpose rub with the recipe here, or you can order the BBQ Shack All Purpose Barbeque Rub from Rick on the Internet. Get it and you will enjoy it!

18

"CHECKPOINT CHICKY" WINGS

Serves 4

¼ cup white cane sugar

2 tablespoons onion salt

2 tablespoons garlic salt

2 tablespoons paprika

2 teaspoons chili powder

1 teaspoon black pepper

1 teaspoon lemon pepper

1 teaspoon rubbed sage

1 teaspoon dried basil

¼ teaspoon ground rosemary

¼ teaspoon cayenne

3 pounds chicken wings (about 15)

Canola or lard oil, for deep-frying

2 ounces barbecue sauce (optional)

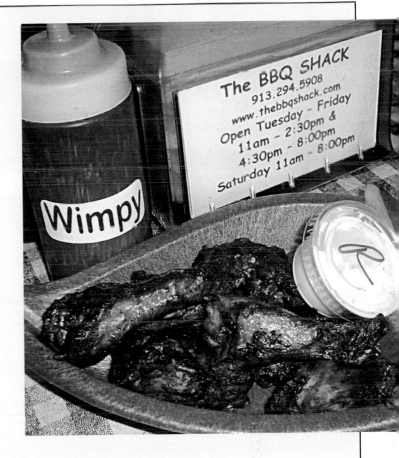

To make the rub, combine the sugar, onion salt, garlic salt, paprika, chili powder, black pepper, lemon pepper, sage, basil, rosemary, and cayenne in an airtight container and blend well. Set aside until ready to use.

Rinse the wings with cold water and pat dry with paper towels. Cut into 3 sections, discarding the tips or saving them for another use.

Place the chicken wings in a large bowl or plastic tub large enough to permit mixing the wings and rub together. Sprinkle a liberal amount (1 to 2 ounces, or 2 to 4 tablespoons) of the rub in with the wings and mix by turning the wings over and over. You still want to see plenty of skin through the rub, so add the rub a little at a time. Place the wings on a smoker at 275°F for approximately 1½ hours, or until the wings reach 165°F on an instant-read thermometer. If you want a crispier skin on the finished wings, cool them down in the refrigerator for at least 1 hour or overnight.

Put the oil in your deep-fryer and preheat to 350°F (or put the oil in a deep pot and measure the oil temperature with a deep-frying thermometer). The fry basket in a turkey deep-fryer works great for these wings. Deep-fry the wings for 1½ to 2 minutes, until they brown and float to the top.

If you want hot wings or barbecue wings, put a dozen wings in a stainless-steel or ceramic bowl, pour the barbecue sauce over the wings, and toss and shake to coat with sauce.

Fried Cheese Stick Grits

Memphis Minnie's
Barbeque Joint & Smoke House

576 Haight St.
San Francisco, CA 94117
415-864-PORK (7675)
http://www.memphisminnies.com

ob Kantor, Memphis Minnie's proprietor, has "rubbed shoulders with the big hogs," as they say in Memphis. We've seen him visiting with Julia Child, R. W. Apple, Jr., Ed Mitchell, Lolis Elie, Calvin Trillin, and many other famous pitmasters and foodies. As an active member of the Southern Foodways Alliance, Bob keeps in touch with a vast network of people who care about good food, especially southern food, and the important role it plays in our culture. His very successful barbecue joint is a beacon to California swine diners who yearn for some South in their mouth. The joint's bright colors on the walls and furniture evoke a nouveau-hippie feel instead of southern barbecue joint, but it fits the neighborhood. You're in San Francisco, after all.

Besides the barbecue, the fried cheese grits are a best-seller, and we knew why with the first bite. We were ready to arm-wrestle Bob for the recipe, but he gave it up with southern-style generosity. Bob credits his son, Ben, for developing it. Thanks, Bob and Ben. Peace!

FRIED CHEESE STICK GRITS

Serves 8 to 12

1 quart milk

2 cloves garlic, minced

5 cloves smoked garlic, mashed (page 21)

2 cups grits (not instant)

¾ pound sharp cheddar cheese

½ cup freshly grated Parmesan cheese

1 teaspoon salt

1 teaspoon black pepper

2 large eggs

3 tablespoons milk

1 cup cornmeal

1 cup corn flour

Canola oil, for deep-frying

Bring 4 cups water, the milk, and the minced fresh and smoked garlic to boil. Add the grits, stirring constantly, and simmer for 6 to 8 minutes. Remove from the heat and stir in the cheeses, salt, and pepper.

Pour the mixture evenly into a parchment-lined 9 by 13-inch pan and chill until very cold, 4 to 6 hours or overnight. Turn out, peel off the parchment, and cut into 1 by 1 by 4-inch sticks.

Combine and beat the eggs and milk in a small bowl. Combine the cornmeal and corn flour in a medium bowl. Coat the grit sticks in the egg wash and then in the cornmeal mixture. Place on a parchment-lined sheet pan and chill until ready to fry.

Put the oil in your deep-fryer and preheat to 370°F (or use a skillet and measure the temperature of the oil with a deep-frying thermometer). Fry the sticks for 3 to 5 minutes, until golden brown. Serve with your favorite dipping sauce, salsa, or barbecue sauce.

SMOKED GARLIC

½ cup extra-virgin olive oil

1 pound peeled garlic cloves

Sea salt and freshly ground pepper

Preheat your smoker 230°–250°F.

Heat an ovenproof saucepan on the stovetop over medium-high heat. Starting the garlic on the stove saves roasting time. When it's hot, add the extra-virgin olive oil. Next, add the garlic cloves and season with salt and pepper. Let the cloves begin to caramelize, then put the pan in the preheated smoker.

Smoke roast the garlic cloves for about 1½ to 2 hours or until they are nicely browned. Let cool. This makes more than you'll need for the Fried Cheese Stick Grits recipe, but you can store it in an airtight container in the refrigerator for up to a week and use it in a variety of dishes.

To make a garlic paste: When cool enough to handle easily, put the roasted garlic into a small bowl, mash with a fork, and add oil from the pan until a paste forms. This paste makes great garlic bread!

Vidalia Onion Dip

Country's Barbecue

3137 Mercury Dr.
Columbus, GA 31906
706-563-7604
http://www.countrysbarbecue.com

 ountry's Barbecue, which is now a small chain, opened for business in 1975 in an old country store. The food quality and family-friendly ambience quickly caught on. Of the nine Country's today, we like the original on Mercury Drive best. It features a gigantic red wooden rocking chair, very popular with kids of all ages. Of course we can't resist saying that the food at Country's rocks, too!

Chopped pork sandwich, or chopped pork, is what Country's does best—barbecued pork, cooked over hickory and oak, chopped and served with Country's own sauces. Country's does several nontraditional barbecue items such as smoked turkey and homemade corn bread dressing, with a sweet potato soufflé. Its hot roast beef sandwich is topped with Vidalia onions and gravy. It's what we'd expect at a diner instead of a barbecue joint, but it's delicious!

VIDALIA ONION DIP

Makes 5 cups

2 sweet onions, minced

1 cup mayonnaise

1 cup freshly grated Parmesan cheese

1 cup shredded Swiss or cheddar cheese

In a large bowl, combine the onions, mayonnaise, and grated cheeses and stir until well blended. Place in a large baking dish or divide among 4-ounce individual ramekins. Cover and refrigerate for 2 hours or overnight. Bake at 325°F for 1 hour, until bubbly and light brown on top. Remove from the oven and let stand for 10 minutes. If there is too much grease, spoon off and discard or absorb the excess in paper towels and discard. Serve with fresh bread or crackers.

One of Country's interesting appetizers is a Vidalia Onion Dip with Frito Scoops. Since the recipe is a trade secret, we will venture this very close adaptation. It's also good as a dip for veggies, potato chips, fries, and onion rings.

Eesti Barbecue Assotsiatsioon
Estonian National Barbecue Association

FANTASY BARBECUE

Barbecue lovers often have adventurous taste buds and appreciate an innovative approach to food. We're no exception. We've heard of a few dishes that we think would be a nice complement to barbecue and a welcome change from the standard fare. Don't get us wrong—we like the onion rings, fries, slaw, and potatoes as much as anyone, but if we saw any of the following things on a barbecue menu, we'd jump to try it.

- Smoked pickled baloney
- Pig cigars (pulled pork wrapped in a wonton wrapper and fried until crisp)
- Pig fries (testicles)
- Turkey fries (testicles)
- Lamb fries (testicles)
- Smoked chicken liver pâté
- Smoked pickled eggs

BAR-B-Q SANDWICHES		
PORK, BEEF	2.35	
BOLOGNA	2.35	
HAM	2.35	
TURKEY	3.06	
POTATO SALAD & SLAW		
PINT	1.70	
8OZ	1.15	
SERVING	.80	

PORK, BEEF		
BOLOGNA	7.55 LB	
HAM		
TURKEY		
HOT SAUCE		
5 OZ	1.70	
10 OZ	2.45	
LITER	5.30	

DRINKS	
RC COLA	ICE TEA
SUN DROP	
UPPER 10	1.05
DIET RITE	
MILK	.78
COFFEE	.55

Blue Cheese Bowl Appetizer

Ridgewood Barbecue

900 Elizabethton Hwy.
Bluff City, TN 37618
423-538-7543

Our good friend Fred Sauceman has sung the praises of Ridgewood for years. When Ardie was the official Curator of Sauces at the Southern Foodways Alliance symposium on barbecue, Fred readily volunteered to bring a fresh quart of Ridgewood Bar-B-Que Sauce. We can still picture Fred holding that jar carefully and reverently. He handed the jar to Ardie like it was a sacred object—which to many Ridgewood fans it is. All but a few drops of Grace Proffitt's famous sauce were consumed that night by enthusiastic symposium participants. We still have the empty jar. The remnants that went begging aren't safe to eat now, but the empty jar with the Ridgewood label is a treasure we cherish.

Besides our friendship with Fred, we have our own history with the Ridgewood. In 1984, when Ardie founded the Diddy-Wa-Diddy National Barbecue Sauce Contest, he wrote to Grace Proffitt and asked her to enter her sauce in the contest. Grace herself replied, with a nice letter, a newspaper article about the Ridgewood, and a bottle of sauce. We've been Ridgewood fans ever since!

Grace and one of her two sons, Terry, have since passed away. To the relief of thousands of Ridgewood fans who worried that the restaurant would close, Grace's surviving son, Larry, and his daughter, Lisa Peters, have stepped up to the pit. Larry, a pharmacist, owns Burgie Drugs in nearby Elizabethton, but he doesn't mind wearing two hats by helping Lisa and the twenty-seven Ridgewood staffers live up to the Ridgewood's reputation for quality.

Only two living persons know the Ridgewood sauce recipe—Larry and Lisa. It is committed to memory, true to the Proffitt tradition. That's no small task, as there are more than two dozen ingredients! You'll believe that when you taste it. We chuckle when reading the ingredients listed on the label: tomato catsup, salt, sugar, and spices.

Unlike most Tennessee barbecue joints, the Ridgewood serves hickory-smoked fresh ham instead of shoulders. You can taste the difference. With the generous portions of meat, homemade fries, slaw, and Grace's barbecue beans, you will not leave hungry.

When you can't enjoy the Ridgewood's popular Blue Cheese Bowl appetizer in person, try ours. Just remember, there's none better than the original Ridgewood Blue Cheese Bowl. Saltine crackers are served with this at the Ridgewood. You can stick with that out of tradition, or add baby carrots, broccoli florets, celery sticks, and other munchy, crunchy dipping foods. This recipe also works well as a salad dressing.

SMOKED BONE RIBS

ALL YOU CAN EAT... Baby

24

BLUE CHEESE BOWL APPETIZER

Makes 2 cups

½ cup Danish or other blue cheese, crumbled

½ cup mayonnaise

½ cup dairy sour cream

¼ cup buttermilk

1 tablespoon Worcestershire sauce

2 teaspoons fresh lemon juice

1 teaspoon grated onion

1 large clove garlic, pressed

1 teaspoon Lawry's Seasoned Salt

Black pepper, to taste

In a medium bowl, combine all the ingredients and blend well. Cover and chill for at least an hour to allow the flavors to blend.

Rocky Mountain Oysters (a.k.a. RMOs)

Hoke's Genuine Pit BBQ

9134 W. 88th Ave.
Westminster, CO 80005
303-424-QPIT (7748)
http://hokesbbq.com

oke's opened in 1996 as a catering business, and the restaurant opened in 2002. The reason Hoke's barbecue is constantly good is that they stay true to their one mission to keep their barbecue genuine.

You understand why there's a line out the door when you slice into the tender prime meat with its smoke-concentrated beefy taste. We were impressed that it came with real beef juice for dipping and pureed horseradish—not the tamed creamy type—for adding another level of zip.

The thing we especially liked was the Rocky Mountain Oysters appetizer. No, they aren't oysters harvested from a fresh, cold-water mountain stream in the Colorado Rockies. Yes, they are what you think they are: bull testicles. They are rich and good! Some call them country caviar. Here's our version, compliments of our barbecue buddy Steve Holbrook, who also cooks up a mean batch of pig fries. If you can't find the breader at your local store, you can order online or substitute your own favorite breader. You can also order bull testicles online.

ROCKY MOUNTAIN OYSTERS (A.K.A. RMOS)

Serves 20 to 24

5 pounds frozen bull testicles

2 to 4 cups Atkinson's Flowering Onion Breader

Plenty of cold beer—Hey, it's a very hot job!

Morton's Hot Salt

Canola oil or lard, for deep-frying

To prep the golden nuggets: Thaw just enough to be able to skin them. While the testicles are still semifrozen, slice them into coin shapes about ⅜ inch thick and then let them thaw completely.

In the meantime, put 1 cup of breader in a medium bowl and blend in enough beer to make a runny batter. Place 1 cup of dry breader in another medium bowl. If you run out of either the wet mixture or the dry batter, remix and refill the bowls as needed.

Use paper towels to dry the testicle coins, season them with Morton's Hot Salt to your liking, and then drop them into beer batter to cover. Lift, let drain slightly, then drop into dry batter to cover with a dry outer coating.

Put the oil in your deep-fryer and preheat to 350°F (or fill a skillet and use a deep-frying thermometer). Drop in the RMOs and fry until they become floating golden nuggets, 3 to 5 minutes, working in batches if necessary.

Fried Green Tomatoes

Williamson Bros. Bar-B-Q

1425 Roswell Rd.
Marietta, GA 30062
770-971-3201
http://realpagessites.com/williamsonbros

sk your taxi driver in metro Atlanta where to eat the best barbecue in town, and the odds are high that the reply will be "Williamson Brothers." The place has become very popular since Jack Williamson and his two sons, Danny and Larry, decided to move their Talladega, Alabama, restaurant to metropolitan Atlanta in 1989. They have since opened Williamson Bros. restaurants in Canton and Douglasville, Georgia. The menu is extensive enough to appeal to everyone who likes barbecue. People who don't especially like barbecue—unimaginable to us—will find enough delicious appetizers to make a feast, plus salmon, catfish, burgers, and hot dogs. A platter of Williamson Bros. barbecued pork ribs with a side of Brunswick stew, okra, and corn on the cob is a memorable feast. Start with a fried green tomato appetizer. Here's our version of the southern classic.

FRIED GREEN TOMATOES

Serves 6 to 8

4 to 6 medium green tomatoes

Salt and black pepper

2 cups all-purpose flour

2 cups cornmeal

2 cups cold milk

2 large eggs

2 tablespoons bacon grease, or more if desired

Slice the tomatoes ¼ to ½ inch thick. Salt and pepper them to taste on both sides. Place the flour and cornmeal in separate shallow dishes for dredging. In a medium bowl, combine the milk and eggs, beating until incorporated. Place the bacon grease in a large skillet and heat over high heat. When the skillet is hot, dust each tomato slice with flour, then dip it into the egg wash, and then into the cornmeal. Fry some of the battered tomato slices for about 3 minutes, or until golden on the bottom. Gently turn and fry the other side. Repeat with the remaining tomato slices.

Main Dishes

With main dishes, eye appeal is important. Barbecue needn't be served on fine china, but it should be presented with care. Whether it's served on butcher paper, on a plastic plate, in a plastic basket or a paper boat, or on a Styrofoam or paper plate, the food has to look good! Our good Texas buddy John Raven, PhB, has an opinion about the many barbecue joints in Texas and elsewhere that serve their barbecue on butcher paper. When John was a human rocket at chili contests, he was Daredevil Bad McFad. Today we call him Bad. Here's how Bad puts it as no one else can: "One problem I have with just about all the barbecue joints I have visited is that unforgivable butcher paper. I take my brisket to the table, and by the time I have cut one or two slices I am eating through the hole in the butcher paper and onto the top of a table that could use a good steam cleaning. I want a real plate, and I want a real fork. I carry a knife.

"The butcher paper serving that so many find so cute dates back to when minorities were not allowed in the barbecue joints. They were served at the back door and their food wrapped in butcher paper. Although I now qualify as a minority, I still want a plate or at least a clean tray."* John knows more about barbecue than anyone, and you can read more of his recollections on Jim Crow and barbecue on page 96.

Beyond looks, the meat should be packed with smoked meat flavor and easy to chew. Ribs should be moist, tender, and done enough that they pull apart easily, but not so done that they fall off the bone. Pork should be moist and tender, not dry and stringy. Beef should also be tender and flavorful. House Park puts it best in their slogan: "Need no teef to eat my beef." The spices on the meat should complement the meat flavor, not overpower it. When it comes to sauce, we prefer ours on the side. Others like their meat basted and slathered with sauce before serving.

With a few exceptions, the dishes in this chapter reflect regional tastes and availability. You'll find beef in Texas, pork in the Carolinas, mutton in Kentucky, a little bit of bison in Colorado, and a variety of meats in the Midwest and elsewhere. We even threw in some fish and seafood from a couple of our favorite joints. Dig in!

*Quoted with permission from the book Bad is writing, *I Know More About Barbecue Than Anyone.*

Smoked Barbecue Beef Ribs

The County Line Bar-B-Q

6500 Bee Cave Road
Austin, TX 78746
512-327-1742
http://www.countyline.com

Is it legendary? We can go along with that. County Line Barbecue has been up on the hill since 1975. This is the original location. On the outside it looks like a Texas roadhouse.

The huge, meaty beef ribs, slow-smoked for 18 to 20 hours, are what put County Line on the map. When you're eating County Line beef ribs, you're going to want to "Get It All Over Ya!"—the trademark barbecue sauce, that is.

Although Country Line won't or can't divulge too many of their cooking secrets, they were eager to tell us how to smoke ribs at home. Trim some of the fat from the back side of the ribs before you put them on the smoker. An oak-wood fire is preferred for smoking at County Line, and that's our choice at home, too. Season the ribs all over with salt, freshly ground pepper, or perhaps a little garlic powder before placing them in the pit. We suggest seasoning with garlic salt and freshly ground

SMOKED BARBECUE BEEF RIBS

Serves 7 to 10

2 to 3 (5- to 7-pound) slabs beef back ribs

¼ cup garlic salt

3 tablespoons black pepper

Prepare a mesquite charcoal or oak-wood fire in your smoker; let burn for 1 hour or until the flames disappear. The temperature should be 200°–225°F. Place the water pan in the smoker and fill it with water.

Season the ribs all over with the seasoning, sprinkling it on and not rubbing it in.

Place the ribs in the smoker and cover with the smoker lid; cook for 6 to 8 hours, or until an instant-read thermometer registers 180°F or the ribs pull apart, adding wood and water as needed.

black pepper. You don't need a hot fire; you do need to keep the ribs as far away from the fire as possible. Ribs are not as tough as brisket, but they need to smoke for a long time. When we tested this recipe for beef ribs in a backyard smoker, it took 6 to 8 hours to cook a slab of ribs; 1 to 1½ hours per pound is a good rule of thumb to follow.

Barbecued Beef Shoulder Clod

Smitty's Market

208 S. Commerce St.
Lockhart, TX 78644
512-398-9344
http://www.smittysmarket.com

he first time Paul went to Smitty's Market he got it right! He parked in the parking lot at the back of the building and went in the back door. He had actually driven by earlier, and the line was out the door (and it was February!), so he took care of another task and came back later.

At Smitty's, you go in the back door and into the pit room, where you'll find one of the oldest barbecue pits in use in Texas and most likely in the entire United States. That's where you order the barbecue that you want to eat. Paul ordered a good slice of beef shoulder clod and wanted to taste Smitty's famous sausage but wanted only half a link. He was willing to pay for a whole link, but he couldn't eat all of it, so he asked them to please give the other half to someone who would eat it. The pitman said, "I'll cut it in half, but you have to take the whole thing." For them to get paid for the sausages and barbecue, you have to take it into the restaurant to get weighed and priced out to you. This is also where you order your side dishes and drinks. So all Paul got was the slice of clod and a smoked sausage, each cut in half as promised, with half a package of soda crackers, all served on butcher paper. Why crackers? That's what the locals in the general area order, but go for bread if you like.

BARBECUED BEEF SHOULDER CLOD

Serves 35 to 40

1 (18- to 22-pound) beef shoulder clod

Salt and black pepper

Season the shoulder clod all over with salt and pepper and place on an indirect fire built with post oak and heated to 400°F. Cover and cook for 4 to 8 hours, until tender.

Note: On a Weber Smokey Mountain, you'd probably have to cut the beef clod in half.

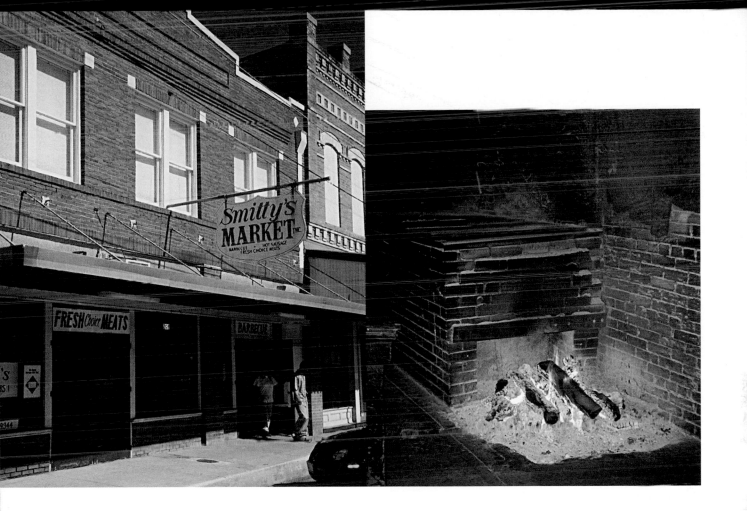

Paul introduced himself to John Fullilove, the pitmaster and Smitty's grandson. John is a big, easygoing, "this is the way it is" type of person. When someone says "barbecued beef" to Paul, he sees only brisket, but John told him the way it is: beef shoulder clod is better. Why? According to John, simple beef clod has more marbling and therefore more flavor, and the yield for the clod is better. You lose at best 50 percent of brisket, where the shoulder clod will lose 40 to 45 percent, and it just tastes better.

Smitty's has four pits plus a smoke room. The two pits on the old side were built in 1924 and the newer ones were built in 1972 and 1978. Paul noticed the pits had no thermometers, so he asked John how long he cooks the shoulder

clod and at what temperature. The answer put Paul into a mild state of shock. John said they cook at about 400°F for 4 to 8 hours, depending how soon they need the meat. Paul would have cooked them at 250°F for 12 to 14 hours, so he just had to ask John why. According to John, when you cook hot for a short time, it seals in the juices and you don't get them too smoky, and that's the way Smitty's prefers them.

Brisket is the meat of choice in Texas, and Smitty's sells more brisket and ribs than they used to. Clod, big pork chops, and sausage used to be the leaders, but things and tastes change, and Smitty's keeps rolling along. And, Paul might add, with great barbecue. Paul thanked John and went on to his next barbecue adventure.

Cooking Method

Cooper's Old Time Pit Bar-B-Que

505 W. Dallas St.
Llano, Texas 78643
877-533-5553 or 325-247-5995 (for mail order)
http://www.coopersbbq.com

Cooper's is considered one of the Meccas of barbecue, and Paul would agree. The Cooper's in Llano has no real ties to the one in Junction (page 35) except they were taught the same way. Cooper's in Llano is more rustic and has a little more ambiance, but they are set up almost identically.

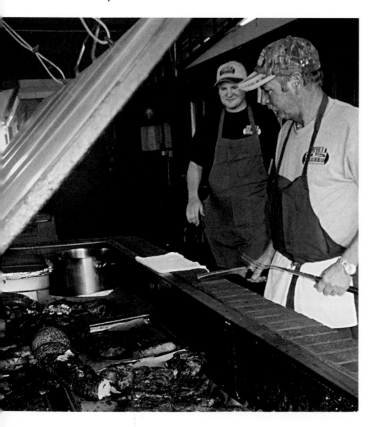

At one end of the parking lot is an enormous pile of mesquite logs. Next to that is the barbecue smokehouse with five old rectangular closed steel pits lined up in a row. At the pit closest to the door, customers choose their meat.

The barbecue at Cooper's is cooked cowboy style, that is, directly over smoldering hardwood coals. The logs are burned down to embers in a big enclosed fireplace, then transferred to the pits by wheelbarrow. The pitman shovels the coals under the meat. The brisket takes six to eight hours and is outstanding, with the robust flavor of meat and smoke. Everything else is fabulous, too: the huge pork chops, which are one of Cooper's signature items (hence the motto "Cooper's Old Time Pit Bar-B-Que, Home of the Big Chop"), the sirloin, the pork sausage, the chicken, the pork ribs, the goat, and on Tuesdays and Fridays, the beef ribs.

In its March 2001 issue, *Texas Monthly* stated that number three of the top fifty things that any good Texan should do before dying is to pick a piece from one of Cooper's Old Time Pit Bar-B-Que pits in Llano. Paul doesn't usually like mesquite-smoked meats, but he likes the way Cooper's cooks theirs, and he would have to agree with *Texas Monthly*. He'd also include the Cooper's in Junction.

BETTER THAN A $162 DUCK!

Cooper's Bar-B-Q & Grill

2423 N. Main St
Junction, TX 76849
325-446-8664

The first time Paul went to Cooper's in Junction, he and his friend Stuart Carpenter traveled there from Houston just to have some barbecue, not realizing or caring that it wasn't the famous Cooper's in Llano, Texas.

When they pulled into the parking lot, the view was amazing. In the back were fifty some cords of mesquite stacked for aging (drying), a pit house that held five old rectangular pits with steel lids, and a 500-gallon fire barrel standing on its side with a four-foot opening in it and a roaring fire burning away.

Paul and Stuart went inside, where displayed in the counter were samples of all the barbecue—brisket, ribs, two types of sausage (smoked and jalapeño), big thick pork chops, and *cabrito* (baby goat), as well as side dishes such as pinto beans, potato salad, and slaw. Their order went something like this: the point of that brisket, a link of smoked and jalapeño sausage, some ribs (the serving lady started

cutting off of the short end, but Paul and Stuart wanted them off the long end, so they just took all of them), and a couple of pork chops. They each also had beans and split an order of potato salad and slaw with two large drinks. The bill came to $85, and when they left, they ordered another $80 worth of barbecue to send to a friend in New York.

Paul and Stuart's trip to Cooper's in Junction always reminds Paul of the old country song "The $162 Duck," which is about a man with a duck and who basically swindles a guy out of $162. Few people remember the song, but the analogy is this: the gasoline for the trip cost $77, and the lunch was $85, for a grand total of $162. But the analogy ends there, because there sure wasn't a swindle involved with Cooper's. Paul likes to tell people that the worst thing he can say is that he would go back, and he has been back four more times and if he is in the area he will go back again.

Beef Brisket

Head Country Barbecue

1217 E. Prospect Ave.
Ponca City, OK 74601
888-762-1227 or
580-767-8304 (for mail order)
http://www.headcountry.com

ead Country Barbecue sauces and rubs are famous throughout Oklahoma and beyond. Being from Oklahoma, Ardie had a liking for Head Country Bar-B-Q Sauce, Original Flavor and Hickory Smoke Flavor, years before meeting Danny Head on the barbecue cooking contest trail. We've both gotten to know and appreciate Danny and his wife, Carey, over the years. They have built an impressive reputation and product line that has been good for the Oklahoma economy as well as the many barbecue lovers who savor the Head Country signature flavors on their barbecue.

When Danny and Carey hired Paul Schatte from his career in school administration, Paul didn't waste any time getting busy with daily restaurant and sauce factory operations, getting acquainted with staff, and putting his leadership skills to work. He also soon became a fixture on the competition barbecue circuit, racking up one impressive win after another, competing as Head Country II. More recently Paul became a part owner of Head Country.

The Head Country Barbecue restaurant outgrew the original smaller joint. The current location could still use some extra tables at the busiest times, but can accommodate seventy-five hungry people at a time. The daily fare at Head Country is a selection of hickory-smoked sliced or chopped beef brisket, pork spareribs, pork shoulder, turkey, ham, chicken breast, and hot links. You can get barbecued baked beans, coleslaw, potato salad, baked potato, french fries, chips, deviled egg, and jalapeño peppers solo or as many as you like on the side. Our favorite Head Country feast is beef brisket with barbecued beans, potato salad, and coleslaw, with a deviled egg starter. You can't go wrong with any choices you make at Head Country, so don't cheat yourself out of grazing your way through the entire menu, one visit at a time, and choosing your own favorites.

After an especially memorable lunch at Head Country one day when we stopped there on our way to Texas, Paul Schatte gave us a tour of the Head Country sauce and rub production and distribution plant, warehouse, and executive offices. Wow! When you walk inside this 25,500-square-foot 22-foot-tall plant bustling with activity, you see why Head Country is able to establish a presence on supermarket shelves, grocery store shelves, and kitchen cupboards all over Oklahoma and elsewhere. We saw orders scheduled for delivery in many parts of the USA.

Before we left Ponca, we got Paul's promise of a Head Country recipe. What follows is what he gave us, and since he has won the brisket category in so many contests, we are pleased and thankful. Oklahoma is cattle country, so of course this is a beef brisket recipe.

BEEF BRISKET

Serves 18 to 20

1 (12- to 14-pound or larger) packer trim brisket aged 35 to 40 days

½ cup Head Country All-Purpose Championship Seasoning

1 (10-ounce) bottle Head Country Premium Marinade

1 (18-ounce) bottle Head Country Original Flavor, Hickory Smoke Flavor, or Hot Flavor Bar-B-Q Sauce

Prepare the brisket the night before you plan to cook it. There are two lean pieces of meat (the "flat" and the "deckle," or "point") sandwiched by fat. Separate the two lean pieces. Leave as much fat on the flat as you like; all of it is best in the cooking stage. The deckle should have as much fat trimmed off the surface as possible. The first time you trim out a brisket it may be difficult to find the two sections of muscle. If you have a good relationship with your local butcher, ask him to show you how to part the brisket. Most people just cook the flat, which is very good. You will be pleasantly surprised at the strong beef flavor the deckle has.

Once the two pieces are trimmed, season both with the Head Country seasoning. The flat portion can be seasoned very heavily, but the deckle should receive a light dusting of seasoning. The fat marbled in the deckle will have a salt flavor to it already. Seasoning this piece too heavily will give the meat a very salty taste. The flat can handle heavy seasoning because it will sweat a lot as it cooks.

After seasoning the meat, shake the bottle of marinade well before opening it. Drizzle some on both sides of the pieces of meat and massage it in. Place the seasoned meat in a plastic container and cover with a lid. Refrigerate it overnight.

The next day, remove the brisket from the refrigerator and allow it to warm up while you prepare the smoker. Build a fire that, when ready for cooking, will be 275°F. Seasoned pecan wood produces a good mild smoke flavor. Unseasoned wood or heavy-smoking wood will leave a creosote/smoky taste on the meat. Allow the fire to burn for 30 minutes.

Place the brisket flat in the smoker, fat side up. The deckle will not have a fat side. Push the muscle together rather than leaving it pulled or stretched out. Cook at 275°F for 3 hours. After 3 hours, check the temperature with an instant-read thermometer. Once the internal temperature reaches 160°F, remove the brisket from the smoker with a fork or heat-rated gloves and place the brisket fat side down on a double layer of aluminum foil cut large enough to seal the brisket tight. Pour ¼ cup of marinade over the top and seal the foil tightly. Do the same with the deckle piece, using a little less marinade. Return the brisket to the smoker and cook at 300°F for 3 to 3½ hours. When the internal temperature of the brisket reaches 200°F, remove the brisket from the smoker with heat-rated gloves. Open the foil and let the heat dissipate for 20 to 25 minutes. Remove the brisket from the foil and slice across the grain of both the flat and the deckle. Compare the taste of the pieces of beef. Serve with plenty of Head Country Bar-B-Q Sauce.

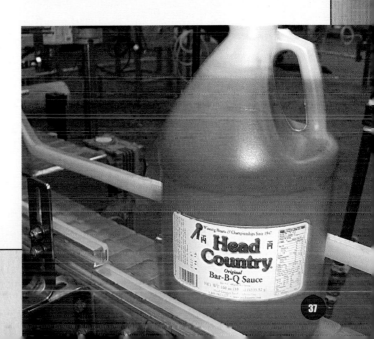

Barbecue Brisket with Pinto Beans

Black's Barbecue

215 N. Main St.
Lockhart, TX 78644
512-398-2712
http://www.blacksbbq.com

Black's is known as Texas's oldest and best major barbecue restaurant continuously operated by the same family. It has been around since 1932. Edgar and Norma Black, co-owners, are assisted by their sons, Kent and Buddy. Paul loves their slogan "Take me back to Black's Barbecue."

Paul went to Black's especially for the sausages and brisket. He ordered exactly that, a big slice of brisket and a sample of each of the sausages: their original, which the Blacks have been making since 1932, as well as the jalapeño/cheddar and the garlic sausage, both of which were introduced in 2003. It all was worth the trip. Black's is a must stop when in Lockhart.

Paul went to the counter and asked to see the owners or manager. Picking up a business card, he noticed that the manager was from Overland Park, Kansas, near where Paul lives. A few minutes later manager Steve Cloud came out. Paul complimented Steve on the barbecue and explained that he was there to steal one of Black's sausage recipes. Steve laughed nervously and said, "I don't think so! I don't think the Black family would go along with that." Paul said, "I understand! But could you give us the procedure for cooking the sausages?" Steve said that he would ask the Blacks if that was permissible.

Paul called Black's later and had the opportunity to talk to Kent Black, and Kent graciously gave us the cooking procedure for their world-famous sausage.

Black's cooks in a rectangular pit with heavy lids, using indirect heat. It has a two-pit setup. The two pits share a common stack, or flue, and cook with post oak. Black's makes, stuffs, and hand-ties the sausages in small sausage rings, places them on sausage rods, and hangs them in the pits to smoke for 3 to 3½ hours at a low 175° to 200°F. We thank Black's for sharing their recipes with us.

BARBECUED BRISKET

Serves 15

¼ cup salt

¼ cup coarsely ground black pepper

1 (9- to 10-pound) beef brisket

Prepare your pit or grill: An indirect-heat pit with a lid is preferred. We recommend using a hardwood such as post oak for heat and smoke. Some woods—mesquite and other types of oak—emit a strong, harsh flavor that is undesirable to many people. Try different hardwoods to suit your taste. Heat the pit or grill to 250°–350°F. The lower the heat, the more smoke, the better the flavor.

Mix the salt and pepper together. Hand-rub the salt and pepper mix into the brisket. Place the brisket in the pit or grill and cook to desired doneness, 8 to 12 hours. Serve with barbecue pinto beans.

PINTO BEANS

Serves 4 to 6

1 pound dried pinto beans, sorted for debris and washed

¼ pound salt pork, chopped

1 teaspoon freshly ground black pepper

2 teaspoons paprika

2 teaspoons salt

1 teaspoon chili powder

Preheat your oven to 450°F. Place the beans in a large pot or cooker with a lid and cover with water. Add the salt pork, pepper, paprika, salt, and chili powder while stirring.

Cook, stirring occasionally and making sure they don't scorch, until the beans are soft, about 3 to 4 hours. The beans can be served immediately or cooled and reheated for use the next day.

Note: You can also use a slow cooker (Crock Pot) and cook the beans for 5 hours on high heat or for 6 to 7 hours on low heat, stirring occasionally.

THE TEXAS CRUTCH

Legend has it that Paul Kirk coined the expression "Texas Crutch" when jesting with barbecue contest cooks from Texas who routinely wrapped their meat in aluminum foil after smoking it a while. Foiling meat betters your odds of getting tender barbecue. The juices steam-tenderize the meat.

In fairness to Texans, not all Texas pitmasters use the crutch, and it's used by cooks all over the country. It works. There's no right or wrong about it. Purists like Paul, however, say it makes "pot roast" out of briskets and butts. To Paul, it's not real, traditional barbecue.

We weaned ourselves from the crutch more than a decade ago. We like bark, and it's near impossible to get bark with the crutch. Nevertheless, you'll see some aluminum foil in some of our recipes, and we guarantee you'll like the result.

Smoked Prime Rib

4 Legs Up BBQ & Steak House

2212 Main St.
Great Bend, KS 67530
620-792-7892

elly and Roni Wertz opened 4 Legs Up BBQ & Catering in McCook, Nebraska, where their award-winning barbecue gave rise to a thriving and growing business. Then they decided to enter the Central Kansas BBQ Cookoff and State Championship in Great Bend, Kansas, where they won "The People's Choice Award." It became a life-changing trip. They liked this Kansas town, and it presented the opportunity to add a steakhouse to their famous barbecue restaurant. With a lot of planning and soul searching they made the commitment to move to Great Bend and open 4 Legs Up BBQ & Steak House.

4 Legs Up is a 70-seat full-service restaurant serving lunch and supper. The Wertzes offer seven different smoked meats plus pork ribs and homemade sides, including their award-winning cheesy potato casserole and barbecue beans. The BBQ Nachos—fresh fried potato chips with your choice of meat smothered in homemade cheese sauce—and their BBQ Burrito, barbecue beans and your choice of meat wrapped in a tortilla, are very popular. And, of course, cold beer always goes well with barbecue. The wood-fire-grilled steaks and burgers are also very popular. At 4 Legs Up they wet-age all-natural, premium Angus beef for a minimum of 30 days before hand-carving each steak for each order. Smoked prime rib is served every Saturday night.

Kelly and Roni have competed in BBQ contests for several years and collectively have won six Grand Championships, two Reserve Grand Championships, and one Reserve Championship, placed eleventh at the American Royal in 2007 and ninth in total points for the KCBS Team of the Year in 2007. Their Royal Red Sauce won the American Royal sauce contest in 2005 and the Colorado State Champion Sauce at Frisco, Colorado, in 2005. Their Chipotle-Raspberry Sauce and Raspberry BBQ sauce have won several awards as well. 4 Legs Up Cow Dust BBQ seasoning has placed third and sixth, respectively, at the Great American BBQ Rub Contest the past two years. In 2008, they were the Grand Champion at the 20th annual Jack Daniel's World Championship Invitational Barbecue.

Paul has enjoyed Kelly and Roni's barbecue at 4 Legs Up BBQ three times. The first time he had a great brisket sandwich, the next time their barbecued ribs, and the third time—wow!—he had their smoked prime rib. The more he thinks about it, the more his mouth waters in anticipation of enjoying the prime rib, which is seasoned a lot differently from any other he has tasted. Here is their recipe. Use premium or certified Angus beef that has been wet-aged for at least 30 days and up to 60 days. You can season the meat up to 24 hours before cooking, but it has to rest for at least 12 hours in the seasoning for good flavor. The horseradish sauce makes a great chip dip, too.

SMOKED PRIME RIB

Serves 10 to 12

HORSERADISH SAUCE

½ cup prepared horseradish

1 cup mayonnaise

1 cup dairy sour cream

2 tablespoons Worcestershire sauce

1 tablespoon fresh lime juice

1 tablespoon black pepper

2 tablespoons Bad Byron's Butt Rub or your favorite barbecue seasoning

SEASONING

¼ cup ground cumin

¼ cup sea salt

2 tablespoons chili powder

2 tablespoons sugar

2 tablespoons garlic powder

2 tablespoons onion powder

2 tablespoons black pepper

1 tablespoon paprika

1 tablespoon dried oregano

2 teaspoons cayenne

1 whole lip-on certified Angus beef rib roast (12 to 15 pounds)

To make the horseradish sauce, combine all the ingredients in a nonreactive bowl. Cover and refrigerate.

To make the seasoning for the meat, combine all the ingredients in an airtight container and blend well. Store in a cool, dark place.

Place the roast bottom side up in a large roasting pan or sheet pan. Season the bottom of the roast heavily with about a third of the seasoning. Rub the seasoning into the bottom side of the roast. Flip the roast so the fat side is up.

With a sharp knife, score through the fat cap just into the top layer of red meat; do not score too deeply. Score every inch or so at a 45-degree angle from the upper left corner to the lower right corner of the roast, going all the way to the lip (the hard fat on the narrow end of the roast).

Season heavily with the rest of the seasoning. You will want to cover the roast thickly, rubbing and pressing the seasoning into the scores. This is a very large roast, so it takes a lot of seasoning. Allow the roast to rest overnight in the fridge—a good 12 hours at least.

Make sure your meat thermometer is calibrated. Preheat your smoker to 250°F, using the wood of your choice. Roast the meat for 4 to 6 hours, until the internal temperature of the meat is no greater than 130°F. This will give you a rare roast in the center.

Remove the roast from the smoker and wrap in several layers of plastic wrap. Allow to rest for at least 1 hour before carving; then place the roast on a cutting board in a sheet pan. Cut the plastic wrap and allow the juice to drain into the sheet pan. The juice can be served straight with the prime rib or reduced by half in a saucepan on the stove with a tablespoon or so of butter added at the last minute to smooth the sauce. Do not use premade or canned beef "au jus." Slice the meat and serve with the juice and the horseradish sauce.

Barbecued Rib Eye

Ranch House BBQ & Steakhouse

10841 Kennedy Creek Rd. SW
Olympia, WA 98512
360-866-8704
http://www.ranchhousebbq.net

my Anderson and Melanie Tapia opened the Ranch House BBQ & Steakhouse in 2004. Amy, a graduate of Paul's pitmaster classes, brings years of world-championship barbecue cooking contest experience to Ranch House. Melanie, with her background in marketing and event planning, plus some impressive barbecue credentials as a competitor and founding member of the Southern California BBQ Association, brings complementary business expertise. Melanie worked for several large companies before starting her own event company in California. She hosted the first barbecue competition ever in Southern California and has organized more than twenty-five other contests. Among the twenty-five teams from four states at that first contest were heavy hitters Bad Byron of Bad Byron's Butt Rub, Mike Scrutchfield of Top Secret, and Amy Anderson's Smokin' Bullet from the Pacific Northwest. That's where Melanie and Amy met. In 2001 Melanie moved to Washington to assist in running Amy's catering business and now the restaurant. The people of Olympia and the many tourists who visit have good reason to celebrate the day Amy and Melanie met. They bring an exemplary commitment to excellence at the Ranch House BBQ & Steakhouse.

The original Ranch House was on the major highway to and from Lake Olympia, a great location. The red wooden shack with checkered curtains had the right aura and world-class barbecue. Word spread, and business was booming when, after 3½ years of growth and a pile of awards, a 100-foot-wide, 15-foot-high wall of mud and debris rumbled through the property, taking everything along with it. Ranch House BBQ was destroyed on the morning of Monday, December 3, 2007, when the mudslide swallowed up the water and septic systems, tore apart the restaurant and outbuildings, destroyed the smokers that made Anderson's signature barbecue meats and even the checkered curtains that made customers feel welcome.

Thanks to the owners' tenacity, with the help of overwhelming community support, Ranch House BBQ arose like the phoenix from the smoke and mud. Within 48 hours, a local hotel had offered use of its vacant restaurant space. Thankful for the opportunity to stay in business, Ranch House BBQ operated temporarily in the Governor Hotel until December 2008. A loan from the Small Business Administration made it possible to rebuild and reopen in a new building at the original location, to the delight of their fans.

Amy's original-recipe dry rub is applied to all Ranch House barbecued meats prior to smoking with apple and cherry wood from the Anderson family farm. Ranch House has been awarded "Best BBQ of South Sound" for several years in a row due to this winning combination of rub and smoke.

Ranch House BBQ offers a full range of championship barbecued ribs, brisket, pulled pork, and chicken, along with excellent charcoal-grilled steaks. One of its signature items is smoked rib eye steak. It is outstanding, especially if you order it medium-rare. Here, thanks to pitmaster Amy, is the recipe.

BARBECUED RIB EYE

Serves 1

PRIME RIB RUB

2 tablespoons white cane sugar

2 tablespoons sea salt

1 tablespoon garlic powder

1 tablespoon paprika

2 teaspoons ground thyme

2 teaspoons ground oregano

2 teaspoons finely ground black pepper

1 teaspoon lemon pepper

1 teaspoon chipotle powder

RIB EYE

⅓ cup yellow mustard

1 whole beef rib eye (about 13 pounds)

Combine all the ingredients for the rub in an airtight container and store until ready to use, or up to 6 months.

Lightly brush the yellow mustard all over your rib eye. Then lightly sprinkle on the dry rub to coat the meat. Preheat your smoker to 225°F. Place the meat fat side up in the smoker and cook for approximately 1 hour. Let cool completely. Cut the meat into the desired steak size. Ranch House keeps it big—a full pound! Grill the steaks over hot coals to your desired doneness. Serve and enjoy.

BBQ HALLS OF FLAME & FAME

Goode Company Barbeque in Houston started the first Barbeque Hall of Flame. Then came the Kansas City Barbeque Society BBQ Hall of Flame. A small committee in Kansas City has been working on a National Barbecue Hall of Fame and Museum since 2003. Meanwhile two virtual online halls of fame are hosted by the North Carolina Barbecue Society and the KC BBQ Forum, respectively.

We applaud these noble efforts and would love to see all real or virtual barbecue halls of fame or flame grow into fully funded, continuously operated institutions. Unfortunately, though, they've been able to reach few, if any, individuals outside the barbecue network. It's OK to preach to the choir, but there's a lot of work yet to be done (and millions of dollars in funding to make it first class) to reach out to the general public and inspire a passion for barbecue throughout the land—a goal we heartily endorse.

To reach that goal the ultimate BBQ Hall of Fame would have to feature:

- **Interactive displays that tell the story of barbecue from thousands of years back to the present—the real history of barbecue as factually as it can be presented**
- **Several dining rooms featuring regional styles of barbecue**
- **National and international guest barbecue pitmasters each month, teaching classes and designing menus for the month—to truly appreciate barbecue you have to get it on your hands and into your belly**
- **Several indoor and outdoor demonstration kitchens equipped with the latest technology**
- **A large auditorium for presentations, movies, and documentaries related to barbecue**
- **A big hotel and conference center**
- **The ability to host four major invitational competitions each year—spring, summer, fall, winter**
- **An archive of barbecue-related books, newspapers, news clippings, videos, DVDs, CDs, tapes, photos, etc.**
- **A gift shop of barbecue memorabilia, grills, pits, books, gadgets, CDs, DVDs, sauces, rubs, posters, and more**

People have to experience barbecue to learn to love it. Can it happen? Yes! Will it happen? Maybe.

St. Louis Pork Steak

Charlotte's Rib BBQ

15467 Clayton Rd.
St. Louis, MO 63011
636-394-3332
http://www.charlottesribbbq.com

erb Schwarz was known in barbecue circles for his famous St. Louis restaurant, Charlotte's Rib, and for his many cooking and sauce contest awards, including a Grand Champion win at the American Royal, the World Series of Barbecue. Herb's barbecue handle was "Dr. Rollin' River," and his barbecue legacy is mighty, like the river that runs through St. Louis. After 25 successful years at Charlotte's Rib, Herb and his beloved wife, Pat, turned Charlotte's Rib over to their children. Today their daughter, Lisa, with co-owner Scott Brown, runs Charlotte's Rib, and their son, Joe, runs C. B. Joe's in Bon Terre, south of St. Louis.

One of Ardie's favorite memories of Herb is of sharing a barbecue tour of the best barbecue restaurants in St. Louis. The last stop was Charlotte's Rib. Ardie was so full of barbecue that he couldn't imagine eating another bite. Herb ordered ribs and a huge pork steak. As his guest, Ardie felt like he had to take at least a token bite and thank Herb for his hospitality. After a bite of rib and a bite of steak, he threw politeness to the wind and ate the whole thing. Charlotte's was the best barbecue on the tour!

We're proud to report that Lisa, Scott, and Joe learned their lessons well. Charlotte's Rib is still one of the best barbecue restaurants in America. Here, thanks to Lisa and Scott, is Dr. Rollin' River's Charlotte's Rib St. Louis Favorite Huge Hand-Cut Pork Steak.

ST. LOUIS PORK STEAK

Serves 8 (or 1 with a hearty appetite)

¼ cup canola oil

8 (¾-inch-thick) pork steaks

Seasoned salt to taste

Charlotte's Rib Mild Hickory or Spicy Southern Barbecue Sauce or your favorite sauce

Set up and preheat your smoker to cook indirectly at 230°–240°F. Meanwhile, heat the oil in a large skillet over high heat until hot. Sear each steak on both sides, about 3 minutes per side. Sprinkle seasoned salt all over the steaks. Smoke for 3 to 4 hours, until fork-tender, then brush on Charlotte's Rib Mild Hickory or, for a little kicker, Charlotte's Rib Spicy Southern Barbecue Sauce to taste for a finishing touch. Then get ready for some of this world's greatest eatin'.

Rib-Eye Steak

Louie Mueller Barbecue

206 W. 2nd Street
Taylor, TX 76574
512-352-6206
http://www.louiemuellerbarbecue.com

Ardie's father-in-law, the late Leopold Walter Mueller, from the small town of Buffalo Lake, Minnesota, would have loved this place. The name from his heritage, of course, would be an obvious draw, but once inside he would have taken to the people, the food, and the small town friendly feel of Louie Mueller. After finishing a generous spread of brisket, pork ribs, sausage, pinto beans, German-style potato salad, raw onions, pickles, and a cold Shiner Bock, he would have mingled with other customers as if they were old friends.

Louie Mueller's exterior looks like a set from a Hollywood western. A weathered sign above the sidewalk roof reads "Louie Mueller Barbeque." You know the joint is open for business when a big American flag is waving from a pole stuck in the conduit pipe in the front sidewalk.

To us the joint feels like a shrine each time we open the screen door and step inside. It's a special place for sure—a stone, brick, and wood structure with tall ceilings, an assortment of tables and chairs, smoky walls, and a counter in the back for taking orders. A big doorway opens to a more recent addition, an annex converted from the adjacent corner building to handle the overflow from the main dining room. It has taken on the smoky patina and has been installed with enough signs and other memorabilia from the mother building that a newcomer would assume the place has always been this big.

Taylor is our buddy John Raven's hometown, and John is no stranger to Louie Mueller. The first time Ardie met John in person, after many years of exchanging snail mail and, later, e-mail, John was sitting in a chair against a wall in Louie Mueller. There was no doubt when Ardie saw him, a big fellow in a bright yellow long-sleeved T-shirt, wide red suspenders, long white hair, and bushy mustache, that he was looking at Daredevil Bad McFad, Commissioner of Barbecue—the man who knows more about barbecue than anybody.

John told us, "Were I to recommend Louie Mueller's to a stranger, I would tell him it is a Texas tradition. It is as Texas as the state capital. Much of the 100-year-old building is still in its original condition. It is just a unique place. You need to go there even if you are a vegetarian."

Featured in two documentaries—*Barbecue: A Texas Love Story* and *The Masters of Texas Barbecue*—plus appearances in three feature films—*Hot Spot* (1990), *Flesh and Bones* (1993), and *The Rookie* (2002)—Louie Mueller has more cinema credits than any other barbecue joint we know about.

Responsibility for daily operations is now in the hands of Wayne Mueller, the third generation of Muellers to run the place. It goes back to 1949 when founder Louie Mueller started cooking barbecue and selling in the alley behind his grocery store. He moved to the present location in 1959. Louie's son, Bobby, joined the business full-time in 1965, and took full ownership in 1974 when Louie retired. The joint has received many accolades in print and TV media over the years, with the crowning achievement being a James Beard Award in the "America's Classic" division in 2006. When Bobby died in 2008, Wayne took

RIB-EYE STEAK

Serves 4

4 (12-ounce) bone-in rib-eye steaks

Coarsely ground black pepper

Salt

Set up your smoker with post oak or oak wood to cook indirectly at 375°F. Season the steaks all over with salt and pepper to taste. Place in the smoker and cook for 45 to 60 minutes or to the doneness you desire. Enjoy—this is a classic!

over. We and thousands of other Louie Mueller fans are grateful to Wayne for continuing the legacy.

A standard introduction to the meats of Louie Mueller should include brisket, sausage, pork ribs, and beef ribs, but we heartily recommend a return visit for the 12-ounce rib-eye steak. It is a smokehouse steak—slow smoked to medium-well—not a grilled hot and fast steak-house steak. We're fans of the latter style as well, but there's something special about a Louie Mueller smoked rib-eye seasoned with a simple mix of pepper and salt; it is a special culinary pleasure not to be missed. It's good enough to make a former omnivore turned vegetarian go into a temporary relapse. Here is our version, but there's no duplicating the atmosphere and flavors from sitting at Louie Mueller on location and savoring the experience.

The steak, like the other meats at Louie Mueller, is served on butcher paper. This is one of John Raven's pet peeves, but he's a regular at Louie Mueller nonetheless.

Slaughterhouse Five Ribs

Oklahoma Joe's Barbecue and Catering

3002 W. 47th Ave.
Kansas City, KS 66103
913-722-3366
http://www.oklahomajoesbbq.com

The dream in sport barbecue is to go from grand champion pitmaster to successful barbecue restaurateur. It has happened in Tennessee, Texas, Illinois, Missouri, Kansas, and elsewhere. Kansas City, Kansas, is where the dream is coming true for Joy and Jeff Stehney. After years of winning trophies and ribbons with Jeff's Slaughterhouse Five competition barbecue team, Joy and Jeff jumped into the barbecue restaurant business. They brought two differences to the table from others who have pursued the dream: (1) They set out to offer championship contest–quality barbecue instead of restaurant-quality barbecue. (2) Instead of a roadside shack, greasehouse, or standard table service restaurant, they converted a gas station and former auto parts dealership into a barbecue restaurant. Yes, you *can* eat here and get gas. The place started out as a Western Auto store, then a convenience store with gas and liquor, then a Go Chicken Go restaurant, before it became famous as Oklahoma Joe's.

Most days you'd best arrive early (they open at 11:00 A.M.) or later, past the lunch and dinner rush, unless you don't mind standing in line for 30 to 45 minutes. Finding a vacant table by the time you get your order usually isn't a problem. Sometimes you'll share a table with strangers.

People aren't strangers for long, however, when barbecue is on the table.

The walls are covered with sport barbecue photos, banners, and other memorabilia. Shelves next to the cash register feature trophies, gift baskets, sauces, and rubs for sale. A corrugated metal canopy over the order line displays a variety of T-shirts you can buy. The most popular says, "I can't believe my favorite barbecue place is in a gas station." Service at the order/pickup line is fast, friendly, and efficient. They want to help you and will honor special requests or substitutions.

Our favorites at Oklahoma Joe's are the ribs, the beef, and the Carolina pulled pork. The best sides are the rub-seasoned fries (one order easily serves two) and the spicy coleslaw. The ribs are pull-off-the-bone tender (as opposed to fall-off-the-bone) and flavorful with the right kiss of smoke and seasonings. The brisket is lean, tender, and smoky—exactly as you'd want it if you were judging in a barbecue contest. The pulled pork is juicy, tender, and not overpowered by seasonings. The spicy coleslaw is a perfect complement. The chicken is moist, flavorful, and pleasingly crispy on the outside. The popular Z-Man Sandwich, barbecue beef garnished with an onion ring, provolone cheese, and barbecue sauce, is a faux fast-food novelty sandwich that has its fair share of fans. Locally brewed Boulevard Wheat Beer goes well with any of the Joe cuisine, as do the soft drinks, water, or iced tea.

Joy and Jeff also run a popular Oklahoma Joe's in Olathe, a suburb on the Kansas side of the KC metro area. Nestled in a busy shopping center, the decor is more upscale but echoes the home location with strategically placed corrugated roofing metal and walls adorned with barbecue contest memorabilia. The Olathe Joe's does feature a full-service bar.

Two essentials for success in Kansas City barbecue are outstanding brisket and ribs. Here's the secret to the outstanding ribs at Oklahoma Joe's.

SLAUGHTERHOUSE FIVE RIBS

Serves 4 to 8

2 tablespoons white cane sugar

1 tablespoon light brown sugar

2 tablespoons Hungarian paprika

2 tablespoons Lawry's Seasoned Salt

1½ teaspoons chili powder

1½ teaspoons ground cumin

1 teaspoon granulated onion

1 teaspoon white pepper

1 teaspoon finely ground black pepper

2 (2½-pound) slabs spareribs

In a small bowl, combine the sugars, paprika, seasoned salt, chili powder, cumin, onion, white pepper, and black pepper and blend well. You can do this ahead of time, cover, and store in a cool, dark place until ready to use.

To prepare the ribs, remove the membrane from the back of the slab and trim any excess fat. Season the slabs all over with all of the rub. Cover and let rest in the refrigerator for at least 2 hours or overnight.

Cook the ribs using the indirect method at 275°F. Jeff says that cooking the ribs at the higher temperature does two things: it renders the fat better, and you get more flavorful ribs. Cook the ribs for 5 to 6 hours, turning them every 2 hours.

The ribs are done when you can easily tear or pull two ribs apart.

Memphis-Style Barbecued Ribs

Jack's Bar-B-Que

416 Broadway
Nashville, TN 37203
615-254-5715
http://www.jacksbarbque.com

Jack Cawthon is known as the "Bar-B-Que King of Nashville," and he has earned the title. He has been in the barbecue business for 20 years, catering and running a succession of Nashville restaurants. There's a popular Jack's in Nashville's historic Talbot's Corner, but Jack started Jack's Bar-B-Que on the corner of Broadway and 1st Avenue in a tiny concrete block building. Jack later renovated the building and added a patio overlooking Riverfront Park and Broadway.

The Broadway location couldn't be better. It's a few doors down Broadway from Tootsies Orchid Lounge, the famous honky-tonk where legendary Grand Ole Opry stars lingered in the radio show's Ryman-based heyday. Like Tootsies, Jack's enjoys an unobstructed view across Ryman Alley to the arched, stone-and-brick stage entrance of Nashville's famous Ryman Auditorium. After decades of minimal use, the rejuvenated auditorium began hosting performances again. Jack spruced up a former loading zone behind his place, set out tables, and kept doing what he does well in the kitchen.

Customers lately have recognized Lyle Lovett, Emmylou Harris, Merle Haggard, Lorrie Morgan, Garrison Keillor, and many others among the luminaries dashing toward those venerable steps. But seeing the occasional country star among the flow of stagehands, backup bands, and hit-maker wannabes aren't the only attraction at Jack's Bar-B-Que. Jack also serves fine plates of smoked pork and beef brisket.

The food is good—basic, flavorful, filling. Variety counts, too. In his formative years as a barbecue connoisseur, Jack couldn't settle on one idea. So he studied techniques for smoking

Tennessee-style pork shoulders, Texas-style beef brisket, St. Louis–style dry ribs, and sausage and chicken treatments drawn from his travels in the Carolinas, Georgia, and Kentucky. If you get a table on the back patio, kick back and enjoy the show. There's no playbill. You watch whoever happens down the alley—just as Jack does.

Jack serves some of the finest barbecue ribs in the South. Here is Jack's recipe.

MEMPHIS-STYLE BARBECUED RIBS

Serves 4 to 6

HAND RUB

2 tablespoons salt

1 tablespoon sugar

1 tablespoon paprika

¼ cup chili powder

1 tablespoon cayenne

¼ cup black pepper

2¾ pounds Curly's (a.k.a. St. Louis) spareribs

Using hickory wood, preheat an enclosed pit with a flat rack to 250°F. In a small bowl, combine the hand rub ingredients and mix well. Generously rub the mixture into the ribs. Place the ribs in the pit and cook them for approximately 4 hours. After the ribs are done, wrap them to keep them tender until serving.

Hogmatism: **Specifically, the belief that pig barbecue— not beef, lamb, chicken, or other meats— is the only true barbecue. Generally, a set of rigid, narrow-minded beliefs about barbecue.**

Glazed Barbecued Ribs

North Main BBQ

403 N. Main
Euless, TX 76039
817-267-7821 or 817-283-0884
http://www.northmainbbq.com

Founded in 1981 by Hubert Green, Dollie Green, Ray Green, and Eddie Kelsey, North Main BBQ claims to be the "Home of the World's Best Ribs," backed by more than 27 years of barbecue experience. Paul has been enjoying North Main BBQ for over 18 years and will be going back whenever he's in the Dallas/Forth Worth area.

North Main BBQ serves an all-you-can-eat lunch and dinner buffet that includes it's award-winning ribs, chopped and sliced beef brisket, chicken breasts and quarters, pork shoulder, sausage, ranch beans, potato salad, and cole-slaw. The meats are slow-cooked with hickory smoke for 4 to 12 hours. If you want any drink other than iced tea, you'll have to BYOB.

In the early 1980s the Greens owned and operated a very successful trucking company, the Green Trucking Company. The trucks made early deliveries and returned by late morning or early afternoon on Fridays, and after that the employees would sit around and have a few Lone Stars and some iced tea, starting their Friday nights early and socializing. This went on for some time. Then one Friday Hubert decided to barbecue some ribs, which everybody enjoyed. This went on for a short time, and the group grew and grew. People they didn't know were invited by their friends, friends would chip in money for the ribs, and eventually it was getting, shall we say, out of hand, going from two slabs to two cases of ribs in a very short time. Figuring that this was a lot more fun than the trucking business, but not wanting to give up a good company, they started the restaurant and kept the trucking company rolling. Now it was work, but it was also fun, and it was making money. They ran both businesses for a while, but eventually the barbecue won out.

One night while sitting out back enjoying the shade, Hubert was asked, "If you get more successful, are you going to open on Sunday?" Hubert calmly said, "No, I'll probably close on Saturday or maybe close for lunches!" That was Hubert's original feeling, but he later reconsidered, saying they needed to take care of the people getting out of church on Sundays.

Anybody in the restaurant business who sees North Main's buffet would say the buffet is set up backward, with the meat first. And the Greens' answer to that is, "No, it isn't." It's set up to give their customers the best barbecue North Main has, and then people can have the salads and beans if they want. And that's one reason they have such good barbecue: the customer comes first and always will.

North Main's boast of having the world's best ribs might be true. We'll let you decide. You can order the real North Main Secret Spice through the Web site. The spice recipe here makes more than you'll need, but you can store leftover spice in an airtight container for up to 6 months. Here is our adaptation of the Greens' recipe.

GLAZED BARBECUED RIBS

Serves 6 to 8

SECRET SPICE

Makes about 1½ cups

½ cup sugar

¼ cup seasoned salt

¼ cup garlic salt

3 tablespoons chili powder

1 tablespoon paprika

1 tablespoon finely ground black pepper

1 teaspoon cayenne

2 slabs St. Louis–style spareribs

FINISHING MOP AND GLAZE

¼ cup ketchup

¼ cup yellow mustard

¼ to ⅓ cup distilled white vinegar

1 cup packed light brown sugar

To make the secret spice, combine all the ingredients in an airtight container and blend well. Store in a cool, dry place until ready to use or up to 6 months.

Preheat your smoker to 230°–250°F. Season the ribs all over to taste with the secret spice. You can store the rest of the secret spice for up to 6 months. Place in your smoker and cook for 4 to 6 hours, or until done.

While the ribs are smoking, make the finishing mop and glaze. Combine the ingredients in a small saucepan over medium heat, stirring occasionally, and simmer for 15 minutes. Remove from the heat and cool to room temperature.

In the last 10 minutes of cooking time, mop the ribs all over with the finishing sauce. Remove from the smoker and let rest for 15 to 30 minutes. Slice and serve.

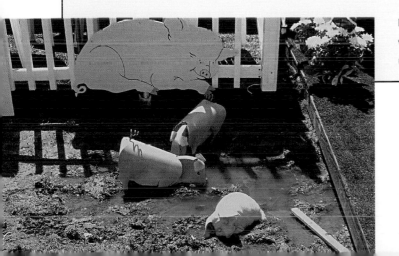

Rib Tips

Lem's Bar-B-Q House

311 E. 75th St.
Chicago, IL 60619
773-994-2428

Lem's and Barbara Ann's are the two best reasons we can think of for a trip to Chicago. Barbara Ann's links and Lem's rib tips with fries make a feast fit for royalty, and that's how you'll feel from first bite to last.

James Lemon, proprietor, has lived on Chicago's South Side since he moved from Mississippi in 1942. Later he joined his other brothers to help run the barbecue joint established by the oldest brother, Miles, a.k.a. "Lem," in 1951. The brothers had a history of barbecuing hogs in a homemade brick pit their father built in their hometown, Indianola. Today James is the only surviving brother, and we're thankful he is still running the business.

We're big fans of rib tips. There's no duplicating Lem's rib tips with "spicy gravy"—that's what Mother Lemon called her special barbecue sauce—but when you can't be in Chicago, we hope our rib tips and spicy sauce will provoke some good memories.

RIB TIPS

Serves 4 to 6

DRY RUB

¼ cup packed light brown sugar

2 tablespoons seasoned salt

1 tablespoon chili powder

2 teaspoons finely ground black pepper

1 teaspoon cayenne

1 teaspoon Old Bay seasoning

1 teaspoon rubbed sage

1 teaspoon onion powder

BARBECUE SAUCE

⅓ cup ketchup

¼ cup packed light brown sugar

2 tablespoons granulated sugar

2 tablespoons apple cider vinegar

1 tablespoon chili powder

1 teaspoon dry mustard

2 tablespoons Worcestershire sauce

1 teaspoon sea salt

1 teaspoon finely ground black pepper

½ teaspoon garlic powder

½ teaspoon ground celery seeds

4 pounds rib tips

To make the dry rub, combine the brown sugar, seasoned salt, chili powder, pepper, cayenne, Old Bay, sage, and onion powder and blend well. Store in an airtight container in a cool, dark place until ready to use, for up to 6 months.

To make the barbecue sauce, combine the ketchup, sugars, vinegar, chili powder, dry mustard, Worcestershire sauce, salt, pepper, garlic powder, and celery seeds in a saucepan over medium heat, stirring to dissolve all the sugars. Heat, stirring occasionally, for 30 minutes. Cool to room temperature.

Set up your smoker to cook indirectly at 250°F. Season the rib tips all over with the barbecue rub. Place on the smoker and barbecue for 4 to 5 hours, or until the ribs tear apart easily, basting with the sauce during the last 30 minutes of cooking.

Pigot:

An individual who is hogmatic, i.e., believes that the only true barbecue is pig barbecue; usually exhibits other hogmatic beliefs and behaviors.

Barbecue Pork Butt

17th Street Bar & Grill

32 N. 17th St.
Murphysboro, IL 62966
618-648-3722
http://www.17thstreetbarbecue.com

his is Mike Mills's home base and the birthplace of a barbecue dynasty. Mike's other barbecue joints are listed in the box on page 59. Mike is also the barbecue guru and partner in Blue Smoke Restaurant in New York City.

Mike is humbly known as "The Legend." We have no idea where that title came from, but we assume it was due to his great success in the Memphis in May World Championship Barbecue Cooking Contest. For 13 years he was the only person whose team won three times. His record was tied in 2006. Mike had said that if that happened he would come out of retirement and compete at Memphis in May again, but we think he has better sense than that. Mike is one of the most knowledgeable persons in barbecue, and he is not afraid to share his knowledge.

When Paul went to 17th Street, he was treated like a king (or a baron). Did that sway his critique? Not at all. Paul had some of Mike's outstanding ribs, brisket, chicken wings, and pulled pork. Then, while getting a tour of the kitchen, he saw a great meal being served, one he couldn't believe was intended for a single individual. Mike said, "That's what we call a 'pounder.'" Listed on the menu as a pound of pork shoulder, it's a pound-plus of pulled or

Is Barbecue Better Than Sex?

Ardie and his barbecue buddies Phil and Cheryl Litman were on the bank of the Mississippi at Apple City Smokers chewing on some of the best baby back ribs any of them had ever tasted. Julia Rose Sampson, a Judge's Chairperson at Memphis in May that year, was with them, and Mike Mills and Pat Burke gave her a few ribs to try hot off the smoker. She began moaning and groaning and said that the ribs were better then sex. Cheryl, with her quick wit, responded immediately,

"All depends who you're having sex with or whose barbecue you're eating."

chopped pork served with two side orders. Here Mike shares the recipe with us. You can order the Magic Dust from 17th Street's Web site.

BARBECUE PORK BUTT

Makes 15 to 18 good-size sandwiches

1 (5- to 8-pound) pork butt

½ cup 17th Street Bar & Grill Magic Dust (recipe follows) or your own rub

MOPPING SAUCE

2 cups apple cider vinegar

2 tablespoons dark brown sugar

1 tablespoon canola oil

1 tablespoon sea salt

1 tablespoon chili powder

1 teaspoon cayenne

GLAZE

1 cup Apple City Barbecue Sauce (recipe follows)

PULLED PORK FINISHING SAUCE (OPTIONAL)

½ cup Apple City Barbecue Sauce

¼ cup apple cider vinegar

1 to 2 tablespoons 17th Street Bar & Grill Magic Dust (recipe follows)

Pierce the pork butt all over with a dinner fork and season all over with the Magic Dust. Pierce it again to get the rub to penetrate, place the pork butt it in a pan, cover, and refrigerate for 4 hours or overnight.

Remove the meat from the refrigerator and let it come to room temperature, about an hour. Heat your smoker to 230°–250°F. Mike uses a combination of charcoal and apple wood, which gives the meat a sweeter taste. "Don't oversmoke the meat," cautions Mike. "Smoke should be an ingredient, not

an overwhelming taste." Place the pork butt, fat side up, in the smoker and cook it indirectly for 8 to 12 hours, or until the internal temperature of the meat reaches 165°–175°F on an instant-read thermometer if you're going to slice the meat, 185°–195°F if you're going to pull the meat.

Right after you put the meat in the smoker, make the mopping sauce. Place the vinegar, ½ cup of water, brown sugar, oil, salt, chili powder, and cayenne in a saucepan. Bring to a boil, stirring constantly to dissolve all the ingredients. Set aside to cool to room temperature.

After 1 to 1½ hours, start mopping the pork butt with the mopping sauce every 30 to 45 minutes, or as necessary. Turn and rotate the pork butt as necessary to avoid hot spots in your pit.

After 5 hours, check the internal temperature. The higher the internal temperature, the more tender the meat will be. When the internal temperature is where you want it for slicing, using a pastry brush to brush the pork butt with barbecue sauce and cook it for 10 to 15 minutes, repeating the process as many times as you like to glaze. Mike suggests only twice. Remove the pork butt from the smoker, place it on a cutting board, and let it rest, covered, for 15 to 20 minutes. Remove the bone and slice and serve with barbecue sauce on the side.

If you are going to pull or chop the pork butt, take it out of the smoker when the meat is in the higher temperature range, put it in a large pan, and let it rest, covered, for 15 to 20 minutes. Using heavy-duty dinner forks, pull the pork butt to shreds. Mix the finishing sauce ingredients and add half of this sauce to the pork. Blend it in, adding more as needed without overdoing it; you don't want the pork to be sloppy.

Make sandwiches with the sliced or pulled pork and finish with a swizzle of Apple City Barbecue Sauce or your favorite barbecue sauce.

Many thanks to Mike and Amy for sharing their recipes, which have been adapted and reprinted with permission from their book *Peace, Love, and Barbecue* (Rodale, © 2005 Mike Mills).

APPLE CITY BARBECUE SAUCE

Makes 3 cups

1 cup ketchup (they use Hunt's)

½ cup seasoned rice vinegar

½ cup apple juice or cider

¼ cup apple cider vinegar

½ cup packed brown sugar

¼ cup soy sauce or Worcestershire sauce

2 teaspoons prepared yellow mustard

¾ teaspoon garlic powder

¼ teaspoon ground white pepper

¼ teaspoon cayenne

⅓ cup bacon bits, ground in a spice grinder

½ cup grated onion

Combine the ketchup, rice vinegar, apple juice, cider vinegar, brown sugar, soy sauce, mustard, garlic powder, white pepper, cayenne, and bacon bits in a large saucepan. Bring to a boil over medium-high heat. Stir in the onion. Reduce the heat and simmer, uncovered, 10 to 15 minutes or until it thickens slightly. Stir often. Allow to cool, then pour into sterilized glass bottles. A glass jar that used to contain mayonnaise or juice works well. You can store the sauce in the refrigerator for up to 2 weeks.

VARIATION: To make this sauce a little hotter, add more cayenne to taste, approximately another ¼ to ½ teaspoon. Be careful; a little cayenne goes a long way.

MAGIC DUST®

Makes about 2½ cups

½ cup paprika

¼ cup kosher salt, finely ground

¼ cup sugar

2 tablespoons mustard powder

¼ cup chili powder

¼ cup ground cumin

2 tablespoons ground black pepper

¼ cup granulated garlic

2 tablespoons cayenne

Mix all ingredients and store in a tightly covered container. You'll want to keep some in a shaker next to the grill or stove. Keeps indefinitely but won't last long.

MIKE MILLS'S BARBECUE EMPIRE

17th Street Bar and Grill
32 N. 17th St.
Murphysboro, IL
618-684-3722

2700 17th Street
Marion, IL
618-998-1114

1711 W. Hwy. 50
O'Fallon, IL
618-622-1717

World Shooting & Recreational Center
One Main Event Lane
Sparta, IL
618-295-2754

Memphis Championship Barbecue
2250 East Warm Springs Rd.
Las Vegas, NV
702-260-6909

4379 Las Vegas Blvd. at Craig
Las Vegas, NV
702-664-0000

1401 South Rainbow Blvd.
Las Vegas, NV
702-254-0520

Barbecued Pork Steak with Chunky Applesauce

2801 Hwy. 49 North
Paragould, AR 72451
870-239-9758

Dave and Lynn Aronson started the Ironhorse Barbeque Co. in 1999, and it's a good example of what good food, good service, and great barbecue can do to build a business. Their slogan: Our butts are smokin' for you.

Dave is a meat cutter, so he knows good meat and knows how and where to buy. He cuts all his own meat, grinds the burger meat, and makes the burgers. All the meat is fresh at Ironhorse, never frozen.

The Ironhorse is a converted convenience store and gas station that is also Paragould's first and only motorcycle-themed restaurant. We sat down and asked to see Dave, and he came out and gave us the grand tour of his very clean kitchen. We told Dave we had heard great things about his pork steaks and asked to try one. In our barbecue travels, we had already had five meals that day, including four pig sandwiches, ribs and brisket, beans, and potato salad, so we were just going to taste his pork steak, not eat a whole one. Dave's staff generously brought out a slab of ribs and two pork steaks, with sides. We reluctantly sent one of the steaks back. We each tried a delicious rib and then cut a small portion of pork steak (which was tender enough for a plastic fork), and it was great. That was all we thought we could eat since we had one more place to taste, but we sat and talked barbecue for another 30 minutes, and we ended up picking at that pork steak until it was gone. It was that good! Here is Dave's recipe. He slices his own steaks from a nice square-cut pork butt, and he uses a Southern Pride smoker.

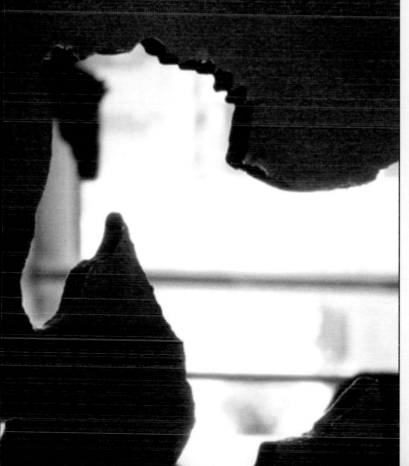

BARBECUED PORK STEAK WITH CHUNKY APPLESAUCE

Serves 1

8 (1-inch or ½-inch) pork steaks (as tender as a mother's love)

Barbecue rub of your choice

CHUNKY APPLESAUCE

2 tablespoons canola oil

8 tablespoons (1 stick) butter

3 or 4 Granny Smith apples, peeled and cut into ¼-inch slices

1 cup raisins

1½ cups packed light brown sugar

½ cup Captain Morgan's spiced rum

Season your steaks on both sides with the rub. If you're using Ironhorse's seasoning, it's not real salty, so be generous with it. Cover the seasoned steaks with plastic wrap and refrigerate overnight.

Preheat your smoker to 225°F. The steaks need to be cooked low and slow with moist heat. A 1-inch steak takes about 6 hours to cook, and a ½-inch steak takes about 4 hours. When the steaks come off the smoker, they should be so tender you can cut them with a plastic fork. Place the steaks in a cooler or plastic container with a lid for 30 minutes before serving to allow them to steam and tenderize further.

While the steaks are resting, make the applesauce by placing the oil and butter in a large skillet over medium heat. When the butter melts, add the apple slices and cook until soft, 10 to 15 minutes. Add the raisins, brown sugar, and rum and cook over low heat until you get a chunky sauce consistency, about 30 minutes. Serve on the side with the pork steaks or pour it over them.

Barbecued Pig Snoots

Smoki O's
1545 N. Broadway
St. Louis, MO 63102
314-621-8180

Smoki O's is a small barbecue joint just up from the football stadium area of St. Louis. In business for more than 11 years, Smoki O's seats only about 10 customers, but takeout is also available. The side dishes here are homemade—and good. Their specialty is a pig snoot and rib tips combo. Because Paul grew up eating pig snoot sandwiches, he favors the snoots sans rib tips. Ardie likes the combo, a perfect combination of tender pork rib meat with crunchy snoot.

We regret that Kansas City has no joints with pig snoots that compare to Smoki O's pig snoots. We (especially Paul) consider ourselves fortunate that there's one joint in KC that serves pig snoots, thanks to Ricardo Herrera, proprietor of the Tenderloin Grill on Southwest Boulevard, home of "Pig Snoot Heaven."

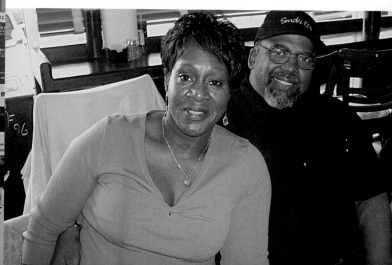

Although Ricardo doesn't serve barbecue, and his snoots are a world away from Smoki O's in cooking method, we like to go there for tenderloin sandwiches, burgers, and snoots. Ardie hasn't made it through a whole snoot sandwich yet, even after downing a shot of Pig's Nose Scotch first. Paul downs them with gusto reminiscent of a New Yorker eating clams or oysters on the half shell. Ardie says they taste like bacon fat with barnyard rub. When he gets to the whiskers, he stops and orders a tenderloin sandwich or a cheeseburger.

Smoki O's snoots are different in that Otis doesn't cook the nostril, and by the time the snoots are smoked to a crisp and soaked in warm barbecue sauce, there is no hint of fat or barnyard flavors. You also won't find any bristly whiskers. Otis cooks them whole, then breaks them up. Smoki O's barbecue sauce, served warm, is a tomato base with a mix of sweet and sour.

Paul first met Otis and Earline Walker in New York City at the Big Apple Barbecue Block Party, which is an invitational, charitable barbecue party put on by Danny Meyers, owner of several restaurants and a major restaurateur in New York City. One of his restaurants is Blue Smoke BBQ. The whole city is welcome to come to the block party and buy samples of barbecue from as many as 10 invited barbecue pitmasters from around the country. Paul was invited as the Kansas City Baron of Barbecue, cooking certified Angus brisket. This was the birth of RUB—Righteous Urban BBQ—but that's another story. Otis was invited for his barbecued snoots and rib tips, the best in St. Louis.

BARBECUED PIG SNOOTS

Makes 12

12 pig snoots

Barbecue sauce

First, wash the snoots well with cold water, then slice them with a very sharp knife into strips about 2 inches wide. Place the strips in a large pot of water, bring it to a boil over medium-high heat, and boil for about an hour. The water will develop a white foam or skin, but don't worry, that's the fat cooking out of them. After they hard boil for about an hour, rinse them off well with cold water.

Set up your grill to cook on low, direct heat (see page 206). If your grill will allow it, it's best to cook the snoots 12 to 14 inches from the coals. The snoots drip a lot of grease, and you have to watch them closely as they can flame up and be ruined in a brief moment if the coals are too close. If the coals are farther away, the flame-up just burns itself out without burning the snoots. If you can't keep the snoots far enough from the coals, just use a small amount of charcoal or briquettes to keep the heat low.

Grill the snoots, turning them often, until they crisp, 1½ to 2 hours. Don't put any sauce on them while they are cooking, but cover them with sauce as soon as you take them off the grill if they are to be eaten immediately. They keep well in the refrigerator and will immediately crisp up again if you don't put sauce on the ones you aren't eating immediately. Just take them out of the refrigerator and put them in the oven at 350°F for 15 to 20 minutes, uncovered. Top with sauce and serve.

Paul talked with Otis about his technique for smoking snoots. The recipe is above. When you want rib tips with your snoots, try the Lem's Rib Tips recipe on page 54.

Jamaican Jerk Hog Wings

Gordon's on the Green

**13500 Interurban Ave. South
Tukwila, WA 98168
206-267-7427
http://www.gordonsonthegreen.com**

Several years ago, while Paul was traveling with Bob Lyon, the power who created the Pacific Northwest BBQ Association (PNWBA), Bob told Paul, "Tonight we are going to have some of the best barbecue in the Pacific Northwest." That got Paul's attention. "Where?" he asked, as did Bob's wife, Sandra. "Gordy's Steak and BBQ Smokehouse in North Bend, Washington," Bob replied. They call it "a classy barbecue joint with great steaks." Gordy's was set on the edge of the fifth hole of the Cascade Golf Course, and it was indeed a classy barbecue joint. When Gordy's lease there expired, Gordon

and his wife, Kathy, chose to move and change the name to Gordon's on the Green, located adjacent to another golf course, the Foster Golf Links municipal golf course. Like Ted's in Minneapolis (page 124), Gordon's on the Green serves golfers and other hungry customers with cuisine worthy of a nineteenth hole, although the physical settings are very different.

In the starters chapter of this book you'll find a fantastic appetizer recipe from the old Gordy's Steak & BBQ Smokehouse, Volcanic Goat Cheese (page 16). Here's an unusual main dish from the new Gordon's on the Green. The pig wings are packaged ham shanks from Farmland, trimmed down to a single bone with meat and fat. Gordon's serves pig wings three ways—in a classic Hunter Sauce with mashed potatoes, glazed in a spicy bourbon barbecue sauce, or as Jamaican Jerk Hog Wings. Gordy says, "The one that works the best is the jerk we use as an appetizer in both the bar and the restaurant."

JAMAICAN JERK HOG WINGS

Serves 4 as a starter or 2 as an entrée

MARINADE

⅓ cup fresh lime juice

¼ cup dark rum

3 tablespoons firmly packed dark brown sugar

1 bunch scallions, both white and green parts, roughly chopped

4 cloves garlic, chopped

1 habanero or Scotch bonnet chile, stemmed, seeded, and minced, or 2 chiles if you want it hotter

1 tablespoon ground ginger

1 tablespoon ground allspice

¼ teaspoon pumpkin pie spice

4 pork shanks

FRESH FRUIT SALSA

1 cup diced watermelon

1 cup diced orange

1 cup diced pineapple

3 tablespoons chopped cilantro leaves, or more to taste

¼ cup diced red onion

¼ cup diced red pepper

¼ cup light rum, or more to taste

2 tablespoons lime juice

3 tablespoons vegetable oil

¼ cup dark rum

Put all the marinade ingredients in a food processor and pulse to make a slightly chunky sauce. Rub the jerk paste all over the pork shanks, cover, and refrigerate for 2 to 24 hours.

To make the fresh fruit salsa, combine all of the salsa ingredients in a medium bowl and mix well. Cover and refrigerate for 45 minutes to 1 hour before serving.

To prepare the wings, you can sauté or use the broiler. To sauté, heat the vegetable oil in a large skillet over high heat until very hot. Place the shanks in the oil, always at a safe distance to avoid burns. Cook for 4 minutes on each side, or until the shanks lift from the pan without sticking and have reached an internal temperature of 150°F on an instant-read thermometer, 3 to 5 minutes. Deglaze the pan by adding the dark rum to the pan and stirring it in with the drippings. Pour the sauce over the shanks and serve.

To broil, place on a cookie sheet lined with parchment paper or aluminum foil and broil until well browned on all sides, 3 to 5 minutes. Drizzle with a little rum and serve.

Old-Fashioned Southern Pit Barbecue

The Dixie Pig

701 N. Sixth St.
Blytheville, AR 72315
970-763-4636

There's more than one Dixie Pig around the country, but this is the best and has no ties to any of the others. Back in 1923, when they started serving their genuine Old-Fashioned Southern Pit Sandwich in Blytheville, they were a big hit. For many years, people visited the Dixie Pig to enjoy their barbecue, and the Dixie Pig built a reputation that spread far and wide. Today it's run by Buddy "Pops," and Wanda and Bob Halsell, and they are still very proud of that reputation and continue to serve the same quality sandwich that made the Dixie Pig so well known, or as we would argue, famous. Their slogan: "When you feel piggish, come to the Dixie Pig for the best of old southern-style barbecue."

They cook pork butts on an old-fashioned southern barbecue pit, which is usually a concrete block and/or brick pit, 30 inches high and anywhere from 6 feet to 10 or more feet long, with a lid. It's fueled with charcoal and cooks using the direct method. Buddy said that they don't use any seasoning on their pork butt, they just cook and turn them for anywhere from 8 to 12 hours, depending on the size of the butts.

Since we were pacing ourselves when we visited the Dixie Pig (we planned to visit six other places) we had a small pig sandwich, cut in half. It was chopped pork butt, topped with a slaw with Dixie Pig hot sauce on it. Paul can say without a doubt that that was some of the finest chopped pork he has ever put into his considerably large mouth. The slaw was lightly salted with vinegar on it, and the hot sauce had a slight sweet bite that complemented the meat. If you're anywhere near Blytheville and feeling piggish, don't forget the Dixie Pig.

This is a simple-looking recipe that might be a little challenging to execute, since it uses both the direct and indirect methods (page 199). You'll need a charcoal fire that is at least 30 inches from the cooking grate, and you'll need a lid, so a pit is ideal.

OLD-FASHIONED SOUTHERN PIT BARBECUE

Serves 24 to 30

2 (6- to 8-pound) pork butts

Hamburger buns, for serving

Coleslaw, for serving

Hot sauce, for serving

Prepare a medium-hot charcoal fire 30 inches from the grates. Place the butts, fat side up on the grill, cover, and cook for 1 hour and turn. Repeat every hour until the internal temperature of the meat reaches 180°F on a meat thermometer, 10 to 12 hours. Remove the meat from the pit. Remove the bone from the meat and place the butt on a cutting board. Use one or two French knives or cleavers to chop the pork into small pieces. Place some meat on half a hamburger bun, top with coleslaw and hot sauce, and serve.

BREAD IN THE 'CUE.S.A.

When we talk about "barbecue bread" or "Bunny bread" and you wonder, "What's that?!" here's the answer. A long-standing tradition in American barbecue joints is to serve cheap white mass-produced bread with the barbecue. It serves two purposes. It is cheaper than whole wheat or multigrain breads, and the spongy texture soaks up excess fat and sauce.

In some Texas barbecue joints you can tell the locals from the tourists by their bread of choice. Locals choose the unleavened saltine crackers instead of bread. They're cheap, but they don't soak up the juices and sauce like bread. Southern joints will serve you corn bread and/or hushpuppies, but your sandwich will be on cheap white bread.

Garlic bread is a good accompaniment to barbecue. Here's a good garlic cheese spread recipe:

GARLIC CHEESE SPREAD

2 cups grated Pecorino Romano

2 cups mayonnaise

2 tablespoons chopped parsley

2 heads roasted garlic

2½ tablespoons lemon juice

Pinch of cayenne pepper

Dash of hot red pepper sauce

Combine all ingredients and blend well. The spread is also good on baked potatoes.

BBQ Pig Salad

Short Sugar's Drive-In

1328 S. Scales St.
Reidsville, NC 26992
336-342-7487
http://shortsugarsbar-b-q.com

You expect good food when you step inside a place as busy as Short Sugar's. People from all over have stories to tell about eating at Short Sugar's from their childhood, teen, and adult years. Our barbecue buddies David Bailey and Carl Rothrock, who grew up in this area, had shared so many fond memories of Short Sugar's that we had to try it. We were lucky and got a booth right away.

The place is an old drive-in. On one end is counter service; booths and table service are on the other end. Busy staffers, diners visiting and having a good time, and the familiar chop-chop-chop is what you'll hear. We got so conditioned to that sound that our mouths watered every time we heard it, and of course we ordered a chopped pork sandwich with hushpuppies and slaw. Every bite was delicious!

BBQ PIG SALAD

Serves 2

1 (10-ounce) bag prewashed salad greens of your choice

2 cups pulled or chopped barbecued pork shoulder (page 191)

Salad dressing of your choice, homemade or store-bought

Put half the greens on each plate. Top with meat. Serve with dressings on the side.

We noticed that Short Sugar's, like many other barbecue joints, has a barbecue pig salad on the menu. B. B. Perrins in Decatur, Alabama, calls its barbecue pork salad "Pig in the Garden." We haven't tried either one yet, but in the interest of providing a public service to diet-conscious readers, here's a BBQ Pig Salad that's easy to make at home.

Barbecued Baloney

Mac's Barbeque

1030 W. Rogers Blvd.
Skiatook, OK 74070
918-396-4165

Some folks call barbecued baloney "Okie Steak." We've enjoyed some excellent barbecued baloney at Ozzies Bar & Grill on Monkey Island, Oklahoma, on the shore of the Grand Lake of the Cherokees. At Ozzies the King Kong of Hot Dogs is perfectly married to hickory smoke and Head Country Bar-B-Q Sauce. Starnes in Paducah, Kentucky (see page 70), also serves a great barbecued baloney sandwich. Matter of fact, hundreds of places in Oklahoma, Texas, Tennessee, Kansas City, and elsewhere serve barbecued baloney worth writing home about. Our favorite, however, is at Mac's in Skiatook.

We met Mike and Vickie McMillan, pitmaster/proprietors of Mac's Barbeque, on the barbecue contest trail several years ago. They won so many awards for their barbecue and sauce that they decided to open a barbecue joint. It's a small place, but they do a booming business, eat in or carry out, and they still manage to do some competing on the barbecue contest circuit.

All of Mac's barbecue is prize-winning quality—brisket, pork butt, ribs, and chicken. Mac's all-beef baloney stands above the crowd. Many places fry the baloney slices after smoking; Mac prefers it as it comes out of the smoker. If you can't make it to Skiatook (near Tulsa) soon, try barbecuing baloney at home. Here's how Mac does it.

BARBECUED BALONEY

Serves 6 to 8

1 (5-pound) stick all-beef baloney, cut in half lengthwise

Preheat your smoker to 225° to 250°F. Place the halved baloney in your smoker with no seasoning and smoke for about 1 to 2 hours, or until the outside is dark and crusty. Slice the baloney into 1/4-inch-thick slices and serve on a bun.

Pulled Pork Sandwich

Starnes BBQ

1008 Joe Clifton Dr.
Paducah, KY 42001
270-444-9555

If you think you'll be more likely to get a seat at the counter by waiting three hours past noon, don't count on it. The counter stools at Starnes get warm as soon as the doors open at 11:00 A.M., and most days they stay warm until closing time.

Starnes offers a no-frills menu: hickory-smoked pulled pork, mutton, baloney. No ribs. However, if you miss Starnes because they don't serve ribs, you've missed one of the best bar-becue restaurants on earth. Go to Paducah and eat at Starnes and we'll bet you a MoonPie that you'll agree.

Starnes is definitely not the product of chic food marketing experts. It looks like a textbook example of how not to package a restaurant. It is small. The pit and supply rooms are bigger than the dining room. It seats maybe twenty people on stools that line the U-shaped counter, and there's room for two in each of the two little booths that cap the ends of the U. The walls are cinder block, painted green; plate-glass windows don't offer a scenic view, except the park on the other side of Joe Clifton Drive. It hasn't changed its 1950s diner look since it opened in 1954, and the only idle days it has seen since then are Sundays and a few holidays. There's a hodgepodge of MoonPies, sauce, and snack foods filling shelves in the middle of the U, leaving enough space along the counter for the wait staff to serve your food and beverages. Formica countertop, linoleum tile floor, and a large framed gallery of past generations of Starnes proprietors lend atmosphere, but it's the food and the people that make it work. The wait staff and customers, mostly regulars and in-the-know travelers, give Starnes a friendly ambience that makes you feel welcome and glad to be there.

Sandwiches are served between two slices of white bread, toasted on one side. Inside, your order of pulled pork, mutton, ham, or sliced baloney will be slightly seasoned with a kiss of hickory smoke. The first time we ate at Starnes, the waitress asked if we wanted our sandwich "hot" or "mild." Mild was three shakes from the sauce bottle; hot was six shakes. The last time we ate there, the saucing was up to us. An abundance of the delicious hot tomato/vinegar/pepper sauce is within reach of all the customers, where they can shake it on as they wish. Ardie takes several bottles home and uses it on a variety of foods in addition to barbecue.

PULLED PORK SANDWICH

Serves 1

2 slices white sandwich bread

1 cup hickory-smoked tender moist pulled pork shoulder (page 191)

Starnes Bar-B-Q Sauce as desired

Put the bread on a lightly greased hot grill or cast-iron skillet until lightly toasted on one side, less than 1 minute. Place one slice of bread, toasted side down, on a plate. Top the bread with meat. Add the other slice of bread, toasted side up. Press down firmly on the sandwich, then slice in half diagonally. Serve with sauce on the side.

Starnes barbecue is also sold downtown near the river at D Starnes at 108 Broadway. It has a separate owner and features some menu items not served at the original Starnes, such as soups, corn muffins, vinegar slaw, baked beans, and coconut cream pie, but the meat and sauce come from the original Starnes. It is also more roomy, with counter and booth space to accommodate tourists and *Delta Queen* stopovers.

Even if you're dead set on getting ribs at a barbecue joint, give Starnes a try. After eating a Starnes sandwich, we think you'll exclaim, "No ribs? No problem!"

Pig in a Puppy

Kings Restaurant

405 E. New Bern Rd.
Kinston, NC 28504
800-332-6465
http://www.kingsbbq.com

Wilbur King, Jr., a true southern gentleman, family man, and Civil War buff, has a barbecue pedigree that is second to none. The King legacy began in the 1850s, when R.W. King opened a country store in Kinston. The country store tradition continued with R.W.'s son, Richard, whose son, Frank, opened a store in 1936 that became Kings Restaurant.

Our favorite swine dining experience at Kings is a cup of Brunswick stew appetizer, followed with a Pig in a Puppy and cold, sweet iced tea. There are times when you want wine or beer with your puppy, and you can get that at Kings as well. You can order a hog heavenly feast from Kings, delivered fast and easy via the Carolina Oink Express. Get the works in a Pig Out Party Pack, or smaller portions of chopped pork, sausage, country ham, center sliced ham, chitlins, collard greens, black-eyed peas, hushpuppies, delicious Brunswick stew, coleslaw, potato salad, pecan, apple, chocolate chip, or sweet potato pie, and—most important for making your own Pig in a Puppy—Kings own hushpuppy mix and the famous sauce we have savored for years, King's Delight BBQ Sauce. The sauce is classic eastern North Carolina vinegar with some signature ingredients that make it stand above the crowd. We like it on everything short of ice cream! If you can't make it to Kings, you can call their toll-free line or order online.

How did Wilbur King, Jr., get the idea for the Pig in a Puppy? He told us that one day when business was slow in the restaurant (had to be between lunch and dinner, as Kings is a popular, busy restaurant), he was messing around in the kitchen. He dropped some hushpuppy mix in the shape of a hot dog bun into the deep-fryer and fried it until crisp and golden on the outside. When he removed it and let it cool a bit, he sliced it in half. Some of the mix was uncooked and soft, so he scooped it out and filled the cavity with chopped pork, sauce, and coleslaw. The Pig in a Puppy was born!

Wilbur mixes large amounts for the hungry crowd at Kings, and it's hard to put an exact formula on this because the cornmeal mix varies depending on the corn crop and what company makes it. Wilbur uses a white corn hushpuppy mix from Lakeside Mills, and you can order it from Oink Express. Thanks to Wilbur, inventor of the Pig in a Puppy, here's a home version recipe.

PIG IN A PUPPY

Makes 4

HUSHPUPPY BATTER

2 cups self-rising white cornmeal

1 medium onion, minced

1 teaspoon salt

1 teaspoon finely ground black pepper

1 large egg, beaten

¾ cup milk or buttermilk

Canola, peanut, or vegetable oil, for deep-frying

1 cup chopped barbecue pork (page 191)

½ cup King's Delight BBQ Sauce

1 cup coleslaw (see recipes in chapter 3)

To make the hushpuppy batter, mix the cornmeal mix, onion, salt, and pepper together in a large bowl until well combined. Stir in the egg and milk or buttermilk to form a thick, moist batter. Let the batter rest for 30 to 45 minutes to allow the self-rising mix to work.

Fill your deep-fryer with enough oil for the hushpuppies to float and heat the oil to 350°F (or use a deep pot and measure the oil temperature with a deep-frying thermometer). If you'd rather make traditional hushpuppies, use a teaspoon or scoop to drop batter by teaspoons into the oil. Fry until the puppies turn golden brown and float to the top, turning the puppies once so that they brown evenly on both sides. Drain on paper towels.

For pigs in a puppy, mold a large piece of batter into a round ball, lay the ball in one palm, and use your other hand to gently flatten the ball into a thin oblong shape (think flat football) the size of a hot dog bun. Dampen your free hand and move the batter to the dampened hand so it will slide off the dampened hand into the oil. Move your hand as close to the oil as is safe and let the puppy slide off into the hot oil. Cook for about 4 minutes, or until the outside is crisp and golden, turning the puppy once for more even browning. Remove from the fryer, drain, and let cool.

When the puppy is cool, slice it in half. If it didn't cook completely through, you may want to scoop out some of the doughy part and discard it. Fill the puppy with chopped pork, sprinkle with sauce, top with coleslaw, sandwich it, and serve. It's a delicious plate of "Southern Goodness" that you'll not soon forget!

Barbecue Hash

Maurice's Gourmet Barbeque

1600 Charleston Hwy. West
West Columbia, SC 29169
800-MAURICE (628-7423) (to order)

Maurice Bessinger's legendary Piggie Park Barbeque is known worldwide. The recipe for his Gourmet Blend BBQ Sauce was given to him by his father. Maurice also learned cooking and restaurant management from his father. According to the company story, it took Maurice 55 years to build the Piggie Park chain and the Flying Pig Express into the "largest barbeque operation in the country."

The original Piggie Park sports a huge Confederate battle flag on a pole in the parking lot. Inside, in addition to great food and friendly service, you'll find religious and political pamphlets and a book written by Maurice, *Defending My Heritage*.

On the walls you'll see framed photos of Maurice with famous dignitaries and entertainers. If Maurice got the same admonition from his parents that we did—"Never discuss politics or religion with friends or strangers"—he didn't heed it. Fortunately our parents didn't forbid eating barbecue where the owner's views on politics and religion are freely dispensed!

When you sit down to enjoy a pulled pork sandwich or a slab of ribs with Carolina Gold

BBQ Sauce, your mind won't be on politics or religion, just good food. The mustard-based sauce is said to have been inspired by a reference to mustard seed in a biblical passage.

A dish the Piggie Park is famous for and that's found all over South Carolina is barbecue hash. Here's our recipe.

BARBECUE HASH

Serves 6 to 8

2 pounds barbecued pork shoulder (page 191)

¼ cup white vinegar

2 tablespoons packed light brown sugar

1 tablespoon rubbed sage

2 teaspoons ground ginger

1 cup diced onion

8 tablespoons (1 stick) unsalted butter

Salt and black pepper

Cooked rice for serving

Cube the meat and place it in a heavy cast-iron pot or a Dutch oven with enough water to cover. Add the vinegar, brown sugar, sage, and ginger. Simmer over medium-low heat until the meat falls apart, about 1½ hours, adding water as needed. Transfer the meat to another pan, add the onion to the pot, and bring to a gentle boil. When the meat is cool enough, remove and discard any connective tissue, veins, bone fragments, etc., and pull the meat into small bits. Return the meat to the pot and add the butter. Continue stirring and cooking to combine the meat and onion. Season with salt and pepper to taste. Serve over rice.

Pit Ham

Clark's Outpost BBQ

**101 N. Hwy. 377
Tioga, TX 76271
800-932-5051 or 940- 437-2414
http://www.clarksoutpost.com**

lark's Outpost was founded by Warren Clark in 1974. It's known for genuine slow-smoked Texas barbecue. Barbecue historian Dr. Howard Taylor (above) told us we had to stop at Clark's Outpost, and we're glad he insisted. The main thing that got Paul's attention was the smoked ham—something dear to his heart and that most barbecue joints don't do. He prefers the good old bone-in cured ham but will take a PIT ham (one that is *p*artially *i*nternally *t*rimmed) next.

Clark's has some of the best ham in the universe, and it's really easy to do. It just takes a lot of patience. Here's how Clark's does it.

PIT HAM

1 (12- to 14-pound) PIT ham

Prepare a hickory fire in your smoker and heat it to 190°F. Place the ham in the smoker and smoke it for 18 hours. Let rest for 30 minutes; then slice and serve.

Hash on Rice with Carolina Coleslaw

Melvin's Legendary Bar-B-Que

538 Folly Rd.
Charleston, SC 29412
888-MELVINS (635-8467) or 843-762-0511
http://www.melvinsbbq.com

 elvin Bessinger of Charleston, South Carolina, is the elder brother of Maurice Bessinger of West Columbia, South Carolina (see page 74). Each has attained fame in his own right for many years of selling millions of pounds of tender pork barbecue with a mustard-based sauce to a barbecue consumer public that keeps coming back. We won't take sides. We like both!

The South Carolina Bessinger barbecue legacy began with Melvin and Maurice's father, Big Joe Bessinger. Big Joe was born in 1891 in Orangeburg, South Carolina. His lifelong career was in farming, but his legacy was the barbecue sauce he invented and the interest in the barbecue restaurant industry that he inspired in his sons. Big Joe invented a mustard-based barbecue sauce in 1933. He called it the Golden Secret Recipe BBQ Sauce. Melvin, age 10 at the time, learned the secret recipe from Big Joe. Big Joe opened the Holly Hill Café in 1939 and later the Eat at Joe's café with Melvin when Melvin came home from World War II.

Melvin Bessinger's impressive restaurant career portfolio includes not only founding Eat at Joe's with his dad but also founding Piggy Park Drive-Ins, Bessinger's BBQ & Burgers, and Melvin's Legendary Bar-B-Que. Melvin retired to the family farm after 71 years in the restaurant business, but his two Melvin's Bar-B-Que restaurants are still going strong, serving barbecued Carolina pork hams, pork ribs, and smoked chicken—all with the famous Golden Secret Recipe BBQ Sauce. The menu also includes much-acclaimed burgers, onion rings, hash on rice, collard greens, lima beans, fried okra, mac and cheese, corn on the cob, baked beans, sweet potato soufflé, and fries.

If you hanker for a taste of Melvin's barbecue, you can order ribs, pulled pork, chicken, and a variety of mustard-based sauces online. We recommend starting with the original 1933 Golden Secret Recipe BBQ Sauce before trying the newer varieties. You can barbecue your own fresh ham until tender enough to be pulled by hand and then serve it with Melvin's original sauce. Save enough for making hash on rice, a South Carolina tradition. We don't have Melvin's secret recipe, but we think you'll like our version here, and we threw in a recipe for homemade Carolina coleslaw to go with it.

HASH ON RICE

Serves 6

1 medium sweet onion, minced

2 tablespoons canola oil

4 pounds barbecued fresh ham, chopped

Black pepper and salt

2 cups mustard-based barbecue sauce

4 medium russet potatoes, peeled and chopped

2 cups long-grain white rice, cooked according to package instructions

In a large soup pot over medium heat, sauté the onion in the oil until soft, 3 to 5 minutes. Add the meat and pepper and salt to taste; stir the meat with the onion until mixed. Sauté for 6 minutes. Add 2 cups of water and the barbecue sauce and bring to a boil; then turn the heat down to low and simmer for 10 minutes. Add the potatoes and simmer until tender, 15 to 20 minutes. Serve over hot long-grain rice.

CAROLINA COLESLAW

Serves 10 to 12

1 large head green cabbage (about 3 pounds), shredded

3 to 4 celery ribs, diced

1 medium Spanish onion, diced

1 small green bell pepper, seeded and diced

3 medium carrots, grated

2 cups white cane sugar

½ cup white vinegar

½ cup apple cider vinegar

½ cup olive oil

1 teaspoon celery seeds

1 teaspoon kosher salt

In a large bowl, combine all of the vegetables and mix in the sugar. Set aside. Combine the vinegars, olive oil, celery seeds, and salt in a medium saucepan, bring to a boil, and pour over the cabbage mixture. Toss to coat all the ingredients. Cover and chill overnight before serving.

Greetings from American Royal Kansas City, Mo.

Loaded Pork-Stuffed Potato

Curtis's BBQ

40 Old Depot Rd.
Putney, VT 05346
802-387-5474
http://www.curtisbbqvt.com

You have to admire Curtis Tuff. There he is, a barbecue pitmaster in rural Vermont, where New England cuisine runs more along the lines of fresh baked bread from King Arthur Mills, dairy fresh butters and cheeses, including the world's best goat cheese, Grade A Vermont Maple Syrup, fresh micro brews from Harpoon, Long Trail, Magic Hat, Otter Creek, Rock Art, or Trout River, plus fabulous fresh seafood from the nearby coastal waters of Maine.

There is reason to believe, however, that barbecue is indigenous to Vermont and other New England states. Some think Native Americans in the area engaged in some form of barbecue cooking prior to the arrival and settlement of Europeans. Be that as it may, Curtis Tuff certainly deserves credit for his key role in introducing modern-day New Englanders to real barbecue over the past four decades. His customers rave about the quality of Curtis's ribs, chicken, sauce, stuffed potatoes, potato salad, coleslaw, macaroni, baked beans, sweet yams, corn on the cob, corn muffins, and homemade root beer.

Christine Tuff, co-owner of Curtis's BBQ, and Curtis's wife, also plays a key role in the success of the restaurant. Curtis and Christine's daughter, Sarah, and son-in-law, Chris Parker, run a second Curtis's BBQ in Chester, Vermont. They learned the cooking techniques, recipes, and business from Curtis and Christine. For a masterly online introduction to Curtis and his cuisine, go to our barbecue buddy Mark Dolan's Barbecue Pilgrim Web site and click on the Curtis stories: www.bbqpilgrim.com.

Chris Parker told us the story of how Christine Tuff invented their popular stuffed potatoes: "According to Christine, it started as a way to use up the meat that fell off the rib bones and was not usable for much else. So she tried it as a snack and thought that she had struck gold, and some 20 years later we can't make these fast enough to keep up with the demand."

LOADED PORK-STUFFED POTATO

Makes 1 potato

1 (9-ounce) Idaho baking potato

Pat of butter (optional)

6 ounces chopped barbecued pork (page 191)

3 ounces Vermont cheddar cheese

2 tablespoons sour cream

1 tablespoon bacon bits

¼ cup sliced mushrooms, or more to taste

Curtis' own award-winning Southern Style Bar-B-Q Sauce (we like the Spicy)

1 tablespoon dried chives

Using hardwood, such as hard maple or oak, preheat the grill to 250°F. Grill the potato for about 1 hour over indirect heat, or until it is soft when you squeeze it. Remove the potato from the grill, cut the potato open, and add the pat of butter. Fill the potato with the chopped pork, then top with the cheese, sour cream, bacon bits, mushrooms, barbecue sauce to taste, and chives. Grab a fork and maybe a friend, because you may need help eating all of this!

Bar-B-Q Spaghetti

The Bar-B-Q Shop

1782 Madison Ave.
Memphis, TN 38104
877-DSAUCES (372-8237)
or 901-272-1277
http://www.dancingpigs.com

From the atmosphere to the friendly service and the outstanding food, the Bar-B-Q Shop is a place that makes you feel good. No wonder it's a Memphis favorite! Dark red walls, lots of wood, and subdued but sufficient lighting give the place a warm, inviting feel. If you're faced with a wait, and you're starving, see if there is a place for you at the bar. The last time we were there that's exactly what we did, and it was our honor to be served by Mrs. Hazelteen Vernon

herself—a kind, strong, beautiful, and dignified lady. Competence, friendliness, and dedication to serving customers with care must run in the family, because Frank and Eric Vernon are the same way.

Once you've dined at the Bar-B-Q Shop, you'll be back. Graze your way through the menu. Ribs come wet or dry. Try both. The pork sandwiches are some of the best we've ever eaten. Get barbecued beans on the side. You'll order those beans at each visit! And you have to try the Bar-B-Q Spaghetti, a Memphis classic. Although the recipe here is available online from the Bar-B-Q Shop, it's a must-have dish for any book about American barbecue. Bobby Flay also featured this recipe on a Food Network show on barbecue specialties. Since we're so partial to the way the Vernon family cooks and serves this dish, here's the recipe.

BAR-B-Q SPAGHETTI

Serves 6 to 8

1 cup chopped onion

¾ cup chopped green bell pepper

1 pint Dancing Pigs Original Bar-B-Q Sauce

1 cup sugar

2 tablespoons Liquid Smoke

½ cup cooking oil

Pinch of salt

1 pound spaghetti, prepared according to package directions, rinsed, and drained

Chopped barbecued pork shoulder, for serving (page 191)

In a large skillet, combine the onion, green pepper, barbecue sauce, sugar, liquid smoke, oil, and salt. Cook for 30 minutes, stirring occasionally. Pour the sauce over the cooked spaghetti and stir. Top with pork shoulder and serve hot.

WHERE ARE THE BARBECUE POLICE?

Kansas City artist and cartoonist Charlie Podrebarac has created many classic "Cowtown" cartoons with a barbecue theme. One of our favorites is titled "Most Cowtowners Travel Well. Others......" Pictured is a backyard cook, dressed in chef gear, standing at a grill. There are two hot dogs on the grill and one hot dog skewered on a grill fork. The chef is holding the skewered dog upward. He says, "Who wants some Bar-B-Q?" The "other" Cowtowner, dressed in red with "K.C." on his chest and a righteous scowl on his face, is pointing at the hot dog. He says, "If I want 'Barbecue,' I'll go to Kansas City and order some. That, sir, is a grilled wiener!"

Some people hold to strict differences between barbecuing and grilling. Barbecue is slow and low. Grilling is hot and fast. We accept and understand the difference, but backyard cooking is as American as apple pie. If some Americans want to call a backyard hot dog party or a hamburger or steak party a *barbecue*—gas grill or charcoal grill—we're OK with that. The accepted term has evolved from *cookout* to *barbecue*.

The U.S. government, on the other hand, has defined barbecue in a way that leaves no room for grillers or cooking with gas.

Here's the government definition:

Barbecued meats, such as product labeled "Beef Barbecue" or "Barbecued Pork," shall be cooked by the direct action of dry heat resulting from the burning of hard wood or the hot coals therefrom for a sufficient period to assume the usual characteristics of a barbecued article, which include the formation of a brown crust on the surface and the rendering of surface fat. The product may be basted with a sauce during the cooking process. The weight of barbecued meat shall not exceed 70 percent of the weight of the fresh uncooked meat.*

It is our understanding that federal regulations are, in effect, laws. If this is so, the federal government is not enforcing the law as it applies to barbecue. There are restaurants, for example, that label any item with barbecue sauce on it "barbecue": pizza, burgers, oven-baked ribs or beef or chicken, slathered with barbecue sauce and sold as barbecue. Where are the Barbecue Police? We have yet to see or hear of any. We hope we never read a newspaper headline that reads like this: "Local man arrested in backyard by FBI. Grilled burgers and called them 'barbecue.'"

*Code of Federal Regulations, Title 9, Chapter III, Part 319, Subpart C, Section 319.80, revised: 1/1/1985

Smoked Garlic Sausage

Meyer's Elgin Smokehouse

188 Hwy. 290
Elgin, TX 78621
800-MRS-OINK (677-6465)
or 512-281-3331
http://www.cuetopiatexas.com

eyer's is billed as "The Capital of 'Cue-Topia, Texas," which, according to R. G. Meyer, is "the perfect state of barbecue." A strong case can be made for naming the Elgin/ Lockhart area a barbecue capital. Although we have our favorites, you can't go wrong in your search for great barbecue in this legendary section of lower central Texas.

Our good barbecue buddy John Raven told us that for a Texas commercial product today he likes Meyer's sausage out of Elgin. John keeps some Meyer's hot sauce in his cupboard, too, just waiting for the right moment.

We didn't even try to get an original sausage recipe from Meyer's or any other sausage kings in Elgin. Although the recipe we're sharing with you makes darned good sausage, the easiest way to get a taste of true Texas smokehouse sausage is to go to Elgin in person or online. Make sure you allow enough time to prepare the casings the night before.

SMOKED GARLIC SAUSAGE

Serves 12 to 24

4 yards hog casings

Apple cider vinegar

4 pounds pork butt with fat

2 pounds boneless beef chuck or round with fat

1 large onion, minced

6 cloves garlic, minced

2 tablespoons minced fresh sage

1 tablespoon salt

1 tablespoon black pepper

2 tablespoons crushed red pepper

1 teaspoon cayenne

Vegetable oil

The day before you plan to stuff the sausage, rinse the sausage casings inside and out under cold water. Prepare a solution of 1 cup water to 1 capful of cider vinegar. Soak the casings in the solution overnight.

In a meat grinder, coarsely grind the meats and place in a large bowl. Thoroughly mix in the onion, garlic, sage, salt, black pepper, red pepper flakes, and cayenne. Refrigerate overnight. Stuff the casings to 1 inch thick and 5 inches long and tie off. They can be refrigerated for 3 days or frozen for 6 months at this point.

Prepare a smoker with oak or mesquite and preheat to 225°F. Rub the sausages with just a little vegetable oil. Don't overdo it or they'll get messy and then turn to mush. Smoke the sausages for 2 hours, or until the skin looks ready to pop.

Beef PB (Polish Boy) Deluxe

Mt. Pleasant BBQ

12825 Kinsman
Cleveland, OH 44120
216-561-8722

Our friend and barbecue buddy Jeff Sanders of Des Plaines, Illinois, told us about Mt. Pleasant BBQ. Jeff is the inventor and CEO of Roadhouse Bar-B-Que Sauces, Inc., and every sauce he makes is on our faves list. He found Mt. Pleasant BBQ while promoting his sauces one fine day in Cleveland.

Before we found out about Mt. Pleasant BBQ, we thought Cleveland was mostly a rock and-roll rib burner town—home of the Rock and Roll Hall of Fame and Museum and site of the annual Memorial Day weekend Great American Rib Cook-Off & Music Festival. Thanks to Wayne Whitmore and "BuddyRoadhouse," Jeff's handle on the Roadfood.com forum, we've added "great barbecue" to what we think about Cleveland.

Jeff, knowing that we're regulars at Arthur Bryant's, told us that "Mt. Pleasant BBQ is a classic in terms of location and ambience." He went on to say, "The interior makes Arthur Bryant's look like a four-star restaurant in Paris!" That's just the kind of environment we like! You go to Mt. Pleasant BBQ for the food—barbecued ribs, pulled pork sandwiches, fresh-cut skin-on fries, mac and cheese, collard greens, and barbecue beans. If you're not hungry for barbecue (imagine that!), Wayne also has fried fish and fried chicken on the menu. But we agree with Jeff that what brings down the house is Mt. Pleasant's Beef PB (Polish Boy) Deluxe! As Jeff says, it's "an unholy mess that is pure pleasure to eat!" We put together a home version, but the best place to get a Mt. Pleasant BBQ PB Deluxe is to buy one from proprietor Wayne Whitmore.

BBQ PB (POLISH BOY) DELUXE

Serves 1

½ cup barbecue sauce

1 clove pressed garlic

1 (6-ounce) beef kielbasa

1 standard hot dog bun

1 cup barbecued pulled pork butt (page 57)

1 cup creamy coleslaw (page 139)

1 handful fresh-cut fries (page 126)

Combine the barbecue sauce and pressed garlic. Cover and refrigerate overnight.

Lightly oil your grill rack and prepare a charcoal grill for direct-heat cooking over medium-hot coals. Grill the kielbasa, turning once, until sizzling and grill marks appear, about 4 minutes. On a dinner plate, put the kielbasa in the bun; add pulled pork; top with coleslaw and then fries. Sprinkle sauce on to taste. Enjoy the messy feast!

Smoked Hot Links

Barbara Ann's Bar-B-Que & Motel
7617 S. Cottage Grove Ave.
Chicago, IL 60619
773-651-5300

We couldn't stop ourselves from humming the tune to "Third Rate Romance (Low Rent Rendezvous)" when we saw this 'cue joint/motel combo. It's not exactly the kind of place where you expect to find good eats, but the food at Barbara Ann's Bar-B-Que & Motel doesn't disappoint. While the joint is known especially for its Chicago smoked links with regular/hot mixed sauce, the rib tips, ribs, and chicken are customer favorites, too. Barbara Ann doesn't eat pork, so she added turkey links to the menu for herself and like-minded customers and those who want a change from chicken. Jumbo shrimp, catfish, and fries are also on the menu. This is a carryout only joint, so think ahead about where you'll eat your links feast from Barbara Ann's.

When Delars Bracy decided to open a barbecue joint and motel on Chicago's South Side in 1967, he named it after his daughter, Barbara Ann Bracy. Delars settled in Chicago by way of Ruleville, Mississippi, his hometown, and Los Angeles, his college town. He started a family in Chicago after discovering that Bertie, his hometown sweetheart, was also in Chicago. The barbecue joint and motel came later, after Delars had finished a successful career as a criminal defense attorney. Some of his brothers who lived in Chicago helped Delars run the carryout joint in the early years. Now Barbara Ann is in charge, and—other than adding turkey links and chicken to the menu—she runs it just the way her dad and uncles ran it.

Due to flecks of sage in the seasoning, Barbara Ann's links are compared to breakfast sausage. We like them any time of day or night, especially with a mix of her regular and hot sauce. If you're using sausage casings, make sure you allow enough time to soak them overnight before stuffing them.

SMOKED HOT LINKS

Serves 6

9 feet sausage casings (optional)

Apple cider vinegar (optional)

5 pounds pork butt, coarsely ground twice or medium once

2 tablespoons granulated garlic

1 to 2 tablespoons rubbed sage

1 tablespoon dried parsley

1 tablespoon sea salt

2 teaspoons fennel seeds, cracked

1 teaspoon dried oregano leaves

1 teaspoon dried thyme leaves

1 teaspoon black pepper

½ to 1 teaspoon cayenne

1 cup ice water, if needed

Barbecue sauce

Hot sauce (such as Louisiana Hot Sauce or Texas Pete)

If you're using sausage casings, the day before you plan to stuff the sausage, rinse the casings under cold water inside and out. Prepare a solution of 1 cup water to 1 capful of cider vinegar. Soak the casings in the solution overnight.

In a large bowl, mix the pork with the garlic, sage, parsley, salt, fennel, oregano, thyme, pepper, and cayenne. Stir. If using casings, mix in the ice water if the meat mixture is too dry to stuff into the casings.

Stuff the sausage mixture into the casings or make into loaves, sticks, or patties. If you're making sticks, links, or logs, it helps to use plastic wrap to form the meat into the desired shape. Hang stuffed casings for at least an hour in a cool, dry place and then refrigerate at least overnight but for no more than 5 days before using. Sticks, links, or logs can be cooked immediately.

You can fry, smoke, or grill the sausage as desired.

Barbecued Whole Hog

The Pit

328 W. Davie St.
Raleigh, NC 27601
919-890-4500
http://www.thepit-raleigh.com

We haven't visited Ed Mitchell's new place in Raleigh yet, but we've eaten his hickory-smoked barbecued whole hog on several occasions, and it has always been some of the finest hog we've ever tasted. Paul and Ed became instant buddies when they first met at the Big Apple Barbecue Block Party in New York City several years ago. When Ed brought his rolling pit to Oxford, Mississippi, for a barbecue symposium sponsored by the Southern Foodways Alliance, his whole hogs were picked to the bone. We did our share of the picking.

At the Pit, Ed has teamed up with Chef Jaimy Waters, who is known for creative dishes made from fresh, local ingredients. Ed himself is a leading advocate of free-range hogs raised without growth hormones and antibiotics. He has spent the past several years making arrangements with North Carolina pig farmers to raise heritage breeds for a steady supply of quality hogs for North Carolina barbecue.

Ed Mitchell's barbecue pits are 74 inches long and about 6 feet wide and are made with fire brick on the inside, decorative brick on the outside. His mobile pits are a little smaller, at 66 inches long, 60 inches wide, and 26 inches tall.

When we heard that the Pit is a white-tablecloth restaurant, it gave us pause. Does Ed still wear his signature overalls, we wondered, or a tuxedo? No surprise to us, Ed would never give up his overalls.

Our friend John T. Edge, executive director of the Southern Foodways Alliance, has paid a visit to the Pit. His favorite dish is the chopped whole hog accented with Ed's vinegar and pepper sauce. He also likes the Brunswick stew and the Brussels sprout halves blackened in a skillet and tossed with a small portion of prepared mustard. We've heard that the fried chicken, prepared from Ed's mother's recipe, rivals one of our other favorites, Gus's in Mason, Tennessee.

Besides John T's kudos for the Pit, we asked our friends at Ford's Foods in Raleigh, Sandi, Patrick, and Lynn Ford, to check out the Pit for us and take some pictures. They raved about Ed's whole hog and all the sides. We're sure they were too polite to sneak in some of their own classic Bone Suckin' Sauce (one of our favorite barbecue sauces), but it must have been tempting. There were no complaints about Ed's sauce, however.

What will happen to the former restaurant in Wilson where Ed gained his fame? Leave it to Ed to make sure it's put to good use. He's founding a cooking school there, dedicated to teaching and preserving the art and science of cooking hickory-smoked whole hogs and other southern delicacies. Our hats are off to you, Ed. Way to go!

Here's what Ed shared with us about the proper way to barbecue a whole hog. You can get a dressed and butterflied or split hog from a butcher or hog supplier.

BARBECUED WHOLE HOG

Serves 90 to 100

1 (150-pound) dressed hog, butterflied or split

Salt and black pepper

1 gallon Ed's Pepper Vinegar Sauce

Open the pit and take out the grate. Bank about 40 pounds of charcoal around the inside walls of the pit in a big circle. Pour two large chimneys of hot coals around the outside of the charcoal ring. Preheat the pit to about 250°F.

Trim any excess fat from the inside of the hog and season the inside all over with salt and pepper. Put the grate back over the charcoal and top with the hog, close the lid, and cook overnight. With a meat thermometer, check the temperature of the hog in the hams and shoulders. The temperature should be at least 165°F, but most prefer 185° to 195°F. Serve with the sauce.

Rib Gumbo

B. B. Perrins Barbecue a.k.a. Sports Grill

601 Holly St. Northeast
Decatur, AL 35601
256-355-1045

Our longtime friend and barbecue buddy, Ron Harwell, introduced us to B. B. Perrins Barbecue. Ron lives in Decatur, and Ron knows barbecue. An active member of the Kansas City Barbeque Society for many years, Ron is a master certified barbecue judge (CBJ) and CBJ instructor. He has been around the pit many times, for sure. Thanks to Ron's being a regular B. B. Perrins customer and friend of proprietor Benny Perrin, we have the famous Rib Gumbo recipe for you.

Ron says, "B. B. Perrins should really be called the B. B. Perrin Family Sports Grill, because during any given meal you choose to dine with Benny and wife Courtney, there are sure to be families enjoying various entrées on the menu." Locals call it a "sports grill" mainly because Benny was a two-sport All-American in high school. After graduating from Decatur High School, Benny played on the legendary Paul "Bear" Bryant's last two

National Championship football teams in 1978 and 1979. "Of course, Alabama added another National Championship in 1992, but who's counting?" says Ron, a hard-core Alabama fan. In 1981 Benny was the Senior Player of the Year at Alabama and was the Chevrolet Defensive Player of the Game in Coach Bryant's record-breaking win number 315. During that game Benny had two interceptions. He also played in the Senior Bowl that year.

When his impressive four-year stint in the National Football League with the Saint Louis Cardinals ended, Benny opened B. B. Perrins Sports Grill in 1988. More than 20 years later it is still pleasing palates from near and far. On July 4, 2008, it celebrated its 20th anniversary. Yes,

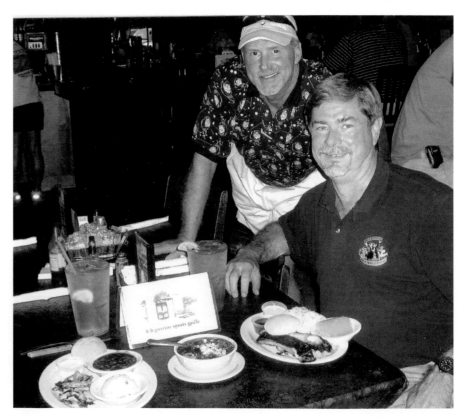

the decor is sports-themed, specifically college football, with a predominate Alabama Roll Tide motif. But don't expect the usual game nosh cuisine here. The menu is all southern barbecue. The pork ribs and tenderloin are served with "the secret sauce," which is a sweet tomato-based recipe handed down through several generations of the Perrin family. And being from this part of the country, no chicken plate would be complete without a signature white sauce. Oh, yeah: on different visits, you may want to sample the Pat's slaw, the jailhouse slaw, or any of several additional appetizers. Complementing the menu is the local favorite, Rib Gumbo, and Benny was gracious enough to share his award-winning legendary recipe with his friends—enjoy!

AWARD-WINNING LEGENDARY B. B. PERRINS RIB GUMBO

Serves 10 to 12

2 cups dehydrated onion

6 quarts cold water

4 cups diced onion

8 cups diced green bell pepper

8 cups diced celery

½ cup chopped or jarred fresh garlic

½ cup Cajun seasoning

10 bay leaves

1 (16-ounce) jar beef base paste

1 #10 (6-pound, 6-ounce) can tomatoes (drained)

1 bag frozen okra

3 cups cornstarch

1 quart cold water

2 pounds boneless smoked rib meat, straight out of the smoker

Cooked rice, for serving

Place the dehydrated onion in a small bowl, cover with hot water, and let hydrate for about 15 minutes. In a large slow cooker, combine the rehydrated onion, 6 quarts cold water, the onion, green pepper, celery, garlic, Cajun seasoning, bay leaves, and beef base paste. Bring to a boil over medium-high heat and cook for about 20 minutes. Add the tomatoes and okra, bring to a boil, and cook for another 20 minutes.

In a bowl, mix the cornstarch with 1 quart cold water until smooth. Slowly add the mixture to the gumbo and cook until the gumbo thickens. Then add the meat and stir to combine. Serve over a bed of rice and enjoy.

Chili

Iron Works BBQ

100 Red River St.
Austin, TX 78701
800-669-3602 or 512-478-4855
http://www.ironworksbbq.com

Iron Works BBQ is right downtown. With trees growing in the middle of the dining room, its ambience is outstanding, as is the barbecue. It's a unique piece of Texas history Austinites are proud to call their own. Originally an ornamental ironworks shop (hence the name) owned and operated by the Weigl family, this little tin building was converted into the Iron Works BBQ in 1978. Shortly after the restaurant's opening, the state historical commission registered the property as a historical site, honoring the Weigls and their legacy. The Iron Works BBQ has been a family owned and operated business serving real Texas barbecue in a country atmosphere ever since. Many celebrities have walked through the doors, including Kevin Costner, Leonardo DiCaprio, Bob Dylan, and Jay Leno, but most important are the many Austinites and hungry travelers who enjoy the good barbecue and atmosphere every day.

We sat down and sampled our way through the Iron Works menu and enjoyed beef ribs, sausage, brisket, chili, and beans. We asked Charlotte Finch if she would share a recipe with us, but we had never met Charlotte, and she didn't know us from Adam. Charlotte said she gets requests all the time for recipes and just can't give them out because it's their business

and they are very proud of their food and recipes. So we asked if she would give us the ingredients in Iron Works Chili, without the amounts, and she said that she would and if anybody wanted they could order the Iron Works BBQ Chili Seasoning. If you like chili, ordering the seasoning from Iron Works is well worth the small investment.

Now that we have fixed Iron Works BBQ Chili at home using its seasoning, we don't think that Charlotte could give us an accurate recipe for the chili without divulging the contents of the Iron Works seasoning, too. So if you don't order the seasoning from Iron Works, try one of our versions here.

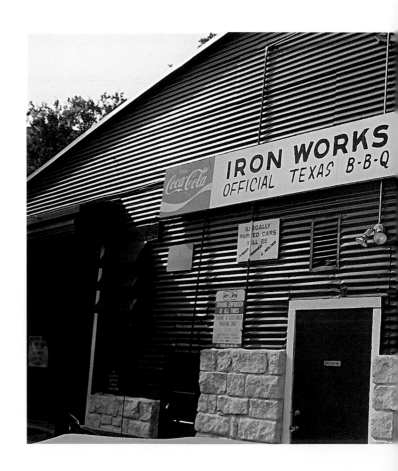

CHILI

Serves 6 to 8

3 pounds coarsely ground chili meat of
your choice

1 medium yellow onion, chopped, plus
chopped onion, for garnish (optional)

2 medium jalapeño peppers, seeded and
minced

1 (14½-ounce) can stewed tomatoes

6 tablespoons Iron Works BBQ Chili
Seasoning or one of the versions that
follow

Grated cheese (cheddar or Jack is good),
for garnish (optional)

Lightly brown the chili meat in a large saucepan over
medium heat. Drain any excess grease. Add the onion,
jalapeño, and tomatoes (save the can). Add the chili seasoning and 2 cans of water and simmer, covered, for 1
hour. Serve as is or top with grated cheese and chopped
onions.

PAUL'S CHILI POWDER

Makes about 1 cup

½ cup ancho chile powder

¼ cup paprika

1 tablespoon ground cumin

2 teaspoons dried oregano leaves

2 teaspoons onion powder

1 teaspoon garlic powder

1 teaspoon salt

In a storage container with a tight-fitting lid, combine all
the ingredients and mix well. You can store the mixture
tightly sealed in a cool, dry place for up to 6 months.

PAUL'S CHILI POWDER II

Makes about ½ cup

2 tablespoons ancho chile powder

5 teaspoons paprika

4 teaspoons ground cumin

1 tablespoon onion powder

2 teaspoons dried oregano

1 teaspoon garlic powder

In a storage container with a tight-fitting lid, combine all
the ingredients and mix well. You can store the mixture
tightly sealed in a cool, dry place for up to 6 months.

Tamales and Beans

McClard's Bar-B-Q

505 Albert Pike
Hot Springs, AR 71901
866-622-5273 or 501-623-9665
http://www.mcclards.com

When you stop at McClard's for barbecue, you're walking into more than 75 years of barbecue history. In 1928, the Westside Tourist Court became Westside Bar-B-Q with *cabrito,* baby goat, as its star menu attraction. In 1942, McClard's moved into its current location—a whitewashed stucco building—and became McClard's Bar-B-Q.

If you get a chance, go to McClard's Web site and read about its history. The story of how McClard's legendary barbecue sauce came into the restaurant's possession is like something you see or hear of only in the movies. The story goes like this: a customer was staying at the Westside for two months and couldn't afford to pay the $10 he owed; he asked them if they would accept instead a recipe for "the world's greatest barbeque sauce." They tried the traveler's sauce, and now everybody knows about the world-famous McClard's Bar-B-Q Sauce.

Fourth-generation McClards now run the kitchen, with some outstanding numbers. Each week they serve 7,000 pounds of mouthwatering hickory-smoked beef, pork, and ribs, along with 250 gallons of spicy barbecue beans, 250 gallons of coleslaw, 3,000 hand-rolled hot tamales, and 3,000 pounds of fresh-cut potatoes french-fried to perfection. The number that intrigues us most is the handmade tamales—that's more than 400 a day!

Tamales are about as basically Mexican as you can get, but they turn up at barbecue joints in the Mississippi Delta, Memphis, and Hot Springs. McClard's tamales are what we call upscale barbecue, and they are a pleasant change at a barbecue restaurant. Making them isn't rocket science, but it is a bit of a fiddle, and it takes some practice to learn how to wrap them. You may put just about any good-tasting filling in your tamales that you want, but McClard's filling of finely ground barbecued meat is different.

We strongly suggest that you make your fillings on one day and then do the wrapping and filling the next. Tamales require a lot of handwork, but these barbecue tamales are worth it! Here is our version thanks to some tips from owner Scott McClard.

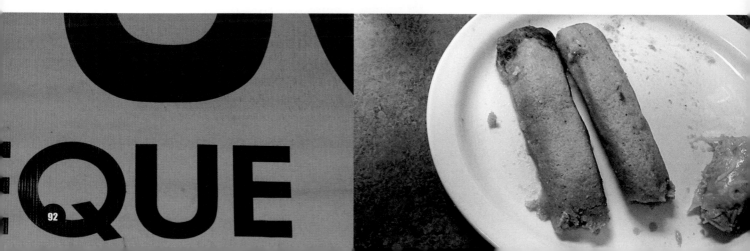

TAMALES AND BEANS

Makes 20 to 24 tamales

CHILI BEANS

1 pound dried pinto beans

1½ cups chopped onion

4 cloves garlic, minced

1 to 2 tablespoons chili powder

1 (6-ounce) can tomato paste

Pinch of black pepper

TAMALE DOUGH

4 cups white masa harina

3 cups warm beef or chicken stock

2 cups lard

FILLING

2½ pounds barbecued brisket (page 38), chopped

2½ pounds barbecued pork butt (page 191), chopped or pulled

¼ cup barbecue seasoning of your choice

1 to 2 cups barbecue sauce of your choice

To prepare the chili beans, wash and rinse the beans well, pick over, and drain. Place in a large kettle and cover with water. Bring to a boil over high heat. Remove from the eat and set aside for 1 hour. Drain the water and add fresh water to cover the beans. Add the onion, garlic, chili powder, tomato paste, and pepper to the beans. Bring to a boil over high heat. Reduce the heat and simmer, covered, until the beans are tender, 45 minutes to 1 hour. Taste and adjust the seasonings, adding salt if necessary.

To make the tamale dough, put the masa harina in a large bowl and reconstitute by adding warmed stock. Beat with a wooden spoon until the dough is thick but smooth. Add a little more stock if necessary, but be sure to keep the mixture firm.

In another large bowl, beat the lard with a mixer fitted with a paddle until it is very fluffy, 3 to 4 minutes. Continue to beat at medium speed and add the masa a little at a time until well combined. The texture should remain light and fluffy. To see if the mixture is mixed well, drop a teaspoon of the dough into a glass of water. If it floats, it's ready. If not, beat it some more. Cover and allow to rest for at least 30 minutes before using.

While the masa is resting, prepare the filling. In a large bowl, combine the beef, pork, and barbecue seasoning and blend well. Place the mixture in a food processor and process to an almost smooth paste, adding barbecue sauce as needed. You can also use a meat grinder to grind it to an almost fine paste. Cover and refrigerate until ready to use.

McClard's tamales are hand-rolled, bigger than most other tamales—5½ to 6 inches long. Spread about ¼ cup of masa dough over a sheet of parchment paper (6 to 8 inches long) and place 3 to 4 ounces of the filling in the center of the masa. Roll the paper lengthwise to seal in the barbecue mixture and tie together on each end with butcher's twine. Repeat with the remaining masa.

Fill a large pot with water and bring to a boil, then reduce to a simmer. Drop the tamales in and boil for 30 to 45 minutes.

To serve, take the tamales out of the parchment paper and top with chili beans.

Smoked Glazed Fresh Pork Ham

Danny's Place

902 S. Canal St.

Carlsbad, NM 88220

505-885-8739

http://www.dannysbbq.com

Paul has known Danny and Carolyn Gaulden for about ten years. Their new digs are a far cry from their original barbecue. On August 1, 1975, Danny and Carolyn opened a Dairy Queen/Barbecue. It was the only one in the whole world. It was also a thorn in the side of the DQ people. It was legal since Danny had one of the original franchise contracts with DQ, and it was permitted, but word started to spread about this Dairy Queen that sold fantastic barbecue. That was the start of a lot of problems. There was too much publicity, and other franchisees wanted to do the same but couldn't. The Barbecue Maverick was the one and only.

There was a lot of pressure on the Gauldens to stop serving barbecue, and it went on until February 2004. Push came to shove, and the decision was made to stop serving a $1.50 sundae and start serving $5.00 hand-cut barbecued brisket sandwiches. They shut down and remodeled and have never looked back. And now the world around Carlsbad, New Mexico, has a new barbecue joint: Danny's Place!

Here's how Danny smokes a fresh ham. His glaze is great for ribs *and* ham. Serve it with some of Danny's potato salad (see page 134).

SMOKED GLAZED FRESH PORK HAM

Remove the rind or the skin (this lets the smoke penetrate more), but leave the fat intact. Put a basic rub on it. If you don't have one handy, some salt, pepper, and a little garlic will work just fine. Cook low and slow at 225°–250°F and keep the smoke going fairly often. Barbecue until the internal temperature of the meat reaches 160°–175°F. The higher the internal temperature, the drier the ham will be. Remember, this isn't as lean as a pork loin, but not as fat as a Boston butt. It's in the middle. This process makes it more tender if you bring it up easy. About 30 minutes before it's done, baste a couple of times with the rib glaze here or your favorite barbecue sauce.

DANNY'S RIB AND PORK FINISHING GLAZE

¾ cup packed light brown sugar

¼ to ⅓ cup yellow mustard

¼ to ⅓ cup apple cider vinegar

Mix all the ingredients in a small saucepan and bring to a simmer. Let cool until you're ready to baste the ribs or pork. The glaze should be at least thick enough to coat a spoon. If the glaze is too thick, add more vinegar or some beer. Apply to the ribs or roast the very second they come off the pit or grill. Or put on a coat of the glaze about 2 minutes before removing the ribs or roast and then another as soon as they are off the pit or grill.

Barbecued Mutton Ribs

Southside Market & Barbeque

1212 Hwy. 290
Elgin, TX 78621
1-877-487-8015 or 512-285-3407
www.southsidemarket.com

Southside Market in Elgin, which was named the Sausage Capital of Texas in 1995, was a must-stop for Paul while making his way through the hill country of Texas. A little more than 1.5 million pounds of hot sausage is made annually in Elgin (pronounced "El-gun"). Elgin sausage is also known by its more affectionate names, Texas Hot Gut and Elgin Hot Guts.

Fresh beef and pork seasoned with secret herbs and spices make Southside Market's sausage unique. Produced since 1882, the original "hot" was toned down in the 1970s to appeal to a broader base of consumers. Forget about getting the original recipe for Southside Market's Texas Hot Gut. It's a trade secret, or at least a corporate secret.

When Paul got in line to order a link of Hot Gut and some brisket, something else caught his eye: mutton. So he ordered a mutton rib. Many Central Texas barbecue joints serve barbecued mutton, as well as goat, a.k.a. *cabrito*. It is usually cut into fist-size pieces called "chuck barbecue."

Here is Paul's version of the mutton ribs he enjoyed for lunch at Southside Market.

BARBECUED MUTTON RIBS

Serves 6 to 8

¼ cup kosher salt

¼ cup coarse ground black pepper

¼ cup paprika

2 tablespoons chili powder

2 tablespoons ground cumin

2 tablespoons granulated garlic

1 tablespoon cayenne

2 mutton breast (ribs), trimmed

Preheat your smoker to 375°F. Combine the salt, pepper, paprika, chili powder, cumin, garlic, and cayenne and blend well.

Sprinkle the mutton breast all over with the rub and rub it in. Place on your smoker and cook indirectly for 4 to 5 hours until done, turning every 1½ hours. The ribs are done when you can take two side-by-side ribs and tear them apart easily.

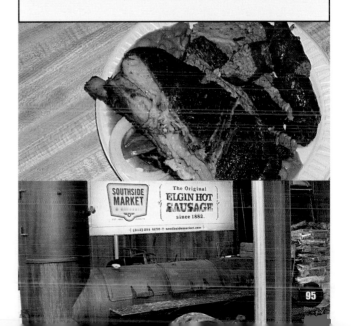

JIM CROW: BLACK, WHITE, AND BBQ

Thomas "Daddy" Rice, a white minstrel performer who blackened his face with burnt cork or charcoal paste, did a "Jump Jim Crow" dance routine in his show. The "Jump Jim Crow" dance caught on with other minstrels. By the mid–nineteenth century Jim Crow was routine minstrel fare. Jim Crow became synonymous with racial discrimination, and race discrimination laws came to be known as Jim Crow laws.

Jim Crow has a history with barbecue joints. We've heard unconfirmed stories about a "Jim Crow Wall" in some barbecue joints. Whites, we were told, were seated on the pit side for warmth in wintertime and on the cooler side opposite the hot pit in summertime. We asked our friend John Raven, PhB, Commissioner of Barbecue, for his recollections of Jim Crow in Texas. He told us:

"All I can report are my observations from around central Texas from the mid-1940s. All public facilities were segregated. The terms used to designate were *white* and *colored*. Mexicans sort of fell in between in a gray area. In some places they could use the white facilities; in some places they could not. Mexicans and colored seldom were put together.

"The first barbecue joint I remember is Novisad's on South Main in Taylor. This was 'across the tracks.' Grandma and Grandpa Veselka (Czech) ran the joint. You would see a lot of Mexicans in there, but I do not recall seeing a colored in there. The storied Taylor Café was segregated by the bar that ran down the center of the big room. Colored on one side of the bar, white on the other. I think Mexicans were seated on the white side.

"There were establishments well into the 1960s where neither colored nor Mexican were served. They went to the back door and sometimes were served in the kitchen if they came in the company of whites. Otherwise they were served at the back door, and no seating was provided."

You'll hear similar stories about Jim Crow and barbecue in Oklahoma, Missouri, Arkansas, Tennessee, Mississippi, Georgia, Alabama, and other states. Most recollections are word of mouth. When Jim Crow was the norm in Kansas City, legend has it that after performing a gig in a white club, Count Basie would pull a late-night jam session in the "Twenty Blocks of Black" East Side neighborhood he had to stay in due to segregation. After losing one too many slabs of ribs while he was focused on music, the Count got wise. He made sure everyone saw him spit on his slab. After that, he didn't lose any more slabs.

Lamb Ribs

Jack Stack Barbecue

13441 Holmes Rd.
Kansas City, MO 64145
816-942-9141
http://www.jackstackkc.com

The Fiorella family has had a major presence in the Kansas City barbecue scene for more than half a century. Russ Fiorella got the family tradition going when he opened the Smoke Stack Barbecue restaurant in 1957. The original building on Prospect Avenue stands vacant and weather-worn today, sporting realtor signs instead of a working smokestack and signs advertising slab specials. Russ's first son, Jack, opened today's famous Jack Stack in Martin City with his wife, Delores, in 1974. Their success with an expanded menu of hickory-grilled steaks and seafood in addition to a complete menu of barbecue meats led to the opening of three more restaurants in Kansas City, each with a popular following of local fans and tourists. They also run a busy online sales business, shipping barbecue and Jack Stack sauces and seasonings nationwide.

We like all four locations, but our favorite, perhaps out of nostalgia, is the Holmes Road store. It is a big wooden structure reminiscent of the Prospect Avenue original. Inside the decor could be described as Ozark Victorian. Some walls are like weathered barn lumber. Others are covered with fancy wallpaper of Victorian design. Framed vintage photos, farm implements, and other memorabilia adorn the walls. It feels warm and welcome and puts you in a good mood for feasting and fun.

Jack Stack is one of the few barbecue restaurants in Kansas City that offers lamb ribs. With Jack's method of cooking them there's no gamy flavor. Be sure to try them on your next visit.

The nice thing about lamb ribs is that they can be barbecued or grilled. Here is our rendition of Jack's lamb ribs. You can order some of Jack's barbecue rub to be more authentic.

LAMB RIBS

Serves 4

4 slabs Denver lamb ribs (6 to 7 bones each), trimmed

1 tablespoon onion salt

1 tablespoon garlic salt

1 tablespoon dried parsley

2 teaspoons herbes de Provence

1 teaspoon black pepper

1 teaspoon kosher salt

Olive oil

To prep the ribs, trim any excess fat and remove the membrane from the back of the ribs. Combine the onion salt, garlic salt, parsley, herbes de Provence, pepper, and salt and blend well. Rub the ribs with olive oil and season all over. Place on a plate, cover, and let rest for 30 to 60 minutes to an hour.

To grill the ribs, cook over medium coals (see page 206) for 45 to 60 minutes, turning every 10 to 15 minutes and taking care not to burn them. To barbecue the ribs, cook with indirect heat for 1½ to 2 hours, turning every 45 minutes. Serve with Jack Stack sauce or your favorite barbecue sauce on the side.

Barbecued Rack of Lamb

Daisy May's BBQ USA

623 W. 46th St. at 11th Ave.
New York, NY 10036
212-977-1500
http://www.daisymaysbbq.com

Chef Adam Perry Lang probably has the best pedigree of any chef we have run across in all of barbecue. He has proven himself in some of the greatest fine dining restaurants in the world and is now creating some of America's best barbecue at Daisy May's BBQ USA. If you can't make it down to the restaurant, and you're out and about in New York City, try one of the mobile barbecue carts located around the city.

The selections at Daisy May's are quite extensive. They include Texas chopped brisket and Carolina pulled pork sandwiches, chicken and rib combinations, and a thorough selection of soulful side dishes. Daisy May's BBQ is a deliciously different way to entertain. The barbecued rack of lamb is a perfect example of that difference.

BARBECUED RACK OF LAMB

Serves 6

MARINADE

2 tablespoons Worcestershire sauce

½ cup chopped sweet onion

10 cloves garlic, chopped

1 tablespoon fresh thyme leaves (about 10 sprigs)

1 tablespoon fresh rosemary leaves (about 10 sprigs)

1 tablespoon ancho chile powder

1 tablespoon black pepper

1 tablespoon hot red pepper flakes

LAMB

2 (8-bone) racks American lamb

SPICE BLEND

½ cup smoked paprika

2 tablespoons chili powder

2 tablespoons garlic salt

1 tablespoon lemon pepper

GLAZE

¼ cup honey

½ cup barbecue sauce of your choice

1 clove garlic, grated

½ jalapeño pepper, grated

Salt

To make the marinade, puree the Worcestershire sauce, onion, garlic, thyme, rosemary, ancho chile powder, pepper, hot red pepper flakes, and ¼ cup water in a blender. Set aside until ready to use.

Trim off as much fat from the lamb as possible, leaving the fat and meat in between the rib bones intact. Place the lamb racks in a resealable plastic bag large enough to hold them and pour in the marinade. Seal the bag and shake it around a little to coat the lamb with the marinade. Refrigerate 3 to 4 hours, or overnight.

Preheat a barbecue to 275°F, using oak wood. Remove the racks of lamb from the refrigerator and wipe off most of the marinade with paper towels; it's OK to leave some on.

In a small bowl, combine the spice blend ingredients and sprinkle it all over the racks until the meat is thoroughly coated.

Place the seasoned lamb racks bone side down in the barbecue and cook over indirect heat until the meat registers 125°F on an instant-read thermometer, about 1 hour 15 minutes. While the lamb is cooking, combine the glaze ingredients. Remove the meat and coat with the glaze. Return the lamb to the barbecue and continue to cook for 20 minutes. Remove, wrap in plastic, and allow to rest for about 5 minutes. Cut into individual chops and season each chop individually with salt.

Butterflied Leg of Lamb with Caramelized Onion BBQ Sauce

Dinosaur Bar B Que

246 W. Willow St.
Syracuse, NY 13202
888-476-1662 ext. 211 or 315-476-4937 or
http://www.dinosaurbarbque.com

Dinosaur Barbecue is a genuine honky-tonk rib joint, and in Paul's humble opinion it is "the Rock 'n' Roll Biker Bar and Barbecue of the Millennium." There are Dinosaur restaurants in Syracuse, Rochester, and New York City, respectively. The original is in Syracuse. All three are popular and busy. You'll know why from your first visit—and you'll be back!

John Stage, pitmaster-founder, with two biker friends, Dino and Mike, started the Dinosaur tradition in 1983 with a cut-in-half 55-gallon-drum pit in Syracuse. They got the idea while full of "rotgut grub and beer." It still felt like a good idea the next day. They were traveling to biker events anyway. They fancied themselves good cooks. Why not sell barbecue and make some money on the road? They took their barbecue on the road for the next five years, showing up at East Coast fairs, festivals, and motorcycle shows. By 1988 John's reputation for great barbecue was established and he was tired of selling it on the road, so he opened a takeout joint in downtown Syracuse. By 1990 he had a sit-down restaurant with waitresses and a full-service bar and thousands of fans. The momentum roars on like a full-throttle hog on a highway.

Inspiration for the name came from two sources: Dino's name and a Hank Williams, Jr., song about the sad transition of his favorite honky-tonk, Dinosaur, to a disco. The business name has evolved from Dinosaur Productions to Dinosaur Concessions and finally to Dinosaur Bar B Que in 1985, when John and Mike came up with the recipe for Dinosaur's famous sauce.

The early fare was grilled meats with Italian accents—such as barbecue-sauced Delmonico sandwiches. Then, thanks to a customer at a Hagerstown, Maryland, gig, John had a barbecue epiphany. In so many words this southern gentleman politely told John the food was good, but it wasn't barbecue. He told John about the barbecue method of cooking as done down South. John took the man seriously, and then he took to the road on a barbecue pilgrimage to Virginia, North Carolina, Tennessee, and Mississippi. He saw, he asked questions, he took notes, and he ate. Last stop: Memphis. By then John was hard-core passionate about real barbecue and bringing it home to New York. Thank you, Mr. Southern Gentleman, whatever your real name is.

Today's Dinosaur restaurants offer a full line of barbecue meats and other great eats—with outstanding beverage choices as well. Their starters, called "Palate Igniters," include catfish or spicy shrimp boil, chicken wings, fried green tomatoes, and deviled eggs, some with several size and flavor options. Pulled pork, spareribs,

continued on page 102

BUTTERFLIED LEG OF LAMB WITH CARAMELIZED ONION BBQ SAUCE

Serves 6 to 8

MARINADE

1 cup plain yogurt

Grated zest of 1 lemon

½ cup fresh lemon juice

1 tablespoon olive oil

4 scallions, both white and green parts, sliced

6 cloves garlic, chopped

¼ cup chopped fresh mint leaves

2 tablespoons dried thyme

2 tablespoons black pepper

1 tablespoon ground cumin

1 tablespoon kosher salt

LAMB

1 leg of lamb, boned by a butcher (4 to 5 pounds boneless)

Salt and black pepper

SAUCE

2 tablespoons butter

1 large onion, thinly cut into half-moon slices

Pinch each of kosher salt and black pepper

Pinch of sugar

1 cup chicken broth or stock

1 tablespoon Dijon mustard

1 cup Dinosaur BBQ Sensuous Slathering Sauce

1 teaspoon ground cumin

3 tablespoons chopped fresh mint

Whirl all the marinade ingredients together in a food processor. Prick the lamb all over with a fork and nestle it in a large nonreactive bowl. Spoon the marinade onto the meat and slather it around until the meat is well coated. Cover and marinate in the fridge for 6 to 8 hours or overnight.

Prepare a hot coal bed and mound the coals on one side of the grill. Preheat it to 325°–350°F When you're ready to cook, scrape off all the marinade and pat the meat dry. Season the lamb with salt and pepper. Lay the lamb, boned side down, directly over the coals. Sear it for 4 minutes. Flip it over and sear the other side for 3 to 4 minutes. Slide the meat away from the coals to cook it with indirect heat. Cover the grill, check to make sure the heat is 325°–350°F inside, and roast for 50 to 60 minutes, or until the internal temperature of the meat reaches 145°–150°F on an instant-read thermometer. Remove the meat from the grill and let it rest for 15 minutes before carving.

Start the sauce cooking while the meat roasts. Drop the butter into a saucepan and melt over low heat. Add the onion, season with salt and pepper, and add a pinch of sugar. Cook slowly, stirring every now and then, until deeply caramelized, 5 to 7 minutes. Add the broth, mustard, barbecue sauce, cumin, and any meat juices. Fold in the mint at the end. Keep warm over low heat until ready to serve.

Carve the lamb across the grain (watch for grain changes) into ¼-inch slices. Retain all the juices from slicing, then stir them into your sauce. Top the lamb with the sauce and serve.

brisket, and chicken are the featured barbecue meats. Grilled steaks and chicken, plus specialty sandwiches such as pulled pork with mushrooms or melted cheese, Cuban-style seasonings, a tasty variety of burgers, with sides of beans, fresh-cut fries, salads, mac and cheese, chili, mashed potatoes and gravy—all that and more round out Dinosaur's barbecopia of a menu. All of that great food, plus bands such as Naughty Lil' Pig Show, Silent Fury, Dark Hollow, Greezy Wheels w/Penny Jo, Legendary Jones Gang, and Turnip Stampede give substance and meaning to why Paul calls Dinosaur "the rock 'n' roll biker bar and barbecue of the millennium."

Paul has been a Dinosaur diner several times in Syracuse and New York City, once when he was preannounced and treated like royalty, and other times unannounced, to get the food that everyone else gets. As expected, he got the same great barbecue on each visit. He has concluded that Dinosaur barbecue is really as good as John has always told him. And everyone gets the royal treatment at Dinosaur.

Paul has asked John for his rib recipe and cooking procedure several times, and he agreed to give both "tomorrow." Tomorrow hasn't come yet, but John did share this fantastic leg of lamb recipe from the fun and fabulous *Dinosaur Bar B Que—An American Roadhouse* (2001) cookbook John wrote with Nancy Radke.

BARBECUE

The barbecue contest circuit is knee deep in rituals. Rare is the team that doesn't perform some kind of rite before sending an entry to the judges. Squeal of Approval does a—you guessed it—squeal ritual.

The eleven o'clock shot ritual has been traveling the barbecue competition circuit since the late 1980s. Rituals vary by team, but the one constant is a shot of Jack Daniel's whiskey, most often Gentleman Jack. It's a good-luck shot meant to increase a team's odds of being invited to the Jack Daniel's World Championship Invitational Barbecue (a.k.a. "The Jack"). World Champion barbecue cook Scotty Johnson of Cancer Sucks invented the Clonesicle for his friends Darren and Sherri Warth of the Smokin' Clones. The Clonesicle is a shot of ice-cold Gentleman Jack from a bottle that has been put in a bucket of water and frozen overnight. Any teams at contests where the Smokin' Clones are competing are welcome to ask for a Clonesicle. Darren told us there have been times when fifty to sixty teams have joined them for a Clonesicle good-luck shot. On those

RITUALS

occasions Darren and Sherri luckily had planned ahead to have enough Gentleman Jack for all. There must be something to it, as the Smokin' Clones are no strangers to the Jack.

We were present at the birth of a ritual for barbecue judges that has become part of the standard operating procedure at barbecue contests sanctioned by the Kansas City Barbeque Society (KCBS)—the official judges' oath. Ardie penned the original oath on a piece of butcher paper from Arthur Bryant's in 1984. It was for the Diddy-Wa-Diddy National Barbecue Sauce Contest judges. Later he changed the wording to apply to barbecue meat judges and donated the oath to the KCBS. Since then tens of thousands of judges have taken the oath. It has a bonding effect. It makes each judge feel official. It reinforces the importance of taking the job seriously while having fun. The Diddy-Wa-Diddy is now part of the Great American Barbecue Festival (www.thinkbbq.com).

Chants, cheers, toasts with beers, and many more rituals abound. Get involved. Invent your own.

OFFICIAL KCBS BARBECUE JUDGES' OATH

by Ardie A. Davis, a.k.a. Remus Powers, PhB

Ardie penned this oath in 1984 for the Diddy-Wa-Diddy National Barbecue Sauce Contest. He adapted it later for barbecue meat cooking contests and donated it to the Kansas City Barbecue Society in 1989 for use at sanctioned contests. The oath was also given by Remus to judges at the Memphis in May World Championship Barbecue from the late 1980s to the early 1990s. Thousands of judges from across the United States take the oath each year.

I do solemnly swear
To objectively and subjectively evaluate
Each Barbecue Meat
That is presented
To my eyes,
my nose,
my hands,
and my palate.

I accept my duty
To be a [name of contest]* judge,
So that truth,
justice,
excellence in barbecue,
and the American Way of Life,
May be strengthened and preserved
    forever.
You're on your oath!

* Ardie says this rapidly and makes it too long for most judges to remember and repeat—e.g., "2011 Tenth Annual Harpoon Brewery New England Barbecue Society Championship Barbecue Judge"

Barbecued Pork Loin and Buffalo (Bison) Bratwurst with Cheese and Jalapeños

Buckingham's Smokehouse Bar-B-Q

2002 S. Campbell
Springfield, MO 65807
417-886-9979

aul has been going to Buckingham's in Columbia, Missouri, for more than 15 years. It's so good he needed to see just how good the original one in Springfield was.

David Campbell started Buckingham's in 1996. It's a chain, but not a typical chain. All of the restaurants are individually owned, not franchises, so it's hard to tell what category they belong to other than good.

Paul sampled their barbecued ribs and then spied two things that are not on many barbecue menus: smoked pork loin and a Buffalo bratwurst. Brandon Grame, the manager, kindly agreed to give us the recipes and procedures for both. He even told us where he gets the bratwurst: Fort Bison Ranch, Attn: Sonny & Melainie Shannon, 507 Rock House Rd., Galena, MO 65656, 417-357-1920. The pork loin is easy to cook and tender. Paul actually made the bratwurst in a barbecue class in Stavanger, Norway, but he used moose meat since bison meat was not available. If you're using sausage casings, make sure you allow enough time to prepare them the night before you plan to stuff them.

BARBECUED PORK LOIN

Serves 25 to 35

1 (8- to 12-pound) boneless pork loin

¼ cup mustard (preferably standard yellow mustard)

½ cup Buckingham's rub or your favorite rub

Trim the pork loin as needed. Using a pastry brush, lightly coat the underside of the loin with half of the mustard and season with half of the rub. Turn the loin over and repeat the process. Don't forget the ends of the loin.

Preheat a smoker to 250°F using apple wood. Place the loin in the smoker and cook for 1½ to 2 hours, or until the internal temperature of the meat reaches 140°–145°F on an instant-read thermometer. Let rest for 15 to 20 minutes; then slice and serve.

BUFFALO (BISON) BRATWURST WITH CHEESE AND JALAPEÑOS

Serves 20 to 24

5 to 6 feet hog casings or large sheep casings (optional)

Apple cider vinegar (optional)

3 pounds lean boneless buffalo meat, chilled

2 pounds pork or pork butt, chilled

½ cup cold milk

1 cup fresh bread crumbs

¼ cup diced pickled jalapeño peppers

2 tablespoons seasoned salt

1 tablespoon rubbed sage

2 teaspoons ground ginger

2 teaspoons dry mustard

1 teaspoon ground white pepper

1 teaspoon ground coriander

1 teaspoon ground mace

1 teaspoon ground nutmeg

1 cup ice water, or as needed

½ cup diced sharp cheddar cheese

If you're going to make sausage links instead of patties, the day before you plan to stuff the sausage, rinse the sausage casings under cold water inside and out. Prepare a solution of 1 cup water to 1 capful of cider vinegar. Soak the casings in the solution overnight in the refrigerator.

Grind the meat twice through the sausage plate of a meat grinder or in a food processor and place it in the bowl of a stand mixer. Combine the milk, bread crumbs, and jalapeños in a small bowl and set aside. Combine the seasoned salt, sage, ginger, dry mustard, white pepper, coriander, mace, and nutmeg in a small bowl and set aside.

Fit the stand mixer with a dough hook, add the bread crumb mixture to the meat, and blend on low speed for 2 minutes. Slowly add the dry ingredients and mix on medium for about 5 minutes, or until well blended, adding ice water as needed. Add the cheese and blend in for 1 minute. Stuff the mixture into the casings or make into patties and cook as desired.

Panfried Chicken Livers

Jack Stack Barbecue

13441 Holmes Rd.
Kansas City, MO 64145
816-942-9141
http://www.jackstackkc.com

Jack Stack gave us several recipes, including Jack Stack Lamb Ribs (page 97) and Jack Stack Cheesy Potato Bake (page 129). To our regret, the fabulous panfried chicken livers that were once served at the original Jack Stack on Holmes Road are no longer on the menu. However, Jack Fiorella and his son-in-law, Case Dorman, were kind enough to share the recipe with us. Now you can enjoy them at home.

PANFRIED CHICKEN LIVERS

Serves 6

HORSERADISH SAUCE

¾ cup mayonnaise

¼ cup drained prepared horseradish

1 tablespoon dried parsley

CHICKEN LIVERS

1 pound fresh chicken livers

1 cup all-purpose flour

3 tablespoons cornmeal

2 tablespoons cornstarch

2 tablespoons Lawry's Seasoned Salt

1 tablespoon baking powder

1½ teaspoons dried parsley

2 teaspoons onion powder

1 teaspoon black pepper, or to taste

1 quart whole milk

Vegetable oil, for frying

To make the horseradish sauce, combine the mayonnaise, horseradish, and parsley in a small bowl and mix thoroughly. Cover and refrigerate until needed.

Clean and rinse the livers and pat dry. In a large bowl, thoroughly mix ½ cup of the flour with the cornmeal, cornstarch, seasoned salt, baking powder, parsley, onion powder, and pepper. Add the milk to this mixture and mix with a wire whisk until well combined.

Heat ¼ inch of vegetable oil in a large skillet until sizzling, about 325°F. Thoroughly coat the livers in the remaining ½ cup flour and shake off the excess. Dredge the floured livers in the batter and place half of them in the oil, one at a time, being careful not to crowd them. Cook the livers for 5 to 7 minutes, until golden brown, turning once halfway through. Remove the livers from the oil and drain them on paper towels. Repeat with any remaining livers, adding more oil as needed. Serve with Horseradish Sauce.

Barbecue Turkey Breast

Buckingham's Smokehouse Bar-B-Q

3804 Buttonwood Dr.

Columbia, MO 65201

573-449-7782

his Buckingham's is halfway between Kansas City and St. Louis, Missouri, and a must stop when driving on I-70. The original Columbia Buckingham's opened in 1998 and was an old drive-in restaurant. The new Buckingham's is out in the suburbs of Columbia, and it's a little more difficult to find than the original. True, you can't just turn off of I-70 and go a block and a half anymore, but it's worth the extra drive.

The owner, Mark Brown, spent about 24 years as a roadie for the groups Pink Floyd, AC/DC, and Fleetwood Mac. When he decided it was time to get off the road, he hooked up with David Campbell of Springfield, Missouri, the founder of Buckingham's Smokehouse Bar-B-Q, where he honed his passion for great barbecue.

One of Paul's favorite things other than Buckingham's ribs is a pulled turkey sandwich. Yes, a pulled *turkey* sandwich: different but very good. Here's a recipe you can try at home.

BARBECUE TURKEY BREAST

Serves 20 to 24

1 (9- to 12-pound) boneless 3-lobe turkey breast with skin on

Salt and black pepper

¼ cup Buckingham's barbecue seasoning or your own rub

40 to 48 slices white bread

Sliced pickles, for serving

Sliced onions, for serving

Barbecue sauce, for serving

Season the turkey breast with the salt, pepper, and barbecue seasoning. Preheat your smoker to 230°F, place the turkey in the smoker, and cook for about 4 hours, or until the internal temperature of the turkey reaches 170°F on an instant-read thermometer when inserted in the center or thickest part of the turkey. Remove the turkey from the smoker and let rest for 15 to 30 minutes.

Remove the skin from the turkey and discard. Put the turkey in a baking pan or dish large enough to hold it. Using two heavy-duty dinner forks, shred the turkey breast. Serve on white bread or a bun with pickles and sliced onion, with barbecue sauce on the side.

Barbecued Bison Ribs

Big Papa's BBQ

12652 W. Ken Caryl Ave.
Littleton, CO 80127
720-922-3233
http://www.bigpapas-bbq.com

In 2003, when Frank Alfonso moved from his hometown in North Florida to Denver, he decided to venture into the barbecue business. "When you're a southern boy, barbecue is in your DNA," he told us. He designed Big Papa's with good food and fast service in mind but didn't compromise on the traditional slow and low method of cooking barbecue. Frank adapted well to his new environment by putting an item not likely to be seen in North Florida or Alabama on the menu.

At Big Papa's you order your food at the cashier counter, pay for it, get seated, and soon your order is brought to the table. Since it isn't everywhere that you can get barbecued bison ribs, we highly recommend you try them at Big Papa's. We don't know how they compare to the bison ribs at the Fort, which our barbecue buddy Dr. Ira Salmon in New York City told us about, but we're pretty sure he would be just as enthusiastic about Big Papa's ribs.

Here's the basic technique for barbecuing bison ribs that Frank shared with us. A Memphis-style tomato-based, tangy barbecue finishing sauce is recommended.

Thanks to Denverite Adrian Miller, barbecue buddy and Southern Foodways Alliance member, for telling us about Big Papa's. Thanks also to Ardie's friend Linda Ray, of Littleton, for the photos and menu.

...SMOKED OVER SPLIT HICKORY

	Lite with 1 side	Entreè with 2 sides	Just the Ribs 1/2 Slab *no side included	Full Slab
	10.75	16.99	9.99	18.99
	10.99	16.99	11.99	21.99
s	9.99	15.99	9.99	18.99
	12.49	18.99	11.49	21.99

SALADS

with tomato wedges and cheddar	2.25
en tenders served on a bed of greens with tomato wedges and cheddar	8.45
e of smoked meat on a large bed of greens with tomato wedges and cheddar	8.45

OR THE NON-SMOKERS

ky fillet served on top a moist french bread hoagie	6.99
n fillets served with your choice of two sides and hush puppies	9.85
en tenders served on a bed of greens with tomato wedges and cheddar	8.45
fried chicken tenders served with your choice of two sides	8.95

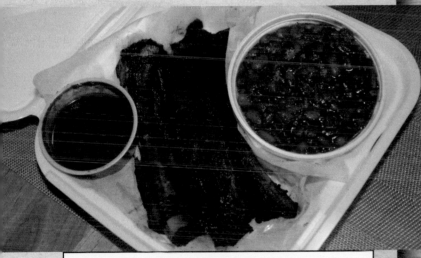

BARBECUED BISON RIBS

Serves 7

1 slab bison ribs (about 7 ribs per slab)

Dry rub of your choice

Barbecue sauce of your choice

Sprinkle the ribs lightly with the rub. Preheat your grill to 225°F and cook the ribs, using indirect heat, for about 4 hours. Remove the ribs from the pit, slather with sauce, and grill both sides directly over hot coals just long enough to crisp the outside. Serve immediately.

FEED THE FAMILY

Picnic (serves 3-4)
$28.95
*from $7.25 per Person

1/2 Slab of St. Louis Style or Baby Ba
1/2 Chicken and 1/2 lb. of any third M
1/2 Pint of BBQ Beans and Cole Slaw
1/2 lb. of Steak Fries

Picnic (serves 6-8)
$57.90
*from $7.25 per Person

Full Slab of St. Louis Style or Baby B
Whole Chicken and 1 lb. of any third
One Pint of BBQ Beans and Cole Sla
1 lb. of Steak Fries

Wings by the Pound

1 lb: 5.99	2 lbs: 11.99	3 lbs: 17.99	5 lbs:

STARTERS

Fried Catfish Nuggets (10 Piece)
Wings (One Whole Pound)
1/2 lb of Baby Back Rib Tips served on a bed of fries

DESSERTS

Brownie a chocolate brownie with chunks of Ghirardelli™ Chocolate
Banana Pudding creamy pudding with fresh bananas a illa wafer
Homemade Cobbler a bed of fruit with a flaky crumb topping

Spatchcock Chicken

B's Barbecue

Hwy. 43 North—751 B's Barbecue Rd.
Greenville, NC 27834
http://www.ncbbqsociety.com/
trail_pages/bs_bbq_large.html

B's is the only barbecue joint we know of that has a road named after it (and one of the few with no phone). B comes from the nickname of the founder, William "B" McLawhorn, who opened B's in 1978. We knew B's reputation for great barbecue, and after our friend Carl Rothrock gave it high marks, we knew for sure we had to eat at B's. Carl lives in Greenville and knows B's well.

As we expected, B's looks like two roadside shacks—one for serving, dining, and carryout and another for the barbecue pits. The restaurant shack used to be a country store, but it works fine as a barbecue joint—friendly, with a good feel to it. If you can't find seating in the spacious, dimly lit inside, there are picnic tables outside. For customers on the run—and there are many—B's does a brisk business at the carryout window.

B's has four big steel box pits with lids. Each pit has a side door for adding coals that are fired up outside the pits in big containers. Two pits are about 5 by 15 feet. The two smaller ones, used for cooking the chickens, are about 4 by 8 feet.

William's daughter, Peggy McLawhorn, and her three daughters—Tammy Godley, Donna

McLawhorn, and Judy Drach—run B's today and do a fine job of it. Pitman Dexter Sherrod cooks the meat the same way it's always been done at B's. That means hardwood charcoal for heat and smoke, with hours of slow and low in the pit. That goes for B's moist, tender, and flavorful whole hog and B's famous chicken, too. B's sauce is the typical eastern North Carolina cider vinegar and peppers with B's special accent. Each dining table sports a Crown Royal whiskey bottle that contains B's sauce. It's one of the best ideas for recycling we've seen.

As for the sauce recipe, we're told that the only way you can get it is to marry into the family. When Carl told Judy that she might expect to get a proposal, she said that she "married for love the first time, but this time it would be for money." Single millionaires should consider taking a trip to Greenville. Matter of fact, everyone who loves barbecue should plan a trip to Greenville. B's barbecue is worth it!

Don't choose between whole hog and chicken at B's. Have both. But get there well before 2:00 P.M. if you expect to eat. It's a busy place, with cars and trucks filling the parking lot and parked along the highway. Carl raved about the chicken, and we see why. Each order is a half chicken. This recipe is our version.

SPATCHCOCK CHICKEN

Serves 4

EAST CAROLINA BASTING SAUCE

3 cups cider vinegar

2 tablespoons black pepper

2 tablespoons sea or kosher salt

2 tablespoons packed brown sugar (optional)

1 tablespoon cayenne

1 large whole fryer chicken

Preheat your pit or grill to 230°–250°F. Combine all of the basting sauce ingredients and whisk to blend.

Remove the giblets from the bird, along with any fat. Rinse the chicken inside and out with cold water. Pat the chicken inside and out with paper towels to dry it. Put the chicken on a cutting board, breast side down with the tail pointing away from you. Pull the chicken to an upright position on its neck end. With a sharp knife, cut down the right or left side of the backbone, through the thigh joint, which is just gristle, then go down the backbone, cutting through the rib bones. Be careful to keep to the backbone, not the breast bone. Repeat the process on the other side of the back bone.

Open the chicken, breast or skin side down, with the breast end pointing toward you. In the middle of the breast you'll see the keel bone. Some people call it the breast bone, but it's the keel bone. At the top of the keel bone, in the center, there is a white piece of gristle about the size of a quarter; with your knife, cut straight down the center of the gristle.

Place your thumbs on either side of the cut, and with your fingers under the keel bone or your fingers on the skin side of the breast, push down with your thumbs and up with your fingers and the keel bone will pop up, you can then pull the keel bone and attached gristle out. Turn the chicken over and press on the breast, flattening the chicken out. Season with pepper and salt. Place the chicken on your pit or grill skin side up and cook indirectly for 3 to 4 hours, depending on the size of the chicken, or until the internal temperature in the thighs are 165°F or higher. Do not turn the chicken. Baste the open side of the chicken with the sauce at 1½ hours, and baste the skin side every 30 minutes until done.

Smoked Catfish

Stevenson Bar-B-Que

114 S. Ash

Paul's Valley, OK 73075

405-238-2040

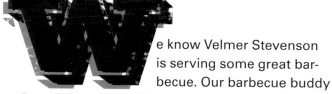

e know Velmer Stevenson is serving some great barbecue. Our barbecue buddy Russ Sifers, CEO of Valomilk Candies, backyard barbecuer, and official Kansas City Barbeque Society Certified Barbecue Judge (pictured on page 113), gave us this report:

Stevenson Bar-B-Que is located in Paul's Valley, Oklahoma, about an hour south of Oklahoma City just off I-35 at Exit 72. In October 2007 it moved into a former Braum's Ice Cream building. The tables sport red-and-white checkered plastic cloths and of course plenty of paper napkins. Velmer Stevenson (pictured above on the left) himself was at the order window, and he greeted everyone as they came in and left. He is a large man with large but gentle hands, like many farmers I know. He has a salt-and-pepper beard, a smile that is infectious, and brown eyes that sparkle with pride over his food. Like most barbecuers, he is friendly and laid back. Each time I speak with Mr. Stevenson I leave feeling happy about the world in general and barbecue in particular.

Velmer's parents, Hilbert and Willie Mae Stevenson, began cooking barbecue at home in the 1950s based on the Louisiana tradition they came from. Later they started selling barbecue "to go." In 1990 Velmer and his brother started serving barbecue on Fridays and Saturdays from a house in the old part of Paul's Valley. Velmer's son Herman, who has master's degrees in psychology and criminal justice, helps out with the cooking. He finds the slow cooking to be relaxing and peaceful, like fishing.

The Stevenson menu sticks with the basics. They concentrate on doing the best with what they offer, and it shows. The smoker is a custom-made five-door cylinder about the size of a van with an offset firebox. The doors open with a pulley system, and the entire rig rolls out for hauling to the car wash every two weeks. They use split pecan logs for heat and hickory for smoke. There are two worn chairs on a deck by the cooker in the enclosed cooking room. They allowed me to sit on one, and I felt like I was the Master of the Smoke and quite honored.

Stevenson's dinner offerings are ribs, brisket, steak, hot and Polish links, chicken, and chopped beef. Those meats also come in sandwiches. They use their own dry rub and baste and turn the meat by hand. The mild and hot barbecue sauces come from Willie Mae's Louisiana tradi-

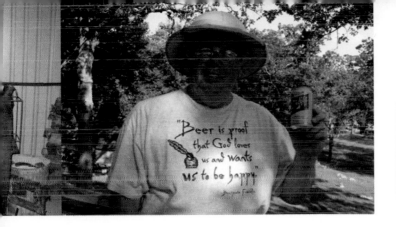

tion: both are vinegary, with the hot sauce being sincerely hot and spicy. Their chicken drumsticks are mild in flavor but lean, moist, and tender. I had two ribs, which might have had a little extra rub. One was tender, lean, and moist, while the other, thicker rib had some fat but was flavorful.

The barbecued steak is something different. It's a big hunk of meat almost 2 inches thick, tender, and moist, with a nice smoke flavor (you could see the smoke ring) and a gentle use of the rub. Velmer has a saying: "If you can't cut it with a plastic knife and fork, it's yours free." Herman adds, "It's tender as a mother's love." They're both right. Stevenson's brisket is also tender and moist. A little sauce (hot) brings it to life. The hot link is standard fare much like you'll find in BBQ contests, and the chopped beef is a little like burnt ends but tender, and it also comes to life with a little hot sauce (maybe it's the Kansas City in me!). I must admit that the smoked steak so had my attention that the other offerings fell by the wayside.

Speaking of sides, the fries at Stevenson's are fresh cut, well seasoned, served hot, and not greasy even at 7:30 P.M. They cry out for beer, but Paul's Valley does not allow beer in its restaurants. Stevenson's offers plenty of cold lemonade and fresh brewed ice tea. I chose the tea, which is clean and full-bodied (I pretended that it was Shiner Bock). The beans are large and cooked in a gray gravy sauce somewhat like Texas ranch beans, though Texas beans tend to have a red

SMOKED CATFISH

Serves 6

6 (13- to 15-ounce) head-on whole catfish

½ cup canola oil

2 cups dry barbecue rub

Preheat your smoker to 225°–250°F. Wash the fish inside and out thoroughly with cold water. Pat dry and then lightly oil the fish with the canola oil. Rub the fish inside and out with a medium to heavy amount of the rub. Place the fish on a screen, cookie sheet, or smoker rack sprayed with nonstick cooking spray. Make sure you have a medium-thick amount of smoke in your cooker; then place the fish in the smoker and smoke for 45 to 75 minutes, or until the fish is opaque and the flesh is just beginning to flake. Watch it carefully. It is better to cook, test, and then finish cooking rather than overcook it.

gravy sauce instead. The coleslaw is homemade, fresh, crisp, and quite good.

When I judge barbecue, I look for something special that gets my attention. Stevenson's bread pudding and banana pudding are both Texas recipes made from scratch by Velmer's wife, Laverne. The banana pudding has fresh chunks of bananas and is creamy but not too rich. The bread pudding is warm and sweet. If I lived in Paul's Valley and ate at home, I think I would still go to Stevenson's just to have Laverne's puddings for dessert.

Russ told us, "Velmer Stevenson talked with me about a smoked catfish recipe he has in mind, and it made me hungry all over again." This isn't Velmer's recipe, Russ, but we don't think anyone will be disappointed.

Beer-Battered Cod with Tartar Sauce, and Marinated Chicken

Smoky Jon's #1 BBQ

2310 Packers Ave.
Madison, WI 53704
608-249-RIBS (7427)
http://www.smokyjons.com

hen most people think of Madison, Wisconsin, cheeseheads, brats, and beer come to mind. Barbecue aficionados familiar with Madison add "Smoky Jon's."

Smoky Jon Olson, avid hunter and "Madison's All-Time BBQ King," has been serving tender smoky barbecue to the citizens of and visitors to Madison for more than 30 years. Now and then he leaves the restaurant in the capable hands of pitmaster Joel Latham and staff while he networks with fellow barbecuers at contests and National Barbecue Association conferences. That's how we met him.

We like Smoky Jon and his barbecue, but since we haven't tried it for a while, we decided to ask Ardie's friends Ron and Mary Buchholz and their son Geof to pay a visit to Smoky Jon's "inhognito" and give us this candid report.

continued on page 116

BEER-BATTERED COD WITH TARTAR SAUCE

Serves 6 to 8

TARTAR SAUCE

1 cup mayonnaise

1 tablespoon Dijon mustard

1 scallion, both white and green parts, minced

1½ teaspoons fresh lemon juice

2 tablespoons minced dilled gherkins

1 tablespoon minced drained capers

2 tablespoons snipped fresh parsley

Pinch each of salt and black pepper

COD

Cooking oil, for deep-frying (about 1 quart)

1 cup all-purpose flour

¼ cup cornstarch

½ teaspoon salt

1 large egg, lightly beaten

1 cup beer, or as needed

2 pounds cod, haddock, or hake fillets, cut into approximately 1½ by 3-inch pieces

Combine all the tartar sauce ingredients in a small bowl. Cover and refrigerate. Preheat the oven to 200°F. Cover a cookie sheet with paper towels and top with a wire rack. In a medium pot or a deep-fryer, heat about 3 inches of oil to 365° (use a deep-frying thermometer if you're using a pot).

Meanwhile, mix the flour and cornstarch with the ½ teaspoon salt. Whisk in the egg. Slowly add the beer while whisking just until the ingredients are incorporated.

Dip the fish pieces in the batter and place on a plate or the wire rack you will be using to drain the fried fish. If you have some batter left over, you can dip the fish in the batter again after the first coat of batter dries on the fish awaiting frying.

Place the fish pieces, two at a time, in the oil. Cook until the fish is done and the crust is lightly golden, about 4 minutes for ¾-inch-thick fillets. Remove the fish with tongs and put on the rack to drain. Sprinkle the salt over the hot fish and put the baking sheet in the oven while you cook the other batches. Serve with the tartar sauce.

MARINATED CHICKEN

Serves 24

¾ cup Whirl liquid butter substitute or drawn butter*

3½ ounces Smoky Jon's Flavor Magic Gourmet All Purpose Seasoning or rub of your choice

24 (5-ounce) boneless skinless chicken breasts

In a small bowl, combine the Whirl or drawn butter and the Flavor Magic and blend well.

Place the chicken breast in a large, deep pan. Pour the Whirl mixture over the chicken breasts. Evenly coat the chicken all over with the paste. Cover the pan with plastic wrap and marinate for 2 hours or overnight in the refrigerator.

Grill over hot charcoal (page 206) just until done. Makes an awesome chicken sandwich on a bun or in a combo with ribs. This recipe makes a lot, but it freezes well.

*To make drawn butter, melt 2 sticks of butter over medium heat in a small saucepan. Bring it to a low boil and boil until the milk solids in the butter separate and sink to the bottom of the pan. Watch carefully so it doesn't burn. Spoon off the clarified butter and use ¾ cup in the recipe.

The exterior of Smoky Jon's leaves no doubt that you're looking at a barbecue joint. Neon and painted signs, with pigs, ribs, and barbecue in a bun will definitely get your attention. Inside, Smoky Jon's "has a rustic North Woods look with pine log walls, rough-cut knotty-pine trim, knotty-pine tongue/groove plank ceilings, and deep burgundy brick paver-type quarry tile floors," as Ron describes it. Awards, a string of small lighted pigs, banners, a Wisconsin "No. 1 BBQ" vanity plate, and other memorabilia add to the feel of the joint.

Is Smoky Jon good enough to wear the barbecue king title? Yes! The marinated barbecued chicken is a house favorite and won't disappoint. The ribs have just the right kiss of smoke, or "smoky undertone" as Ron aptly puts it, and are tender, juicy, and delicious. If you like naked ribs, as we do, ask for sauce on the side or your ribs will be served slathered with Smoky Jon's sauce. It's good stuff, mind you. We just like to decide how much sauce to enjoy with our ribs. The pulled pork sandwich is served with sauce on the side. It's good enough to stand alone, but a touch of Smoky Jon's sharp, tangy barbecue sauce lends a nice complement.

What also catches our attention at Smoky Jon's is the beer-battered cod. As longtime beer-battered Minnesota walleye pike fans, we knew Smoky Jon would make us equally enthusiastic about his cod, and he did! The dinner comes with four pieces of cod, two sides, and a dinner roll with butter. Put some tartar sauce on the lightly coated seasoned battered fish cooked to tender flakiness and enjoy. Any of the sides go well with it—creamy coleslaw, spicy barbecue baked beans, spicy buttered corn, applesauce, fries, and side salad. We agree with Ron that the best of all the sides, however, is the barbecue baked beans.

Smoky Jon's priority is to serve great barbecue in a welcoming setting with friendly service. He delivers that and throws in a moist, rich, flavorful Chocolate/Cherry Bundt Cake for dessert. It is the only dessert on the menu, but it's worth saving room for a few bites. Order

one slice with enough forks for everyone at the table. Our hats are off to Smoky Jon Olson and pitmaster Joel Latham. We thank them for the two recipes.

Barbecue Shrimp

Gridley's Fine Bar-B-Q

6842 Stage Rd.
Bartlett, TN 38134
901-377-8055

Times have changed since the days when we made a point of dining at Gridley's on Summer Avenue during the Memphis in May World Championship Barbecue Cooking Contest. Our feast at Gridley's was capped by a visit to Graceland to pay our respects to the King. Back then Gridley's wait staff wore bow ties and gold jackets. Gridley's was synonymous with Memphis barbecue, and the only sauce packed in a clever cardboard briefcase for Memphis tourism and convention promotions was Gridley's, founded by the late Clyde Gridley. We thought that Gridley's heyday had come and gone, but thanks to Jamie and Doug Walker, we can now say that Gridley's is alive and well and as good as or better than it ever was. Today's Gridley's is farther from Graceland, but the drive to the new smaller Gridley's is worth the adventure.

Jamie and Doug Walker bought Gridley's from Dr. and Mrs. William Coley, who were looking for a buyer at the same time Jamie and Doug were looking for a business to offset losses in their manufacturing company due to competition from China and Mexico. They needed a career change, and since they are one of the hardest/smartest-working barbecue joint couples we've ever met, barbecue lovers are the better for it.

Gridley's walls are decorated with Memphis and Elvis memorabilia, plus some photos of

BARBECUE SHRIMP

Serves 4

2 pounds large shrimp

¼ cup Gridley's Shrimp Seasoning

¼ cup liquid margarine

Preheat your oven to 300°F. Put the shrimp in a shallow baking pan. Sprinkle the seasoning mix on the shrimp and pour the liquid margarine on top. Bake for 3 to 5 minutes, then turn the shrimp over and cook for another 3 to 5 minutes. Be careful not to overcook, or the shrimp will be rubbery. Serve immediately, letting people peel their own shrimp at the table.

CAJUN BARBECUE SHRIMP

Serves 4

2 pounds large shrimp

BARBECUE SAUCE

½ pound (2 sticks) butter

¼ cup olive oil

½ cup beer (not dark)

¼ cup Heinz chili sauce

3 tablespoons fresh lemon juice

2 tablespoons Worcestershire sauce

2 cloves garlic

2 to 3 bay leaves, finely crushed

½ teaspoon dried thyme

Pinch of crushed rosemary or rosemary
 leaves

1 teaspoon dried oregano

¼ teaspoon white pepper

½ teaspoon black pepper

1 teaspoon cayenne

2 teaspoons paprika

2 teaspoons hot pepper sauce

Rinse, peel, and devein the shrimp. Combine all the sauce ingredients in a big pan and simmer gently for about 10 minutes. Cool the sauce to room temperature, then add the washed and cleaned shrimp. Marinate overnight in the refrigerator.

Cook the shrimp on the stove over high heat, stirring just until all the shrimp turn pink, 3 to 4 minutes.

Serve with chunks of crusty French bread to soak up the sauce, a green salad, and lots of napkins. Shrimp must be eaten with your fingers to get the whole experience.

former Gridley's restaurants. Service is fast and friendly. Bow ties and gold jackets just wouldn't fit the new decor, so we didn't miss that relic of bygone days. The barbecue shrimp (not truly barbecue, as everyone knows), ribs, and pulled pork sandwich with slaw are every bit as great as we enjoyed at the former Memphis Gridley's. Jamie and Doug own and operate another Gridley's in Conway, Arkansas. Congratulations and thanks to Jamie and Doug Walker. Surely the Clyde Gridley family would be proud that their legacy continues!

To get the true Gridley's flavor, you have to have the real sauce and seasonings. Thank goodness that's possible! Call Gridley's to put in your order for sauce (mild or hot), Gridley's Rib Rub, and Gridley's Shrimp Seasoning. When you can't go to Gridley's and you yearn for its shrimp at home, try the recipe here. If you're out of Gridley's Shrimp Seasoning, try Paul's Cajun BBQ Shrimp, the recipe here, to get you by until the next shipment of Gridley's seasonings arrives.

Seafood Stuffed Lobster

DennyMike Sherman
http://www.dennymikes.com

Dennis Michael "DennyMike" Sherman caught the barbecue bug in the 1970s from a Texan named Charlie Ariaga. Although DennyMike has since tasted barbecue in Kansas City and several southern states, his barbecue of choice is Texas-style. Like a duckling imprints on a mama duck, young DennyMike imprinted on Texas barbecue. In 2002, he started DennyMike's Smokehouse BBQ and Deli in Old Orchard Beach, Maine, so he could share his love of Texas 'cue with New Englanders. He has since sold the restaurant, and we hope he makes good on his promise to start a new restaurant somewhere along the eastern seaboard. Meanwhile, he is knee-deep in sales of his barbecue products online.

Maine is better known for its rugged coast, lighthouses, and lobster rolls than for its barbecue. But if DennyMike has his way, Maine will also be known for DennyMike's Texas-style barbecue. The recipe here features Maine's specialty—lobster—barbecued to perfection. It calls for apple wood smoke instead of Texas mesquite or oak. This will give our friend Billy Bones in Red Keg, Michigan, a smile, since apple is his wood of choice. Here, with thanks to DennyMike and our barbecue buddies Steve and Hope Rowley, is one of DennyMike's prized recipes.

SEAFOOD STUFFED LOBSTER

Serves 6 to 12

6 (1- to 2-pound) lobsters

SMOKED SEAFOOD

¾ pound bay scallops, with juices

¾ pound Maine shrimp, peeled, deveined, and washed

1½ pounds Alaskan king crab meat, with juices

3 tablespoons DennyMike's Fintastic seasoning or seafood seasoning of your choice

¾ stick (6 tablespoons) butter, melted

SMOKED STUFFING

¾ stick (6 tablespoons) butter

6 tablespoons minced celery

6 tablespoons minced yellow onion

1½ tablespoons minced shallots

3 tablespoons snipped parsley

1½ tablespoons minced jalapeños

3 tablespoons dry sherry

1½ tablespoons Dijon mustard

Juice of 1 lemon

3 sleeves Ritz crackers, crumbled

3 cups Italian bread, cut into ¼-inch cubes

2 tablespoons DennyMike's Fintastic seasoning or seafood seasoning of your choice

3 large eggs

1 lemon, cut into sixths

1 to 2 tablespoons paprika, or to taste

½ cup finely grated Parmesan cheese

Fill a steamer pot large enough for all of the lobster claws with water and bring it to a boil. Kill the lobsters (instructions follow), remove their claws, and toss the claws into the steamer to cook until they turn red. Do not overcook. Use tongs to transfer the claws to a plate to cool slightly, then crack the claws and remove the claw meat in one piece.

Split open the lobsters and remove the bad stuff, saving half of the tomalley (liver) to add to stuffing. Discard the extra half of the tomalley or save it for another purpose. (Or be like Paul and eat it!)

Set up your smoker to cook at 180°F, preferably with apple wood.

To make the smoked seafood, combine the scallops, shrimp, crab and seafood juices with the Fintastic seasoning and butter in a large baking dish or foil pan. Set aside.

To make the stuffing, place the butter, celery, onion, and shallot in a saucepan and sauté until translucent. Add the parsley, jalapeños, sherry, mustard, and lemon juice. In a large bowl, combine the cracker crumbs, bread crumbs, sautéed mixture, Fintastic, eggs, and reserved tomalley. Mix well. Transfer the stuffing to a large baking dish or foil pan.

Place the seafood and stuffing pans in the smoker and cook for about 1 hour, stirring twice. The scallops will take on a nice brown color from the smoke.

Remove the seafood and stuffing from the smoker and increase the heat of the smoker to 350°F. Combine the smoked seafood with the smoked stuffing and mix well. Place the whole lobsters in a large baking dish or foil pan and layer with about ½ inch of the stuffing and seafood mixture. Layer the claw meat on top of that, and generously top with the remaining seafood and stuffing mixture. Sprinkle the lemon juice, paprika, and grated Parmesan cheese over the top.

Put the pan on a baking sheet and place it in the smoker to cook until the internal temperature reaches 180°F on an instant-read thermometer, 1½ to 2½ hours.

Note: The most humane way to kill a lobster is first to render it unconscious by placing it in the freezer for 1½ to 2 hours. When the lobster is cold and no longer moving, place it on a heavy board, take a strong sharp knife and drive it through the center of the cross on the back of its head.

Sides & Condiments

Sides should be outstanding. Since the average adult stomach can hold only a quart of food and beverages at one sitting, it makes sense to be fussy with your ounces.

Our side dish and condiment standards are not complicated. Aside from looking good and tasting great, we want them to be a good match with the meat. To illustrate with some extreme examples, it won't work to garnish barbecued spareribs with pickled herring. Serving New England clam chowder with barbecued brisket is also not a good idea. Maybe that's why most joints seem to serve beans, slaw, and potato salad, though a few feature cheesy taters, and occasionally one heats things up with some jalapeño hushpuppies.

In this chapter, we've chosen side dishes and condiments worthy of sharing plate space with the best barbecue in America or elsewhere. Enjoy!

Jo Jos

Ted's 19th Hole Bar-B-Que

2814 E. 38th St.
Minneapolis, MN 55406
612-721-2023

olf is an eighteen-hole game. The "nineteenth hole" is a refreshment place, usually a clubhouse. Thanks to the late legendary pitmaster and pro golfer Ted Cook, the 19th Hole is also a refreshing barbecue joint.

Ted's neighborhood is poised for change. On our last visit in fact, next door a sign in a cracked glass storefront window proclaimed, "There's Hope Outreach Mission." At a nearby gas station you prepay the clerk stationed behind thick bulletproof glass, and a few tattoo parlors and beer joints echo the past, but coffee shops and ethnic eateries hint of a promising future.

Moses Quartey is a Minneapolin by way of Ghana. He came to the University of Minnesota for graduate studies in microbiology and bio-chemistry. To make ends meet, Moses took a job at Ted's, then owned by mother and son Priscilla and Mike Davis. Moses found a higher calling, and now he owns Ted's. Moses, like Priscilla and Mike before him, prepares and cooks the barbecue exactly as Ted did starting in 1968. He has also kept Priscilla's soul foods on the menu. "We've been doing the same thing for 40 years, over and over again," Moses told us.

Ted's is carryout only. The menu is on the wall behind the white Formica order counter. Framed pictures of menu items adorn another wall. When you're ready, look up to the window, and, like a hungry traveler seeking manna from heaven, tell Moses what you want.

What Ted's lacks in comforts it makes up in food and friendly service. We liked the pork ribs best—spares, lightly rubbed, slow smoked with apple, cherry, and hickory in

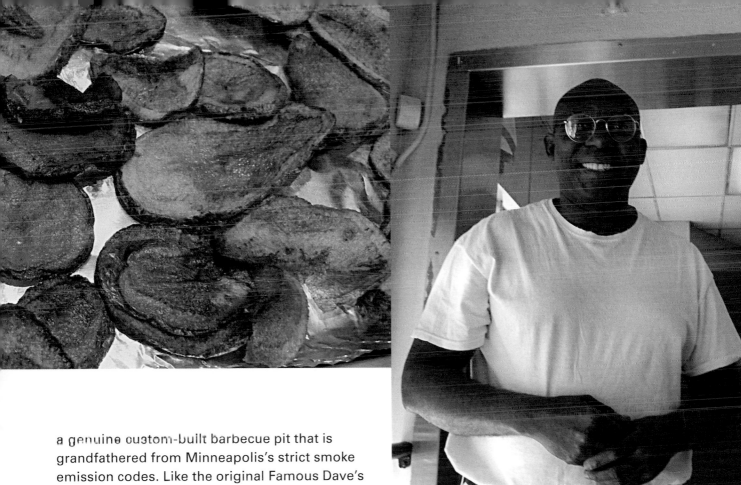

a genuine custom-built barbecue pit that is grandfathered from Minneapolis's strict smoke emission codes. Like the original Famous Dave's in nearby Calhoun Square and the Cozy Corner pit in Memphis, Ted's pit is enclosed with sliding glass walls and a chimney hood that vents from the center. Some pitmasters call it an "aquarium pit." Moses can check the meat without losing heat and smoke. Ted's grandmother's tomato-based tangy sweet sauce with a touch of allspice lends a tasty complement to the barbecue.

For a totally soulful barbecue feast, add beef ribs, sliced barbecue beef, pulled pork, chicken, rib tips, and all the sides—collard greens, red beans and rice, black-eyed peas, baked beans, potato salad, coleslaw, corn muffins. Take home some made-from-scratch 19th Hole peach cobbler and sweet potato pie for a postfeast treat. But most of all, do not leave Ted's without your Jo Jos! Moses Quartey told us how to make them: "Leave the skins on. Wash them up. Cut them up, and deep-fry them." Here's the full recipe.

JO JOS

Serves

4 to 6 russet potatoes, scrubbed but not peeled

Canola oil, for deep-frying

Salt

Pat the potatoes dry, slice them into ⅛-inch-thick rounds or 2½-inch-long wedges about ½ inch wide. Heat the oil in your deep-fryer to 350°–360°F (or use a deep pot and measure the oil temperature with a deep-frying thermometer). Place the potato rounds or wedges in the hot oil and fry until golden brown. Carefully remove them from the hot oil and drain them. Season with salt to taste and serve.

Famous Fresh-Cut Fries

Arthur Bryant's Barbeque

1727 Brooklyn Ave.
Kansas City, MO 64127
816-231-1123
http://www.arthurbryantsbbq.com

There's nothing fancy about this famous "world-class restaurant." The late Mr. Bryant called it simply "a greasehouse." The walls are adorned with framed photos and testimonies by famous and wanna-be-famous customers. There's also a framed portrait of Arthur Bryant and an enlarged cartoon by Lee Judge, local political cartoonist. The cartoon features Saint Peter and Mr. Bryant at the Pearly Gates. Saint Peter wants to know, "Did you bring sauce?" Arthur Bryant's sauces can be purchased at the restaurant, in supermarkets throughout KC, or online.

The menu features barbecued brisket sandwiches, pork spareribs, turkey, chicken, ham, beans, coleslaw, and fries. Arthur Bryant's fries are a favorite, and they are a welcome exception to the ubiquitous precut frozen majority sold at other places. Bryant's fries pair well with all barbecued meats on the menu. Dip them or douse them with Arthur Bryant's Original sauce or Sweet Heat for extra pleasure. Here's how they do it.

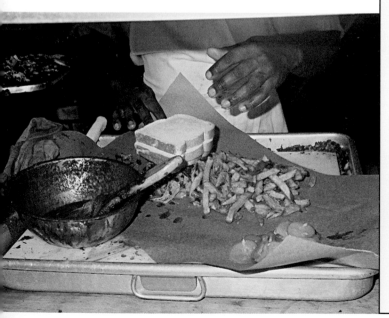

FAMOUS FRESH-CUT FRIES

Serves 4

4 pounds pure lard, such as Armour, or as needed

4 large russet potatoes, washed but not peeled and cut into 5/16-inch french fries or as desired

Salt

Heat the lard to 325°F in a deep-fryer. You could use any frying shortening such as Crisco or a canola oil instead of lard, but you'll lose flavor. Divide the fries into about 8 batches and blanch each batch for about 3 minutes in the hot oil. Drain each batch on paper towels or a wire rack. For best results, put the blanched fries in a cooler until all of the batches are done.

To finish the fries, heat the oil to 400°F. Drop the blanched fries into the hot oil in batches and cook for 4 to 5 minutes, or until they are as crisp as you want. Season to taste with salt. The result is a sweet, crispy-outside/soft-inside mound of fries fit for royalty.

SANDWICHES			MEAT TRAYS
BEEF 5⁴⁵	RIB LONG END 5⁷⁵	NEW ARTHUR BRYANT'S RICH & SPICY BBQ SAUCE NOW AVAILABLE AT YOUR TABLE OR TAKE A PINT HOME $2.65	ANY COMBO OF
HAM 5⁴⁵	RIB SHORT END 6⁷⁵		BEEF, PORK, CHICKEN HAM, SAUSAGE, PORK
PORK 5⁴⁵	½ CHICKEN 4⁹⁵		SERVED BY THE POUND
TURKEY 5⁴⁵	SAUSAGE 5²⁵		MEAT TO GO BY THE
COMBO - ANY 3 MEATS			WHOLE SLAB PORK RI

SIDE ORDER		DRINK	
ARTHUR'S FRIES 1⁷⁵ WITH SAND 85		COKE	LEMON
BAKED BEANS 1⁵⁰ PT 2⁷⁵ QT 5⁰⁰		DIET COKE	RED CR
PICKLES 4		SPRITE	ICE T
ARTHUR'S LEGENDARY SAUCES		SM 95 MED 1¹⁵ LARG
PT 2²⁵ QT 4⁶⁵		BEER
		PITCHER 4²⁵ MU

PORK RIBLET SANDWICH $5.95

WHAT IS THE GREASEHOUSE UNIVERSITY?

The late Arthur Bryant appreciated the fame his barbecue joint attracted, but it never went to his head. Pleased and amused would be the more accurate description. "It's just a greasehouse," he would say.

The Greasehouse University owes its name to Arthur Bryant. It has no physical campus. It has no uniform curriculum. But it's real. It's the barbecue school of hard knocks. Master of Barbecue and Doctor of Barbecue Philosophy degrees are awarded by the university in cooperation with the Kansas City Barbeque Society.

Our hope is that someday there will be an actual Greasehouse University campus.

North Carolina-Style Boiled Potatoes

Stephenson's Bar-B-Q

11964 NC 50 Hwy. North
Willow Spring, NC 27592
919-894-4530

o us an important measure of the character of a community is the quality of its barbecue. We're not saying that a town without barbecue is a town without character. Thanks to Stephenson's Bar-B-Q, however, Willow Spring gets high marks on character, even though the restaurant is 10 miles from downtown. A journey to this rural agricultural area for swine dining is worth your dime.

Founder Paul Stephenson started out as a farmer. He got the inspiration to go into the barbecue business when he figured out that the hogs he was selling to other pitmasters were getting a higher monetary yield as ribs and sandwiches than he was getting from selling the whole animal for someone else to cook. His value-added bulb lit up. Eventually Paul learned how to barbecue, and he made the transition from farmer to pitmaster. Paul and his wife, Ann, managed to raise two boys, Andy and Wayne, thanks to the popularity of the barbecue. The business was also a good venue for teaching and learning business skills, pitmaster skills, and the value of hard work and customer service.

The restaurant has room for lots of hungry customers in a country-style setting. The chopped pork and the ribs are delicious, and the barbecue is what you're there for, but be sure to get potatoes, too. You can't get boiled potatoes on the side at just any barbecue joint, except in eastern North Carolina, where "barbecued potatoes" are standard fare. Our version, with a mix of red and white unpeeled new potatoes, is different from Stephenson's, but it's true to the eastern North Carolina boiled potato tradition. Vinegar, peppers, hot sauce, and salt—the barbecue sauce of choice in these parts—makes it so.

NORTH CAROLINA—STYLE BOILED POTATOES

Serves 6 to 8

1 cup apple cider vinegar

1 teaspoon hot sauce, preferably Texas Pete

1 teaspoon kosher salt

1 teaspoon crushed black pepper

1 teaspoon hot red pepper flakes

3 pounds small new potatoes, red and white

8 tablespoons (1 stick) unsalted butter, melted

Salt and black pepper

Put the vinegar, hot sauce, salt, black pepper, and red pepper in a jar. Screw on the lid and shake the jar to mix the ingredients. Set aside.

Cover the potatoes with cold water. Add the vinegar sauce. Bring to a boil and simmer until tender, 45 to 60 minutes. Drain. Top with melted butter and season with salt and pepper to taste. Serve immediately.

Cheesy Potato Bake

Jack Stack Barbecue

13441 Holmes Rd.
Kansas City, MO 64145
816-942-9141
http://www.jackstackkc.com

Jack Stack gave us several recipes, including its lamb ribs (page 97) and the chicken livers (page 106) it used to serve at its Holmes Road location. These cheesy potatoes are one of our all-time favorites, and we have yet to meet anyone who doesn't like them. You can purchase aged cheddar cheese sauce at the grocery store or online. Enjoy!

CHEESY POTATO BAKE

Serves 6 to 8

2½ cups heavy cream

1 cup aged cheddar cheese sauce

1 cup freshly grated Parmesan cheese

½ cup freshly grated cheddar cheese

½ cup freshly grated Jack cheese

2 tablespoons minced garlic

2 teaspoons onion powder

½ teaspoon garlic salt

2 teaspoons black pepper

2 teaspoons kosher salt

2½ pounds red potatoes

Minced fresh parsley, for garnish

Preheat the oven to 375°F. In a large bowl, combine the heavy cream, cheese sauce, cheeses, garlic, onion powder, garlic salt, black pepper, and kosher salt and mix well.

Wash and slice the potatoes into ⅛-inch-thick slices and place immediately into the sauce mixture. Mix by hand to coat all the surfaces of the sliced potatoes. Place the mixture in a 9 by 13-inch baking dish and cover tightly with aluminum foil. Bake for about 1 hour. Uncover and bake for 20 to 30 minutes longer, until the top is golden brown. Let cool, garnish with fresh parsley, and serve.

Cheesy Taters

Hickory Creek Bar-B-Que

711 High St.
Baldwin City, KS 66006
785-594-RIBS (7427) or 620-228-1328

Ric Gere not only serves top-notch barbecue but does it in a locale that is rich in fame and infamy. Not far from here, in 1856, John Brown answered attacks on abolitionists in Lawrence, Kansas, by dragging five pro-slavery farmers from their homes in the dead of night and killing them. It was called the "Pottawatomie Massacre." Near here also was the 1856 Battle of Black Jack between pro-slavery forces and John Brown's slavery abolition fighters. From Kansas City you'll pass the site on your way into town. So much blood was shed in the Kansas/Missouri border wars in the 1850s and 1860s that Kansas Territory was called "Bleeding Kansas."

Ric always wanted to own a restaurant. He knew the risks. That's why he tested the waters first and didn't jump into the deep end with both feet all at once. For several years Ric held barbecue court with his mobile pit every Saturday in the parking lot of Stan Vicker's Antiques on the Prairie. Customers often said, "Why don't you open a restaurant?" Ric got the same question when he catered and at community events where he sold barbecue. In 2004 the space on High Street became available. Ric and his wife, Angela, decided to take the leap and open Hickory Creek Bar-B-Que.

We like the environment and the friendly service at Hickory Creek. The brick walls lend a sense of history and warmth. Be sure to find out where Tofu is hanging out. From time to time Ric relocates the life-size papier-mâché pink pig known as "The Ugliest Pig in Kansas." Tofu inspired Hickory Creek's annual Ugly Pig Contest. Although the judges pick a new winner every year, Tofu remains the all-time number one. Proceeds from the contest benefit local charities.

Hickory Creek serves excellent beans and potato salad, but the Cheesy Taters get our vote. Eat them with Ric's hickory-smoked pork ribs, pulled pork, lean and tender beef brisket, sausage, or turkey. Ric knows his way around his Southern Pride pit!

CHEESY TATERS

Serves 12

½ cup minced onion

2 cups shredded cheddar cheese

1 (16-ounce) container sour cream

8 tablespoons (1 stick) butter, melted

1 (10¾-ounce) can cream of chicken soup

1 (32-ounce) package frozen shredded hash browns, thawed

Salt and pepper, to taste

Preheat your smoker to 230°–250°F. Combine all the ingredients in a large bowl and mix well. Spray a 9 by 13-inch baking pan with nonstick spray, fill the pan with the mixture, cover, and smoke for about 3 hours, until the top forms a golden crust.

THE BEANS OF BARBECUE

We're told that barbecue was commercialized in the early 1900s of necessity. Recent immigrant butchers, the story goes, discovered that the barbecue method of cooking transformed tough, hard-to-sell cuts of meat such as beef brisket and pork spareribs into tender, juicy, smoky irresistible meat feasts. Tough scraps could also be ground into meat for sausage, burgers, and chili.

It figures that beans are one of the most popular side dishes with barbecue. Dried beans are cheap and tough. When soaked in water, drained, and simmered in fresh water until tender, with a variety of seasonings added, they rock! As with barbecue, you'll find bean side dishes in a variety of presentations in barbecue joints across the country. Pit-baked or oven-baked beans in barbecue sauce with meat scraps and other ingredients such as onion and peppers are very common. In central Texas we found mostly pinto beans with jalapeños, sometimes as a free, help-yourself side dish. Fresh or canned green beans are served in some joints, too.

Vanized Potato

Van's Pig Stands

717 E. Highland
Shawnee, OK 74804
405-273-0000
http://www.pigstands.com

Van's Pig Stands are in the mainstream of American barbecue history, so we couldn't leave them out of the story. "Van" is the nickname of the founder, the late Leroy F. Vandegrift. Today Van's son, Jerry Vandegrift, is the owner, president, and "Head Hog" of the Van's Pig Stands enterprise. Jerry's son Jev is area manager for the Shawnee stores and for retail barbecue sauce sales. They own Pig Stands in Shawnee, Moore, Norman, and Oklahoma City.

We're partial to Van's Shawnee location, due to its history as the oldest barbecue restaurant in Oklahoma owned and operated by the same family. It has been there since 1935. We also like the atmosphere, the service, and the excellent Pig Sandwich® common to all Van's Pig Stands.

Another fun retro perk about the Shawnee joint is the return of the Charcoal Room in the basement. Go down there and have a feast. Start with the chicken liver appetizer. With your charcoal-grilled rib eye or Kansas City strip, get the house salad and Vanized Potato. Save room for key lime pie, pecan pie, or another of the seven delicious dessert choices. You'll want to make some return trips for a rib dinner, brisket dinner, charcoaled tuna, or poached salmon.

With the closing of many original Pig Stands in Texas, we can thank the Vandegrift family for keeping the Pig Stands tradition alive. The first Pig Stand opened in Dallas in 1921, brainchild of Jesse G. Kirby. That's when transportation by private auto was really beginning to take off, and Kirby noticed that people liked their cars so much they were reluctant to get out, even to eat. So Kirby invented drive-ins. You ordered from your car, had your food delivered to your car, and stayed inside the car to eat. Model Ts and other 1920s cars had running boards to make it easier to get in and out. Pig Stand servers—young preteen or early-teens boys dressed in white shirts, white hats, and black bow ties—would hop onto the running board to take customers' orders. Thus they were nicknamed "car hops."

Besides being the first drive-in restaurant, Pig Stands have been credited with several other restaurant firsts in their Texas birthplace. Here's the complete list:

First drive-in restaurants

First curb service with car hops

First drive-through service

First restaurants to use neon signs

First restaurants to use fluorescent lighting

First restaurants to use air-conditioning

Invented Texas Toast

Invented onion rings

Invented chicken-fried steak sandwich

Today's Van's Pig Stands in Oklahoma have added another invention: the twice-baked potato. Predicting how much food a barbecue joint will sell on any given day is always a guess, as it was at Van's Pig Stand in the late 1940s. Instead of having to tell customers who ordered a baked potato that they were sold out, the Vandegrifts started erring on the side of too many instead of too few. Throwing out the extras bothered Grandmother Thelma Vandegrift, so she set her mind to figuring out how to avoid all that waste. And thus the twice-baked potato was born. Here is Van's recipe. For best results, prepare the potatoes at least 24 hours before serving.

VANIZED POTATO

Serves 6 to 8

5 pounds Idaho baking potatoes

½ yellow onion, diced

½ pound bacon, diced

½ cup Milnot or other evaporated milk

1 ½ teaspoons salt

½ teaspoon black pepper

Garlic spread or garlic butter, for serving

Preheat the oven to 400°F. Wash the potatoes and place them directly on a rack in the middle of the oven for at least 1 hour, until soft when pricked or squeezed.

While the potatoes are baking, put the onion and bacon in a small saucepan over medium-low heat and cook, stirring regularly to prevent sticking, until the onions are translucent, 3 to 5 minutes. Remove from the heat and set aside.

Remove the potatoes from the oven. Cut off one side of each potato, keeping your knife as close to the skin as possible, so you don't remove any of the potato inside. Then, using a spoon, remove the potato flesh from inside the skin and place in a large mixing bowl, being careful to not pierce the skin with the spoon. Reserve the skins.

Add the milk, salt, pepper, bacon, and onions, including the bacon drippings, to the mixing bowl with the potato flesh and mix thoroughly until you have a smooth mashed potato consistency. Then, using a pastry bag or a gallon-size food storage bag with a corner cut off, squeeze the potato mixture back into the potato skins. Cover the potatoes and place in the refrigerator to chill for a few hours or overnight.

When ready to serve, place the potatoes on a sheet pan and cook in a 350°F oven for 20 to 30 minutes, until golden brown on top. Serve with a side of garlic spread or garlic butter.

Potato Salad

Danny's Place

902 S. Canal St.
Carlsbad, NM 88220
505-885-8739
http://www.dannysbbq.com

Danny's Place got its start as a Dairy Queen franchise—the only one to serve barbecue. But when owners Danny and Carolyn Gaulden were pressured to stop serving barbecue and start serving standard DQ fare, they decided to remodel and open their own restaurant, Danny's Place. Danny's Place not only makes great smoked fresh ham (page 94) but also serves great potato salad. Here is the recipe.

cor. 8th & Vermont Ave.
LOS ANGELES - "SINCE 1936"

POTATO SALAD

Makes about 6 pounds, serving 12 hungry folks or about 16 average eaters

4 pounds russet potatoes

4 or 5 large eggs

1 medium-small onion, chopped

3 celery stalks, chopped

½ cup chopped pimientos or roasted red peppers

1 cup sweet pickle relish with juice

2 teaspoons salt

1 teaspoon black pepper

3 tablespoons yellow mustard

2 tablespoons apple cider vinegar

1 to 1½ cups Miracle Whip

Paprika, for garnish

Boil the potatoes until fork-tender. Cool and peel. Chop into pieces about fingernail size or smaller. Boil the eggs for 15 minutes, cool, peel, and chop into small pieces. Add the eggs, chopped onion, celery, pimientos, pickle relish, salt, pepper, mustard, vinegar, and 1 cup of the Miracle Whip to the potatoes and mix well. Add a little more Miracle Whip if the mixture seems too dry, but be careful; how much you need will vary depending on how starchy the potatoes are. Turn the potato salad into a serving dish and finish off with a dusting of paprika for a nice presentation. You can also add a couple of sliced boiled eggs on top if you want to get fancy. Refrigerate for 3 to 4 hours or overnight before serving.

Southern-Style Potato Salad

Wilber's Barbecue

4172 US Highway 70 E.
Goldsboro, NC 27534
919-778-5218
http://wilbersbarbecue.com

Many people told us that Wilber's is a mandatory stop if you want the true flavor of eastern North Carolina whole hog. We tried it, and we're glad we did. These days many whole hogs in eastern North Carolina are cooked with gas, but at Wilber's you get it the traditional way, cooked in pits fueled with slow-smoking oak coals. After cooking all night, the meat is separated from the bones and chopped. Some dry seasonings are mixed in, but not enough to overpower the flavor of the hog. Wilber's vinegar-based barbecue sauce is on the table so you can add as much extra seasoning as you wish. Potato salad, slaw, and hushpuppies round out the meal. It's good enough that we wish Wilber Shirley would open a joint in Kansas City. He has been barbecuing pigs in North Carolina since 1962, so it's not likely he would entertain a move. We're just glad he's in Goldsboro, and we've joined the "Wilber's is a mandatory stop" chorus. We'll be back.

Mr. Shirley had left the premises shortly before we arrived, so we didn't get the pleasure of a visit with him. Had we done so, we would have asked for his potato salad recipe. We liked it, and we noticed that Wilber's is one of only a few barbecue joints in North Carolina that serve potato salad. Our version has a few extras that we like in a potato salad.

SOUTHERN-STYLE POTATO SALAD

Serves 6 to 8

2 to 3 pounds potatoes

4 hard-cooked eggs, peeled and chopped

4 celery stalks, chopped

½ cup sweet pickle relish

2 tablespoons diced canned pimiento

½ cup diced sweet onion

¼ cup diced green bell pepper

Sea salt and black pepper

1 cup real mayonnaise

2 tablespoons yellow mustard

Wash the potatoes and cover with water; bring to a boil and simmer for 30 to 40 minutes, until tender. Drain the water from the potatoes and set the potatoes aside to cool. When the potatoes are cool, peel and dice them. Add the eggs, celery, relish, pimiento, onion, green pepper, and salt and pepper to taste. Stir until mixed. Stir the mayonnaise and mustard together until mixed and then add the mixture to the potatoes; mix well. Refrigerate for at least 1 hour before serving.

Barbecue Baked Beans

Boss Hawg's BBQ

2833 S.W. 29th St.

Topeka, KS 66614

785-273-7300

http://www.bosshawgsbbq.com

oss Hawg's BBQ is a family-owned Topeka-based barbecue joint that came about by way of barbecue competition. Hank and Elizabeth Lumpkin decided to take their championship barbecue to the commercial arena in 1986, and it's a winner. Boss Hawg's started out with carryout and catering only. They soon became successful and well known enough to open the present location in a shopping center off Southwest 29th Street. As far as we know, Boss Hawg's BBQ is the only barbecue that has an official annex that's a dining room in a U.S. Navy submarine, the USS *Topeka*.

Shortly before his untimely death in 2003 at age 38, Hank and Elizabeth opened the popular Pigskins Sports Bar adjacent to Boss Hawg's. They used money Hank had won on the TV show *Jeopardy*, to pay for the bar. Fortunately for the barbecue consumer public, Elizabeth carries on the Boss Hawg's tradition. Hank would want it that way.

At Boss Hawg's, knotty pine walls and shelves are adorned with barbecue sauces, trophies, ribbons, and other awards from barbecue competitions, plus artfully framed barbecue memorabilia. The Boss Hawg's liquor license is framed with a picture of Carrie Nation, the famous nineteenth-century hatchet-wielding prohibitionist known for wreaking havoc in saloons. The menu has had a makeover with the arrival of Chef William Fuschino. He has added a gourmet touch to a few new grilled and smoked items—alder-smoked salmon, beef tenderloin, Asian pork ribs with peanut butter sauce, and one we're especially anxious to try, Elizabeth's Smoked Watermelon Rind. The quality of the food is the same, though. Elizabeth will tell you, "We care about you, our guests, in a way no chain or franchise ever could. We care about the quality of service and food you receive."

In our quest for America's best barbecue, asking each and every barbecuer for a recipe that has never been published was a chore in itself. It was even harder to ask for a specific recipe, which was usually not exactly what they wanted to give us. It was easy to get bean and coleslaw recipes, and we wanted some of those things, but in most cases we had to decline those recipes and ask for others. In the case of Boss Hawg's, we really wanted the baked beans! Are these the best baked beans ever? Many people say they are, and we concur. Their baked beans are cooked in the pit for 2 to 3 hours swimming in barbecue sauce with apples, raisins, onions, dark brown sugar, and bacon. Thanks to Boss Hawg's, here is the home version.

Boss Hawg's liquor license is displayed with a picture of Carrie Nation. It has a special irony since Carrie Nation was no stranger to Topeka. In January 1902 she was a guest speaker at a temperance convention there. She branded the hatchet as her saloon attack tool and had souvenir hatchet pins made. Sale of the pins helped further her cause and pay off a slander suit she lost. Carrie once said, "Oh, I tell you, ladies, you never know what joy it gives to start out to smash a rum shop."

BARBECUE BAKED BEANS

Serves 6 to 8

3 (16-ounce) cans pork and beans, rinsed and drained

2 cups dark brown sugar

1 cup cooked chopped bacon, barbecue pork (page 208), or barbecue brisket (page 208)

1 cup diced tart apple, such as Granny Smith

1 cup diced onion

1 cup barbecue sauce

¼ cup golden raisins

2 teaspoons Liquid Smoke

2 cloves garlic, pressed

½ teaspoon ground coriander

Combine all the ingredients in a 2-quart casserole dish and blend well. Bake in a 350°F oven until bubbly, 45 to 60 minutes.

Brown Beans

Rooster's Bar-B-Q

2001 Capps Rd.
Harrison, AR 72601
870-741-5888
http://www.roostersbar-b-q.com/

Rooster's is a dream come true. Rusty "Rooster" Dees was in the construction business but loved to cook barbecue. In the late 1980s Rusty made his first smoker from old metal, including some old road signs. He spent a lot of time perfecting sauce recipes and trying different ways of cooking ribs, pork, and brisket. People said he should open a restaurant, so he opened Rooster's in November 2004.

Rusty's goal was to give people good food at a good price with good service and a good atmosphere. He figured that would bring people back, and he has succeeded. Rooster's was voted the best barbecue in Harrison the last two years.

One of Rooster's side dishes that you don't get just everywhere is brown beans, and here is our adaptation of his recipe. This is the same recipe Paul's mother's side of the family has been making for years, with Paul's own special touch. Serve it with all of the fixin's. It goes great with corn bread, fried potatoes, and fried cabbage, and you can follow it with Rooster's Apple Dumplings for dessert (page 165).

BROWN BEANS

Serves 8 to 10

1 pound dried pinto beans

1 large, meaty ham hock

1 large onion, chopped

2 cloves garlic, minced

1 teaspoon chili powder

1 teaspoon salt, or to taste

¼ teaspoon black pepper, or to taste

Place the beans and 8 cups water in a large stockpot. Add the ham hock, onion, and garlic. Season with chili powder, salt, and pepper. Bring to a boil and cook for 2 minutes. Cover and remove from the heat. Let stand for 1 hour.

Return the pot to the heat and bring to a boil once again. Reduce the heat to medium-low and simmer for at least 3 hours to blend the flavors, adding water as needed. The longer you simmer, the thicker the broth will become. Paul likes to cook his for about 6 hours.

Remove the ham hock from the broth and let cool. Remove the meat from the bone and return the meat to the stockpot, discarding the bone. Adjust the seasonings as needed and serve.

Van's Coleslaw

Bob Syke's BarB-Q

1724 9th Ave.
Bessemer, AL 35020
205-426-1400
http://www.bobsykes.com

Van Sykes grew up in the barbecue business. His parents, Bob and Maxine Sykes, opened a barbecue joint in Birmingham, Alabama, in 1956, a year after Van was born. The combination of Maxine's business savvy and Bob's pit savvy made for a successful barbecue business launch from the get-go. A dozen years after the Birmingham opening Bob Syke's had moved to Bessemer and had spawned fourteen franchises in Alabama and Tennessee. Long hours and extreme stress took a toll on Bob Sykes in 1970. A stroke incapacitated him to the point that he could no longer work in the business. It was up to Maxine and her teenage son, Van, to keep the business going. They dropped the franchise businesses and focused on making the Bessemer restaurant the best it could be. To this day they have lived up to that legacy. Bob Sykes, who died in 1990, would surely be proud of his wife and son.

We have known Van by reputation over the past 25 years. When we tasted his barbecue sauce in 1984 at the first Diddy-Wa-Diddy National Barbecue Sauce Contest, we could tell he knew a thing or two about barbecue. Since then we've gotten to know him as fellow members of the Southern Foodways Alliance. At a symposium on barbecue we shared some bench-shaking belly laughs with Van while Calvin Trillin regaled us with straight-faced humor and insights related to the subject at hand.

Van upholds the high standards he learned from Bob: fresh, quality ingredients and no shortcuts. Van's barbecued pork, beef, and ribs are tender, smoky, and delicious. Try to save room for pie! According to Van, "Everybody loves a good slaw with their BBQ." Thanks to Van for the recipe he shared with us.

VAN'S COLESLAW

Serves 6 to 8

½ **cup real mayonnaise (heavy-duty, not low-fat)**

1½ **tablespoons tarragon vinegar**

1 **tablespoon sugar**

7 **cups thinly sliced green cabbage**

1 **cup grated carrots**

Salt and black pepper

Chopped fresh parsley

Mix the mayonnaise, vinegar, and sugar in a large bowl. Add the cabbage and carrots and toss to coat. Season to taste with salt and pepper. Cover and refrigerate for up to 4 hours. Sprinkle with parsley and serve.

Coleslaw and Baked Beans

Woody's Bar-B-Que

5599 Hwy 14 East
Waldenburg, AR 72475
870-579-2251

ho said you couldn't set up your barbecue rig on a corner, make a living, and get famous too? Woody (William) and Cecelia Wood proved you could when they got into barbecue in 1985 to supplement Woody's crop-dusting income.

Truckers put Woody's on the map; they would pull their big rigs into the parking lot and chow down on his pig sandwich and ribs to go. "How about a bottle of your barbecue sauce?" they'd ask. "We don't bottle it" was the answer. "Well, if you ever do, I want a case to take back to Ohio!" So Woody and Cecelia started making 5 gallons

of barbecue sauce at a time and bottling it, but that made only about 2½ cases. That was OK for the first years; then they graduated to a 20-gallon pot and could make 10½ cases at a time.

Since then those sauces, along with Woody's barbecue and barbecue rubs, have won numerous awards at the National Barbecue Association (NBBQA) contest. Woody has taken home four or five first-place awards more than once and also won first place at the Dallas Gourmet Market. And business is still booming, with the truckers still spreading the word of great BBQ with their CBs blaring, "Good Q—come and get it!"

In fact the barbecue stand was doing so well and demand for his sauces was so high that Woody had several co-packers in the South make a sample of his sauce to make it more widely available. Not one of the five made it like Woody did, though. A close approximation was not what Woody and Cecelia had built their business and reputation on. So they did the only thing they could do: they built their own bottling plant. Now they sell several sauces, rubs, seasonings, and marinades—all award-winning.

Despite having their own plant, Woody's still does all of its barbecue business out of a Winnebago, with everything cooked on a large custom-built Klose barbecue pit. And it's open only three days a week—Wednesday, Thursday, and Friday—plus Saturdays during duck season.

It's worth heading to Woody's on one of those days for the oustanding pork sandwich. The slaw on it is a delicious sweet and sour, not too sweet and not too sour. Here is the recipe,

COLESLAW

Serves 6 to 8

1 head green cabbage, shredded and chopped

½ cup sweet pickle relish

¼ cup Miracle Whip (not mayonnaise)

¼ cup cane sugar

Salt and black pepper

Combine all the ingredients in a large bowl and blend well. Adjust the seasonings to your taste.

WHY PICKLES WITH BARBECUE?

We have eaten at hundreds of barbecue joints across America, and we have seldom found one that doesn't serve pickles with the barbecue. Sometimes it's dill chips, like at Arthur Bryant's, where you help yourself to as many as you want from a big jar at the end of the serving line. Sometimes it's a deli dill spear. Since the custom is near universal, we figured it would be easy to find out when, where, and why it got started, but it was no easy task at all. We called on our barbecue buddy and eminent historian of barbecue, Dr. Howard Taylor of Dallas, Texas, to find out what he knew.

According to Howard, pickles were on deli sandwiches or on the side by the early 1800s and on hamburgers by the early 1900s. In Texas, barbecue workers often ate barbecue, bread, onions, and pickles off butcher paper with no forks. Using sliced white bread or tortillas to eat barbecue was common by the early 1900s. During 1946, Leonard's in Memphis popularized the use of coleslaw on pulled pork sandwiches. Around 1950, some Texas restaurants tried serving pickle relish on barbecued beef sandwiches, but luckily the idea died quickly.

We still don't know the whole story behind the pairing, but we'll keep enjoying pickles with our barbecue.

BAKED BEANS

Serves 6 to 8

2 (16-ounce) cans pork and beans

¼ medium onion, coarsely chopped

1 tablespoon dark brown sugar

1 large green or red bell pepper, chopped

⅓ cup Woody's Original Mild Bar-B-Q sauce

2 teaspoons yellow mustard

Preheat the oven to 350°F. In a 1½-quart baking dish, combine the pork and beans, onion, brown sugar, chopped pepper, barbecue sauce, and mustard, stirring to combine. Bake the mixture for 30 to 45 minutes, until hot and bubbling.

more or less. It's all done to taste, so you be the judge of how sweet or sour you want it and add more or less of anything to taste. The baked beans are also quite good.

WHO IS TEXAS PETE?

Sit yourself down at almost any restaurant in North Carolina and you'll see a bottle of Texas Pete Hot Sauce. Why is a Texas sauce so popular in North Carolina? It's really a North Carolina sauce, made by the Garner family in Winston-Salem. The originators, four brothers—Samuel, Thad, Ralph, and Harold Garner—first settled on the name "Mexican Joe" for their newly invented hot sauce back in 1929. Their dad said no; it needed an American name, like Texas. They could have called it Texas Sam in honor of their father, Samuel, and alluding to the Sam Houston of Texas fame. But Samuel had a better idea. He suggested "Texas Pete," after the nickname for son Harold Garner. Thus it became "Texas Pete," and it has been famous ever since.

Texas Pete's mix of aged hot peppers, vinegar, and salt has become an essential ingredient in hundreds of barbecue sauces, competition and otherwise. We have yet to find a barbecue joint in North Carolina without Texas Pete on the premises. Ardie never leaves home without it. He often tells people he is meeting for breakfast, lunch, or dinner, "I'll bring Texas Pete." They unknowingly ask him upon arrival, "Where is Texas Pete?" at which point he pulls a bottle from his pocket or briefcase. It's a gently hot sauce that won't blast the sensors off your taste buds. If you can't find it where you live, call 800-476-7383, or order online at www.texaspete.com.

Eastern North Carolina Coleslaw

Stamey's

2206 High Point Rd.
Greensboro, NC
336-299-9888
http://www.stameys.com

 tamey's means "barbecue" to residents of Greensboro and the surrounding area. It has been so since 1930. The barbecue comes from a distinguished lineage that started in Lexington, where founder C. Warner Stamey learned the art and business of barbecue from Jess Swicegood and Sid Weaver. When Warner turned the business over to his sons, Keith and Charles, they had big shoes to fill and a stellar reputation to maintain. No problem. Under their leadership the business continued to thrive, as it does to this day with two longstanding locations in Greensboro. Since Keith's death in 2001, Charles and his son Charles Keith "Chip" Stamey have done an outstanding job of running Stamey's, including the Stamey tradition of hickory-smoked barbecue in custom-built pits.

If you've never tried a traditional Carolina pulled pork sandwich, it's time to treat yourself to one. After that, the only way you'll eat pulled pork is with a helping of great Piedmont-style coleslaw slapped on top. The sour notes in the slaw complement the sweetness of the pork. It is one of our all-time favorite flavor combos.

EASTERN NORTH CAROLINA COLESLAW

Serves 8 to 10

½ **cup sugar**

½ **cup ketchup**

½ **cup apple cider vinegar**

2 **teaspoons salt**

2 **teaspoons black pepper**

2 **teaspoons hot sauce, preferably Texas Pete**

1 **medium head green cabbage, coarsely grated**

In a large bowl, stir together the sugar, ketchup, vinegar, salt, pepper, and hot sauce until blended. Add the cabbage to the bowl and toss to coat. Cover and chill for at least 2 hours before serving.

Pink Coleslaw, and Buttermilk Biscuits with Country Ham

A & M Grill

402 E. Center St.
Mebane, NC 27302
919-563-3721

The A & M Grill opened just after World War II, and while it has been modernized since then, it has an inviting, well-weathered feel. Its outside is plain as can be, but before you exit your car the aromas from the barbecue pit tell you that you're in for something special. Inside, tables are covered with checkered blue cloths and outfitted with rolls of paper towels as napkins. A bottle of the ubiquitous Texas Pete sauce is on each table.

When the founder's son, Charles McAdams, Jr., had to step aside for health reasons, the many fans of A & M Grill were relieved that the restaurant would not be shuttered. Thanks to Charles's wife, Donna McAdams, and daughters, Lisa Wright, Charlotte Regans, and Karen Lewis, Mebane's A & M Grill continues to serve its famous pork barbecue with pink slaw and hushpuppies. We had a good visit with Donna and Lisa before our order arrived and are grateful to have their recipe for slaw.

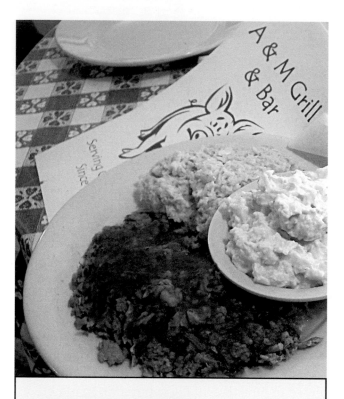

PINK COLESLAW

Serves 6 to 8

½ cup real mayonnaise

¼ cup ketchup

1½ tablespoons white vinegar

1 tablespoon sugar

7 cups chopped green cabbage

Salt and black pepper

Mix the mayonnaise, ketchup, vinegar, and sugar in a large bowl; add the cabbage and toss to coat. Season to taste with salt and pepper. Refrigerate until ready to serve.

Ardie wishes A & M would serve a chopped pork and coleslaw omelet and was disappointed to hear it doesn't serve barbecue for breakfast. Paul came up with a good sub- stitute, one of his southern country favorites that isn't exactly barbecue but is on A & M's menu: country ham on homemade biscuits. Here is Paul's recipe.

BUTTERMILK BISCUITS WITH COUNTRY HAM

Makes 12 biscuits

3 cups all-purpose flour, or more as needed

1 tablespoon baking powder

1 teaspoon sea salt

¾ teaspoon baking soda

¾ cup Crisco or lard

¾ to 1 cup buttermilk

12 thin slices of country ham (or more if desired)

Lard or canola oil, for frying

Preheat the oven to 450°F and put a rack in the middle. Sift the flour to make sure there are no lumps. Add the baking powder, salt, and baking soda. Slowly add the Crisco, working it into the dry ingredients with a large dinner fork or spoon or your hands.

Next add the buttermilk, working it into the mixture and adding only enough to moisten the dry ingredients. After everything is thoroughly mixed, plop it down on a floured counter or cutting board. Knead the dough until it is about the consistency of Play-Doh. If the dough is still sticky, sprinkle more flour on your counter or cutting board. As you knead your dough, it will pick up more of the flour.

When you have it the right consistency, you can shape your biscuits by hand or using a cookie or biscuit cutter. If using a cookie or biscuit cutter, roll the dough ½ inch thick on a lightly floured surface. Place the biscuits on a lightly greased cookie sheet. Bake for 15 to 18 minutes, until golden brown.

While the biscuits are baking, heat a little lard or canola oil in a large skillet over medium high heat. Fry the ham on one side until it just begins to brown, then turn and fry the other side. Remove the biscuits from the oven, split them, fill them with slices of country ham, and serve warm. If it's for lunch, add a side of Pink Coleslaw.

Cast-Iron Skillet Corn Bread

Skylight Inn

1501 S. Lee St.
Ayden, NC 28513
252-746-4113

ational Geographic magazine once called the Skylight Inn the "Barbecue Capital of the World." The late Pete Jones, then owner, was so rightly proud of the distinction that he topped the roof of the joint with a metal dome meant to resemble the nation's capitol dome. The dome is still there, serving as a beacon and an icon.

We can't attest to how the barbecue at the Skylight Inn today compares to how it was when Pete ran the place, but you'll get no complaints from us. It was worth the trip. In fact it was so good we were seriously talking about moving to North Carolina. Well, not so seriously that we would actually leave Kansas City, also dubbed the barbecue capital of the world by other magazines and food writers. But we have no qualms about saying the folks who live close enough to frequent the Skylight Inn are fortunate indeed.

There's nothing fancy about the place, but there's ample seating and the comfortable feeling that you're in the right place, because the door keeps opening to admit more customers and most look like this is business as usual for them. You'll hear the familiar chop-chop-chop of cleavers on a large butcher block lit with heat lamps. Something we liked that not every place

CAST-IRON SKILLET CORN BREAD

Makes 8 wedges

¼ **cup bacon drippings or butter**

2 **cups fine stone-ground white cornmeal**

1 **teaspoon salt**

½ **teaspoon baking soda**

½ **teaspoon baking powder**

1 **large egg**

1½ **cups buttermilk**

Preheat the oven to 450°F. Place the drippings in a 10-inch cast-iron skillet and pop the skillet into the oven to heat. In the meantime, combine the cornmeal, salt, baking soda, and baking powder in a large bowl. In a small bowl, beat together the egg and buttermilk. Add the buttermilk mixture to the cornmeal mixture and stir, using the absolute minimum number of strokes needed to moisten the dry ingredients.

Remove the hot skillet from the oven and swirl it around so the drippings coat the bottom and lower sides of the skillet. Then pour the remainder of the hot drippings or butter into the batter and stir a couple of times. Turn the batter into the hot skillet, place back in the oven, and bake until it is golden brown, 20 to 25 minutes. Remove from the oven, cut into 8 wedges, and serve warm.

does is the addition of pig cracklings to the chopped pork. They must put them in shortly before serving, as they were nice and crunchy in our sandwiches. This is basic North Carolina barbecue goodness: a chopped pork sandwich topped with coleslaw, with a side of skillet corn bread, Texas Pete hot sauce at the ready, and a glass of sweet tea.

Our barbecue buddy Carl Rothrock met us at Skylight. The staff was so busy serving customers none of us could get the recipe out of them, so Paul came up with this home version.

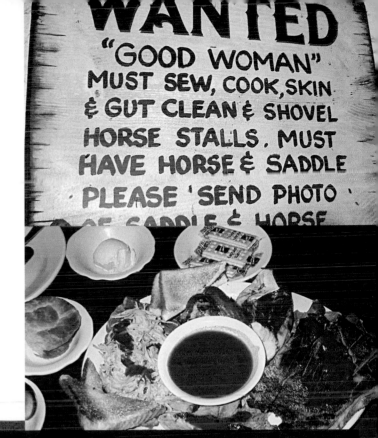

SAUCE MATTERS—

Many pitmasters have told us it's the sauce that matters. "Anyone can barbecue," they say, "but not everyone can make good sauce." On the other hand we've heard—especially in Texas—that "My barbecue is so good it doesn't need sauce." In some places it is house policy to prohibit sauce on the premises. Thus, the barbecue vs. sauce edict is reversed. "Anyone can make sauce, but not everyone can barbecue."

Questions also arise as to what makes a good sauce. Should the base be vinegar, tomato, mustard, mayonnaise, soy, fruit, peppers, or something else? Should sauce be spicy hot, or mild? Are any specific herbs and spices essential? While we can agree on a few objective standards such as barbecue shouldn't taste like lighter fluid and it should be tender enough to chew easily, people part ways on the other questions. Barbecue aficionados debate all of these questions and many others. In the end there are no right or wrong answers when it comes to questions of individual taste.

OR DOES IT?

CINEMA 'CUE

Barbecue is a major or bit player in many famous and infamous movies. Some of our favorites:

Gone With the Wind (1939). There's a barbecue at the beginning of the movie, and the word is uttered eleven times during the 3-hour-and-42-minute movie.

Giant (1956). This blockbuster big-screen drama starring James Dean, Rock Hudson, and Elizabeth Taylor is based on Edna Ferber's best-selling novel. The Barbacoa scene is truly memorable. No "mad cow" scares back then. "And do those brains taste sweet!"

Murphy's Romance (1985). While Sally Field and James Garner romanced each other as Murphy Jones and Emma Moriarty, Kansas City's Rich Davis of KC Masterpiece Barbecue Sauce fame supervised the open-pit barbecue of a steer at Emma's ranch. Notice a bottle of KC Masterpiece on Murphy's kitchen table? This is an early example of the pre-*E.T.* product placement marketing so common in today's movies and TV shows.

Top Gun (1986). Filmed on location in San Diego's Kansas City Barbeque restaurant. The joint, autographed bras, and other memorabilia, burned down on June 26, 2008, due to a pit fire. Like a phoenix, a new joint has emerged from the ashes, just like old times.

Fried Green Tomatoes (1991). Based on Fannie Flagg's best-selling novel *Fried Green Tomatoes at the Whistle Stop Café*, this movie is the Sweeney Todd of cinema 'cue thanks to some Alabama barbecue that you'll see on the screen.

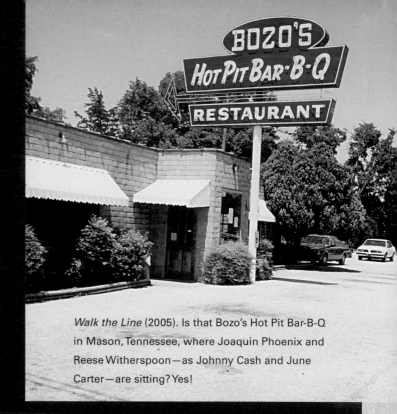

Walk the Line (2005). Is that Bozo's Hot Pit Bar-B-Q in Mason, Tennessee, where Joaquin Phoenix and Reese Witherspoon—as Johnny Cash and June Carter—are sitting? Yes!

Dancer, Texas – Pop. 81 (1998). A bottle of Bone Suckin' Sauce appears on the dining room table in a trailer home. We know it isn't a product placement marketing deal. We asked Sandi Ford at Ford Foods, home of Bone Suckin' Sauce, and she didn't know about the movie. She was happy to know her sauce is in the movie, however.

Primary Colors (1998). Politicking and barbecue are naturals in this story about a former governor of Arkansas, played by John Travolta, in a race for the White House.

The Cookout (2004). Unexpected wildness and confusion occur when Storm P as Todd Anderson hosts a cookout to celebrate a $30 million contract with the New Jersey Nets. The DVD includes a special feature on how to have a good cookout, plus some good recipes from the cast.

Baptists at Our Barbecue (2004). This comedy is about an attempt to bring peace to a divided community by throwing a barbecue with everyone invited.

Corn Bread Muffins

Branks BBQ & Catering
13701 24th St. East
Sumner, WA 98390
253-891-1789

Paul had the pleasure of visiting Branks barbecue at its original location, a nice small, homey barbecue joint in downtown Sumner, Washington. It became very successful, and there was no way to expand, so it moved to the industrial dictrict. The decor is what you might call country with a lot of local history thrown in, things like bucksaws and other old logging items. The staff is young and friendly, the barbecue is cooked in the pit with wild cherry wood, and all of the sides and desserts are made from scratch. Featured here is the recipe for Branks's great corn bread muffins. Paul is good for two or three every time he eats there.

CORN BREAD MUFFINS

Makes 12 muffins

1 cup yellow cornmeal

1 cup all-purpose flour

⅛ to ¼ cup sugar

4 teaspoons baking powder

½ teaspoon sea salt

1 to 1¼ cups buttermilk

1 large egg, at room temperature

11 tablespoons butter, melted and cooled

Preheat the oven to 375°F and place a rack in the middle. Butter 12 regular (⅓-cup) muffin cups. In a medium bowl, combine the cornmeal, flour, sugar, baking powder, and salt, then sift the mixture into a large bowl. In the now empty medium bowl, mix the buttermilk and egg together with a wire whisk. Whisk in the melted butter. Pour the buttermilk mixture into the cornmeal mixture and stir just until incorporated. Do not overmix. Divide the mix equally among the prepared muffin cups. Bake for about 15 minutes, until a toothpick inserted in the center of a muffin comes out clean. The muffins will be a pale yellow. Cool on a rack for 10 minutes. Serve with real butter.

Jalapeño Hushpuppies

Rudy Mikeska's Bar-B-Q

300 W. 2nd St.
Taylor, TX 76574
800-962-5706 or 512-365-3722
http://mikeska.com

Say "Mikeska" to a native Texan, and the reply will be "barbecue." The Mikeska barbecue legacy began in the late nineteenth century, when a penniless family from Czechoslovakia moved to Texas to build a better life. First there was farming, and then there was barbecue—barbecue on a massive scale through several restaurants run by Mikeska family members and through huge catering events in Texas, the rest of the United States, and abroad. This continues today with a third generation of Mikeskas, and a fourth generation is waiting in the wings.

We didn't track down every restaurant in Texas run by a Mikeska, although we'd like to do that someday. Rather, we visited the restaurant, or cafeteria as it is sometimes called, in Taylor, the original Mikeska family home base. We found the ribs and brisket to be downright respectable—tender and flavorful. We couldn't resist the fried catfish, which was good enough to make us plan to come back for more when we're not on a barbecue mission (assuming our lives ever stop being one big barbecue mission!).

We could tell that in addition to the good food, a reason for the phenomenal success of the Mikeska barbecue empire is friendly service. We felt welcome there, although we were strangers and didn't mention we were there to consider putting Mikeska's Bar-B-Q in this book.

Jalapeño Hushpuppies are a popular item on the Mikeska catering menu. We give you our version here.

JALAPEÑO HUSHPUPPIES

Serves 6 to 8

2 cups yellow cornmeal

1 cup all-purpose flour

¾ teaspoon seasoned salt

½ teaspoon cayenne

1 teaspoon baking powder

1 teaspoon baking soda

½ cup chopped scallions

1 or 2 jalapeño peppers

2 large eggs

1 cup buttermilk

2 tablespoons bacon grease

Canola oil or lard, for deep-frying

In a large bowl, mix the cornmeal, flour, seasoned salt, cayenne, baking powder, and baking soda until combined. Add the scallions and jalapeño peppers and stir to combine. Add the eggs, buttermilk, and bacon grease. Stir it all up until the flavors are thoroughly blended.

Heat the frying oil in a deep-fryer to 350°F (or use a deep pot and measure the oil temperature with a deep-frying thermometer). When it's hot, use a tablespoon to drop your hushpuppies in. Allow them to brown on all sides. They will begin floating when done, after 5 to 7 minutes. Be careful not to overcook them.

's Barbecue Pit

Roasted Garlic Chile Morita BBQ Sauce

Josh's Barbecue

3486 Zafarano Dr.
Santa Fe, NM 87507
505-474-6466
http://www.joshsbbq.com

We were saddened when Ardie's friend Elaine Anton decided to shutter her fantastic Santa Fe barbecue joint, R&B. Would anyone else fill the gap Elaine was leaving when the coals went cold in her Southern Yankee? Would anyone else turn out the flavorful, inventive dishes with a Santa Fe accent that R&B's was known for? To our delight, such a place was discovered for us by one of our favorite mystery writers, N.M. Kelby, author of *Whale Season* and *Murder at the Bad Girl's Bar and Grill*—and a BBQ goddess as well. While she was in Santa Fe as artist-in-residence at the Santa Fe Art Institute, Ardie asked her to see if Santa Fe had any good barbecue to offer beyond chain or franchise venues. To our delight, she discovered Josh's! N.M. was kind enough to offer this report, which is followed by a recipe for Roasted Garlic Chile Morita BBQ Sauce that Josh gave us. N.M. Kelby's background in journalism and food writing shines through in this piece. We're proud to share her review with you, and we thank her!

The things people do for love are truly amazing. Josh Baum left behind the world of haute cuisine, working in France at Michelin three-star restaurants, to come to Santa Fe, and eventually he opened up a barbecue joint with a big cowboy boot on its sign. And he did it for love, but not just love of barbecue—it was for the love of his wife.

Josh had always wanted to open his own restaurant, and when the opportunity arose he chose barbecue because the pace appealed to him. It was much more low key than working in the frantic world of fine dining. Josh's uncle owns Steve's Rib and Sports Grill in Oklahoma City, Oklahoma. "I used to watch my uncle at his place, and it was just great. He'd cook everything in the morning and then relax," Josh says. "I really wanted to spend more time with my wife." So, Josh's Barbecue, "Let's meat at the boot," was born.

Even though his work in France is far behind, the haute-cuisine sensibility is not. There is not a single item at Josh's that is bought premade. Everything is made from scratch using the finest seasonal ingredients and hormone-free meats. The fare is mostly traditional, with dry ribs, pulled pork, brisket, and barbecued chicken wings. There's also turkey marinated in red chile, orange juice, and butter—then coated with a mild chile rub. It's difficult to go wrong here. All are standouts in their own right. Josh smokes with a traditional Ole Hickory Pit using Texas oak, anywhere from 5 to 30 hours, depending on the meat, and the results are sublime.

Even the sides are worth driving for. The coleslaw has a nice hit of mustard, rice wine vinegar, and green chile. The Jalapeño Corn Bread is cakelike and more sweet than hot. In fact, most things at Josh's are just hot enough; they won't make you sweat. But, for the chile heads,

continued on page 154

ROASTED GARLIC CHILE MORITA BBQ SAUCE

Makes 4 cups

1 small yellow onion, chopped

2 tablespoons canola oil

4 morita chiles or chipotles in adobo, minced or diced

12 cloves roasted garlic

⅓ cup apple cider vinegar

2½ cups chicken stock

1 (14½-ounce) can diced tomatoes, drained

1½ cups ketchup

½ cup Thai sweet chile sauce

¼ cup molasses

½ cup packed brown sugar

2 tablespoons fresh orange juice

2 tablespoons fresh lemon juice

Salt and black pepper

Sauté the onion in the canola oil in a medium saucepan over medium heat until soft, 5 to 7 minutes. Add the chiles and roasted garlic and toast lightly for 3 to 4 minutes. Add the vinegar and cook until the mixture is reduced by half, 15 to 20 minutes.

Add the stock, the canned tomatoes, the ketchup, chile sauce, molasses, brown sugar, orange juice, and lemon juice. Bring to a boil; then lower the heat and simmer for 30 minutes. Remove the pan from the heat and set it aside to cool. Once the mixture has cooled, puree it in a blender and pass it through a fine strainer. Season with salt and pepper to taste and serve. Goes great on poultry!

ROASTED GARLIC

2 heads garlic

1 tablespoon extra-virgin olive oil

Sea salt and freshly ground black pepper

Preheat the oven to 325°F. Line a small baking dish with aluminum foil. Cut the top quarter from each head of garlic and place the garlic cut side up on the prepared dish. Drizzle with oil and season lightly with salt and pepper. Turn the garlic cut side down, and roast until the cloves are soft and golden brown, about 1 hour. Remove from the oven and let sit until cool enough to handle. Squeeze the garlic from the skins and discard the skins. This makes more than you'll need for Josh's recipe, but you can store it in an airtight container in the refrigerator for up to a week and use it in a variety of dishes.

To make a garlic paste: When cool enough to handle easily, put the roasted garlic into a small bowl, mash with a fork, and add oil from the pan until a paste forms. The paste makes great garlic bread!

sweet chili sauce. The hot version is just that—the same great sauce turned up a notch. Neither is cooked, mostly because he has no room in back, but that's a great decision. The sauces are fresh tasting, and each flavor is married to the other in the French style—which is to say that there is no one dominant taste or overwhelming heat—they are just dang fine sauces and a perfect complement to the moist, smoky meat. The third sauce changes every so often and is usually fruit-based. The one I tried was blackberry and bourbon with a hint of hoisin.

he offers an addictive Jalapeño Cucumber Relish made with shredded carrot, pickles, cucumbers, jalapeños, rice vinegar, and brown sugar. It's so lovely, and so hot, you will weep.

The Santa Fe location puts a regional spin on traditional barbecue offerings. "I really want to cook barbecue for the locals," Josh says. So, not only does he serve a toothsome brisket, smoked for 18 hours and as moist and tender as I've ever had, but he offers a local variation, Green Chile Brisket, in which he resmokes the basic brisket with Hatch chiles for a grand total of 30 hours. The result is as complex as any French sauce. The chiles and brisket become an amazingly complex combination of smoke, sweetness, and heat. Good eats. One of the big "must haves" here is the chips and homemade *queso* with the green chile brisket. If you don't like chips, you can have them pour it over a spud.

Nearly all the meats are served dry (some do have a brush of glaze), so Josh offers three sauces every day. This is where his chef's training truly shows. The "traditional" sauce is anything but. Loaded with flavor, some heat, and only a slight hint of smoke, its base is Thai

Like any good culinary school graduate, Josh believes in specials. During the week he likes to feature meats that are not on the regular menu, including lamb with a jerk rub, beef ribs, and St. Louis–style ribs. When I was there, the special was baby backs with a red chile glaze. Right as he finishes cooking the ribs, he brushes them with the sweet, hot paste and then serves a bowl of it on the side. Totally addictive. I found myself pouring the glaze all over my baked potato.

Don't forget dessert. Every day there's a new cobbler, but I had the white chocolate banana pudding. It was cool and sweet, but not too sweet. It was the perfect foil for perfect barbecue.

For the area, prices are reasonable. They also offer family meals to go. Keep in mind that when Josh runs out of food, he runs out of food. It's just that kind of place.

Goode Company BBQ Beef Rub

Goode Company Barbeque

5015 Kirby
Houston, TX 77098
800-627-3502 or 713-643-5263
http://www.goodecompany.com

Jim Goode, pitmaster at Goode Company Barbeque in Houston, Texas, started the company in 1977. Today there are four Goode Company restaurants, plus a mail-order business called the Barbeque Hall of Flame. Cooking tools, barbecue products, books, pies, and other great products can be ordered from the Hall of Flame online or with a phone call.

To our good friend and barbecue buddy the late Brian Heinecke, a stop at the original Goode Company to dine and to visit with Jim was a favorite highlight of any trip to Texas. We can't think of Goode Company without remembering Brian.

The walls of Goode Company are full of cowboy memorabilia, photos, and taxidermy. Customers line up and order cafeteria style and then find a place to dine at one of the many long picnic tables. It's one of those many barbecue places where the enjoyment of the barbecue brings people from all walks of life together, like a community gathering.

Jim's rub is great for beef, including ribs, roasts, and brisket, but it also enriches pork and lamb. Thanks to Jim, here's the recipe.

GOODE COMPANY BBQ BEEF RUB

Makes ¾ cup

2½ tablespoons packed dark brown sugar

2 tablespoons paprika

2 teaspoons dry mustard

2 teaspoons onion powder

2 teaspoons garlic powder

1½ teaspoons dried basil

1 teaspoon ground bay leaves

¾ teaspoon ground coriander

¾ teaspoon ground savory

¾ teaspoon dried thyme

¾ teaspoon freshly ground black pepper

¾ teaspoon white pepper

⅛ teaspoon ground cumin

Salt

To make the rub, combine all the ingredients in a small bowl. Store the mixture in an airtight container for up to 6 months. There's no need to refrigerate it.

To use the rub, massage it into the meat thoroughly the night before you plan to grill. Wrap the meat well in plastic wrap and place in the refrigerator until grilling time so that the flavors will be absorbed into the meat.

Championship Rib Rub & All-Purpose Seasoning

Johnny's Barbecue

5959 Broadmoor
Mission, KS 66202
913-432-0777
http://johnnysbbq.net

We'll tell you up front that Johnny White is a longtime friend, we eat at Johnny's on a regular basis, and we wrote parts of this book at Johnny's. That said, Johnny's is here because it belongs here. We appreciate the entire Johnny's team, in particular Brian White, Johnny's brother; Mike "Bubba" Brouhard, Johnny's brother-in-law; Terri Brouhard, Johnny's sister; Shannon Hammer, Johnny's niece, who always greets us with smiles and wit; Jason Ossana and Jan Monty, who try to keep a lid on our rowdiness; and Brady Schleicher and Zak Zimmerman.

Johnny has converted this former pizza place into a popular, busy barbecue joint. His son Eric runs another Johnny's, that one in Olathe and of equal quality. Inside the original Johnny's in Mission there's enough southwestern art and artifacts on the walls to make you wonder if you're in Santa Fe. What we like best about the decor is the hundreds of bottles of barbecue sauce on display from all over America and a few other countries. A few years ago Johnny asked Ardie, "Do you have any barbecue sauces you'd give me to display here?" Ardie's wife, Gretchen, had been asking him, "When are you going to get rid of all those barbecue sauces in the basement?" It was a perfect barbecue sauce storm! Ardie told Johnny, "I'll bring sauce. You tell me when to stop." Johnny may not have the world's largest collection of barbecue sauces, but he has several hundred.

Johnny, like about a dozen other successful pitmasters in Kansas City, learned the barbecue method of cooking and how to run a barbecue joint when he worked at Rosedale Barbecue with the founder, Anthony Rieke. Although the Rosedale influence is noticeable, Johnny has developed his own original style of barbecue, and it's a winning formula. His rub is a great all-purpose rub for barbecuing. Here's the recipe for you from Johnny.

CHAMPIONSHIP RIB RUB & ALL-PURPOSE SEASONING

Makes about 6 tablespoons

2 tablespoons kosher salt

1 tablespoon coarse black pepper

1 tablespoon paprika

1 teaspoon sugar

1 teaspoon whole celery seeds

1 teaspoon cayenne

1 teaspoon dried oregano

1 teaspoon garlic salt

1 teaspoon chili powder

½ teaspoon ground cumin

Combine all the ingredients in a tightly sealed clear plastic food storage bag, shaking until blended. If not using the rub immediately, you can store it in a cool, dark place for up to 6 months.

Apply the rub to ribs and refrigerate, covered, for 4 to 6 hours for the best results before cooking as desired.

Fried Okra

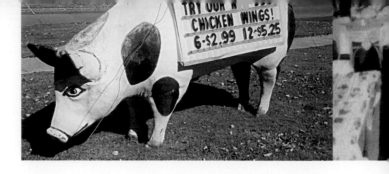

Perry's Original Roadside BBQ

2920 Beneva Rd.
Sarasota, FL 34232
941-724-1702
http://www.perryssauce.com

We're not bona fide snowbirds that head south to Florida annually when winter arrives. We did venture south last winter, however, in search of sun, surf, seafood, and barbecue. We heard there was a man named Perry in Sarasota who cooks outstanding barbecue. Eager to find out, we checked the schedule posted on his Web site and found Perry on a Sunday afternoon on Siesta Key in front of The Old Salty Dog. There he was, at a folding table under a portable tent, wrapping a large order of brisket, ribs, and chicken in aluminum foil for a New York City customer ready to fly home. When it was our turn to order, everything was sold out except a portion of brisket. We took it, Perry sliced it, and it was truly great—moist, tender, and flavorful. Other customers have raved about Perry's chicken and ribs, and we'll be back for that, but on the merits of his brisket alone we can tell Perry knows his way around the barbecue pit.

Washington Perry has been barbecuing for almost 40 years. He learned the basics from his uncle and mother during his growing-up years in Dawson, Georgia.

"I learned how to barbecue the old-fashioned way—out back with a 55-gallon drum and a whole hog," he told us. Perry's longtime dream was to cook and serve the best barbecue possible. His many enthusiastic fans agree that he has achieved that dream. Perry is glad his barbecue is received so well, but he doesn't rest on his laurels. Like all of the best barbecue pitmasters we know, Perry hasn't stopped learning. "There are always new ideas coming up," he said. "My uncle told me, 'I don't care what you do in life—cooking or whatever—your chief occupation is to always be a student.'"

Perry also emphasized that his mother, Alice Perry, "was everything to my success." During the Perry family's early years in Sarasota, Alice opened a café called Alice's Soul Food. All of the items on Perry's catering menu today are from Alice's original recipes. "She was the one to teach us how to do all that," said Perry.

Perry's Original Roadside BBQ is so named "because that's where it all started—selling barbecue on the roadside," he said. He has a kitchen for preparing catered meals and will cook whole hog for special occasions, but when he's on the road at scheduled locations in Sarasota, the customers want spareribs, brisket, and chicken. "There's not much call for whole hog," he said.

Perry uses his own original recipes for rub and sauce. His rub is a mix of granulated garlic, seasoned salt, black pepper, Old Bay Seasoning, and ½ teaspoon ground cinnamon. "The cinnamon gives the meat an apple flavor, like it's been cooked with apple wood," Perry said. Perry's Original Roadside BBQ Sauce is made with tomato ketchup, mustard, vinegar, molasses, peppers, sugar, spices, "and LOTS OF LOVE!" His smoke of choice is a mix of live oak and pecan, with charcoal briquettes to help keep the fire going. "I use no propane at all," he told us. Barbecue "is very simple," he said, "but you must have a lot of love for it." Perry is mentoring his daughter, Lakesha, who definitely has that love. She has taken on the role of marketing Perry's sauce. We like the bold flavor of Perry's sauce. Pepper, vinegar, a hint of sweetness, and some secret spices make it a solid complement to barbecued or grilled meat. Contact Perry or Lakesha to order a bottle or a case. We recommend a case, because after you try it you'll want to share it with friends and keep a supply in the cupboard so you won't run out. "We have a lot of fun," Perry told us. Commitment to excellence, lifelong learning, lots of love, and a lot of fun is Perry's winning formula for life and barbecue. We think he's on to something!

Reading Perry's catering menu could inspire a trip to Sarasota to book an Original Roadside catering event. Besides barbecued pulled pork, beef brisket, ribs, and chicken, your choice of sides is baked beans, mac and cheese, collard greens, Brunswick stew, coleslaw, potato salad, fried green tomatoes, fried okra, or corn bread. We didn't get Alice's original recipe for fried okra, but this is a good one.

FRIED OKRA

Serves 6 to 8

Vegetable oil, for deep-frying

1½ pounds whole fresh okra

1 cup self-rising cornmeal

½ cup all-purpose flour

1 teaspoon salt

½ teaspoon black pepper

Preheat a deep-fryer with vegetable oil to 375°F. If you don't have a deep-fryer, you can use a skillet over medium-high heat. Just be sure to use enough oil to cover the okra.

Wash the okra under cold running water and drain well. Prepare the okra for cooking by cutting off the tip and stem ends. Cut the remaining okra into ½-inch slices. Set the cut okra aside while you prepare the cornmeal coating.

Combine the cornmeal, flour, salt, and black pepper in a brown paper bag or a resealable plastic bag. Shake the mixture well.

Drop the okra into the bag and shake well to coat it uniformly. Drop the okra into the deep-fryer without crowding and fry until the okra turns golden brown and floats to the top for 6 to 8 minutes. If you're using a skillet, once the okra begins to brown on one side, turn it over and brown on the other side for 3 to 4 minutes total. Once the okra is done, remove it from the oil and drain it on paper towels. Serve warm.

Desserts

It isn't easy to save room for dessert when you're eating great barbecue. That's why many joints don't serve dessert. Some do, however, and the ones we give you here are worth your restraint in the earlier courses of the meal. From banana cream pie to fried peach pie, turtle cheesecake, apple dumplings, homemade vanilla ice cream, and more, they look good, taste good, and will bring you back for more. Desserts needn't complement the menu. They are in a category all their own.

Apple Pie

Boneyard Grill

617 S. Division St.
Guthrie, OK 73044
405-293-9615

he City of Guthrie, Oklahoma, has marked a couple of major milestones in the month of April—one territorial, the other culinary. The Great Land Rush for 2 million acres of land in Oklahoma Territory started at noon on April 22, 1899. Some 50,000 individuals took part in the rush, seeking up to 160 acres apiece that could become theirs through homesteading and improving the property. President Benjamin Harrison was authorized by the U.S. Congress to make the land available to settlers. On that day in April, Guthrie blossomed from uninhabited prairie to a city of 10,000 in only 6 hours.

The great culinary milestone in Guthrie happened on April 6, 2007, when Ralph Mann and Wayne Machtolff opened the Boneyard Grill on South Division Street.

As a rule we wouldn't highlight a joint this new, but we liked the Boneyard Grill so much that we believe Boneyard has a winning formula for success: ambience, quality food, and reasonable prices. The two co-owners have enough prior experience as chefs in other restaurants that we're confident Boneyard will grow in reputation and number of loyal customers. The grilled steaks were tempting, but we were on a barbecue mission, so we had ribs, beans, fries, and apple pie. The Boneyard name was inspired by rib bones from a rib-eating and beer-drinking session with friends of Ralph and Wayne. The ribs were so good that we picked the bones clean.

APPLE PIE

Serves 6 to 8

4 Granny Smith apples, peeled and thinly sliced

¼ cup white cane sugar

¼ cup packed light brown sugar

¼ cup dairy sour cream

1 ½ teaspoons ground cinnamon

1 teaspoon ground allspice

1 teaspoon ground nutmeg

4 tablespoons (½ stick) unsalted butter, melted

1 (9-inch) pie shell

1 cup all-purpose flour

8 tablespoons (1 stick) unsalted butter, softened

Preheat the oven to 350°F and place a rack in the middle. In a large bowl, combine the apples, white and brown sugar, sour cream, cinnamon, allspice, nutmeg, and melted butter and gently mix the ingredients together, being careful not to break up the apples. Pour the filling into the pie shell and spread evenly.

In a medium bowl, combine the flour and softened butter and blend with a fork until crumbly. Spread the crumbles evenly over the filling and bake for 1½ hours, turning the pie around after the first 45 minutes for even cooking. The topping should be brown, and the filling should be bubbling. Remove the pie from the oven and cool slightly before cutting into wedges.

From the outside Boneyard looks to us like a former country store or gas station. Inside it feels and looks like an old comfy home, furnished with tables, chairs, and other touches that could go back to Oklahoma's territorial days. Although it seems small, there's enough seating for at least 70. Rapport with Ralph and Wayne was easy, and it was apparent that they are dedicated and talented chefs and pitmasters.

We asked for a recipe, and they gladly obliged with the official Boneyard Grill Apple Pie —the original recipe from Ralph's grandmother, Oma Sczksczeika.

Apple Crisp

Hole in the Wall Barbecue

3200 W. 11th Ave.
Eugene, OR 97401
541-683-7378
http://www.holeinthewallbbq.com

ole in the Wall Barbecue is a perfect example of how the craving and desire for good barbecue can move mountains. In 1992, Richard and Linda Becker returned from Arizona to Oregon, where they grew up. "To satisfy our barbecue cravings, we decided to open our own restaurant," they told us. And their lives were changed forever.

Hole in the Wall Barbecue first opened August 2, 1993, for lunch only on weekdays, from 11:00 A.M. to 2:00 P.M., and on Fridays and Saturdays until 8:00 P.M. The menu was limited, with three sandwiches, chili, barbecue beans, potato salad, and coleslaw—all made from scratch. With their ever-growing barbecue and catering business they "bit the bullet" and expanded their hours to 8:00 P.M. Tuesday through Saturday. They also added St. Louis–style ribs, barbecue chicken, hot links, french fries, and sweet tea, as well as other seasonal items.

Hole in the Wall's reputation has spread far and wide. Paul has enjoyed eating their award-winning barbecue since 1994, when they were only 8 months old. Their outstanding brisket sandwich and barbecue ribs are his favorites, and their award-winning chili is also worth the trip. One of their signature desserts is apple crisp, and as everything else at Hole in the Wall, it's made from scratch.

APPLE CRISP

Serves 8 to 10

FILLING

¾ cup white cane sugar

2 teaspoons ground cinnamon

3 pounds apples, peeled, cored, and sliced

TOPPING

⅓ cup packed light brown sugar

⅓ cup all-purpose flour

½ teaspoon baking powder

¼ teaspoon baking soda

6 tablespoons butter, frozen

½ cup quick oats

Preheat the oven to 350°F. Combine the granulated sugar and cinnamon in a large bowl and blend well. Add the apples and toss until the apples are well coated.

Mix the brown sugar, flour, baking powder, and soda and blend well. Using a metal scraper blade or pastry knife, cut the butter into the flour mixture until it reaches the consistency of peas. Add the quick oats and mix well.

Spray a 9-inch square baking pan with nonstick spray. Add the apple mixture and spread the oat topping evenly over the top. Bake, uncovered, for 20 minutes, rotate the pan, and bake for another 20 minutes, until the topping is golden brown and the apple filling is bubbling.

Apple Dumplings

Rooster's Bar-B-Q

2001 Capps Rd.
Harrison, AR 72601
870-741-5888
http://www.roostersbar-b-q.com/
index.html

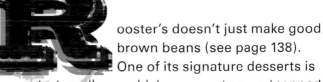

ooster's doesn't just make good brown beans (see page 138). One of its signature desserts is apple dumplings, which are great served topped with cream or ice cream. Here is our version of their trade-secret dumpling.

APPLE DUMPLINGS

Makes about 1 dozen

2 to 2½ cups all-purpose flour

2 teaspoons baking powder

1 teaspoon sea salt

¾ cup shortening

½ cup whole milk

4 to 6 Granny Smith or other cooking apples, peeled, cored, and sliced

About ½ cup sugar, for sprinkling on the apples

Ground cinnamon

Ground nutmeg

8 tablespoons (1 stick) butter, cut into small pieces

SYRUP

2 cups sugar

¼ teaspoon ground cinnamon

¼ teaspoon ground nutmeg

2 cups hot water

4 tablespoons (½ stick) butter or margarine, melted

Heavy cream or ice cream, for serving (optional)

Preheat the oven to 375°F. Lightly grease a 9 by 13-inch baking dish or a 12-muffin tin.

Combine the flour, baking powder, and salt in a bowl. Cut in the shortening until the mixture resembles coarse meal. Gradually add the milk, stirring to make a soft dough. Roll the dough into an ⅓-inch-thick rectangle on a lightly floured surface; cut it into twelve 5-inch squares.

Place 3 or 4 slices of apple on each square. Sprinkle each dumpling with 2 teaspoons sugar and a sprinkling of cinnamon and nutmeg to taste; dot with butter. Moisten the edges of each dumpling with water; bring the corners to the center, pinching the edges to seal. Place the dumplings 1 inch apart in the prepared baking dish.

To make the syrup, combine the sugar, cinnamon, nutmeg, hot water, and butter or margarine; stir to dissolve the sugar. Pour the syrup over the dumplings and bake for 35 to 45 minutes, or until golden brown. Serve hot with cream or ice cream.

Peach Cobbler

Allen & Son

6203 Millhouse Rd.
Chapel Hill, NC 27516
919-942-7576

After a long-awaited visit to the Ginger Young Art Gallery, where they added a couple of treasures to their outsider art collection, Ardie and his wife, Gretchen, told Ginger that their next stop was Allen & Son for lunch. Ginger said, "Oh, yes! That's one of our favorite places." She assured them they were in for a delicious lunch and asked them to give proprietor Keith Allen her hello.

Before eating lunch Ardie and Gretchen wanted to visit with Keith. "He's out back" was the answer. Out back is a working woodpile of huge hickory logs in various states of preparation to become charcoal for cooking some of the best barbecued pork shoulders in the world. A long rectangular building houses the pits on one end and a kitchen/prep room on the other. There was also the unmistakable chopping sound Ardie and Gretchen had become accustomed to already, only two days into their North Carolina barbecue tour.

The man doing the chopping was Keith Allen, the son in Allen & Son. Tall, rugged, handsome, and strong as an ox, Mr. Allen gave Ardie and Gretchen a friendly reception. This is a pitmaster with a passion for serving top-quality barbecue. How he does it isn't easy. "People come here and want to learn how I do it," he said. "But they don't last long." After a few days of getting up at the crack of dawn and doing barbecue the Keith Allen way, they burn out and leave. Doing barbecue eastern North Carolina style as Keith Allen does it demands strength, know-how, long hours, time management, and serious dedication to excellence in barbecue. Keith has all of that. Here is some of what he gets done in a day:

Keeps a steady supply of hardwood on hand

Keeps a steady supply of pork shoulders and other kitchen supplies for made-from-scratch sauce, sides, and desserts

Keeps a steady supply of hot coals at the ready for shoveling under the shoulders every half hour

Saws and chops wood into pieces small enough to fit into his charcoal pit

Converts wood into charcoal

Schedules and plans catering jobs

Chops cooked shoulders for serving

During the 30-minute periods between coal shoveling, he'll be doing a variety of tasks such as making cobblers, making homemade ice cream, preparing sauce or sides—all that and more. Yet, if you catch him at the right time, he is willing to visit with strangers and answer questions.

Allen & Son has a friendly homestyle feel to it. Nothing fancy. A mix of tables and chairs perhaps recruited from yard sales, flea markets, friends, and neighbors. The cinder-block walls are a green color reminiscent of Starnes in Paducah, Kentucky. Pig stuff and a few photos adorn the walls. Brunswick stew, chopped pork, coleslaw, fries, hushpuppies, and iced tea, with peach cobbler topped with homemade vanilla ice cream, made one of the best barbecue feasts Ardie and Gretchen had enjoyed over the years. Just a touch of the homemade vinegar-based sauce with melted butter, pepper, and other spices is a delicious complement to the sweet, smoky pork. The fries aren't stiff like fast-food fries, but they are delicious. Keith told us the basics of how he makes the cobblers, and we're sharing our own similar version here. Our hats are off to Keith Allen. He does North Carolina proud.

PEACH COBBLER

Serves 6

8 tablespoons (1 stick) butter

2 cups sugar

1 teaspoon ground cinnamon

1 cup all-purpose flour

½ teaspoon salt

1 tablespoon baking powder

1 cup milk

3 generous cups peeled and sliced peaches, with their juices

Preheat the oven to 350°F. Place the butter in a 9 by 13-inch baking dish and place the dish in the preheating oven. In a small bowl, combine ½ cup of the sugar with the cinnamon and mix well. Set aside. In a medium bowl, sift together the flour, the remaining 1½ cups sugar, the salt, and the baking powder. Blend in the milk, stirring just until the mixture forms a batter. When the butter in the baking dish has melted, remove the dish from the oven and pour the batter into it. Spoon the peaches and their juice on top of the batter and sprinkle with the reserved sugar and cinnamon mixture. Bake for 35 to 45 minutes, until the peaches are bubbling. As the cobbler bakes, the batter will rise up around the peaches. Remove from the oven and allow to cool for about 20 minutes before serving.

Fried Pies

A&R Bar-B-Que

1802 Elvis Presley Blvd.
Memphis, TN 38106
901-774-7444
http://www.aandrbbq.com

here are two other A&R locations in Memphis, but our favorite has always been on Elvis Presley Boulevard. The first four times we ate there, we were so full from the heavenly chopped barbecue pork sandwiches topped with coleslaw that there was no room for dessert. Lately we've saved room for the homemade crescent-shaped fried pies, and they're so good we now make it a regular practice to save room for fried pie. Sometimes we get it for carryout for later enjoyment, but we don't leave A&R without one unless they're sold out. Like the restaurant, there's nothing fancy about these pies, but the flaky fried piecrust enveloping a filling of your choice—peach, apple, sweet potato—is a treat not to be missed.

To our knowledge no one has explained why fried pies settled in Tennessee and Arkansas barbecue houses. True, you'll find them in nonbarbecue houses elsewhere, including mass-produced versions at fast-food places, but the true southern fried pie is best enjoyed in Tennessee and Arkansas. Some of the finest we've had are at A&R in Memphis.

FRIED PEACH PIES

Makes 10 to 12

2¼ cups all-purpose flour

1 teaspoon salt

½ cup shortening or lard

½ cup milk

1 (21-ounce) can peach pie filling

1 cup vegetable oil or shortening, for frying

To make the crust: In a large bowl, mix together the flour and salt. Cut in the shortening until the mixture is crumbly. Mix in the milk and stir until the dough forms a ball. Roll out the dough and cut it into ten to twelve 6-inch circles. Set aside.

Put the oil or shortening in a small, deep skillet over medium heat (350°F if using a thermometer). Spoon equal amounts of filling into each pastry circle and fold in half. Seal the pastry with a fork dipped in cold water.

Fry the pies one at a time in the hot oil, browning them on both sides, 7 to 10 minutes. Drain the pies on paper towels.

Note: Use fresh oil or shortening for frying. Otherwise, flavors from previously fried fish, onion rings, or fries will be absorbed in your piecrust.

Root Beer Cake

Joe's Real B-B-Q

301 N. Gilbert Rd.
Gilbert, AZ 85234
480-503-3805
http://www.joesrealbbq.com/

he barbecue at Joe's Real B-B-Q is pure Texas and has attracted a large following. We recommend starting with the sampler plate of ribs, chicken, beef, and pork, with a side of cheesy potatoes and pit beans. Root beer aficionados won't be disappointed with Joe's real root beer on tap or with this recipe they generously shared with us.

JOE'S REAL B-B-Q ROOT BEER CAKE

Serves 12

CAKE

1¼ cups (2½ sticks) butter

1¼ cups root beer (Joe's or your favorite)

2½ tablespoons cocoa powder

2¼ cups (4 ounces) miniature marshmallows

2½ cups white cane sugar

2½ cups all-purpose flour

1½ teaspoons baking powder

1¼ teaspoons baking soda

2½ to 3 large eggs

½ cup plus 2 tablespoons buttermilk

1 tablespoon vanilla

FROSTING

3 tablespoons butter

⅓ cup root beer (Joe's or your favorite)

2¼ teaspoons cocoa powder

4 cups (12.8 ounces) sifted powdered sugar

⅓ cup chopped pecans

Preheat the oven to 300°F and put a rack in the middle. Grease a 9 by 13-inch baking dish.

To make the cake, bring the butter, root beer, cocoa powder, and marshmallows to a boil in a large saucepan over medium heat. Cook, stirring, just until the marshmallows melt. Remove the pan from the heat and set it aside.

In the bowl of a stand mixer, combine the sugar, flour, baking powder, and baking soda. Pour in the hot butter mixture and mix for 5 minutes on medium speed until well combined. Add the eggs, buttermilk, and vanilla and mix for 5 more minutes until smooth. Pour the batter into the prepared pan and bake for about 1 hour or until a skewer or toothpick inserted in the middle of the cake comes out clean.

During the last few minutes the cake is baking, make the frosting. Combine the butter, root beer, and cocoa powder in a medium saucepan and bring it to a boil over medium heat. Add the powdered sugar and mix until smooth. Stir in the pecans. Pour the hot frosting over the hot cake and spread it evenly with a spatula. Let the cake cool for at least an hour before slicing and serving it.

Lexington Banana Pudding

Speedy's Barbecue

1317 Winston Rd.
Lexington, NC 27295
336-248-2410 or 336-248-2092
http://speedysbbqinc.com

exington is the pork barbecue capital of America to many—but don't include Memphians among them. All barbecue aficionados, however, agree that Lexington has earned a prominent spot on America's best barbecue map. Wayne Monk, the dean of Lexington barbecue, deserves a great deal of credit for Lexington's famous 'cue. Thanks to that fame, although Wayne's barbecue is still the hallmark, he has some outstanding competition and Speedy's is among them. Speedy's, in our judgment, is a necessary stopping place for swine dining if you're anywhere within 100 miles or more of Lexington.

You can tell by the look of the building and by the logo—a pig on skates with a tray of barbecue—that Speedy's has a history as a drive-in. Today it's a dine-in or carryout joint. Wood-paneled walls, booths and tables, miscellaneous movie posters on the walls—it is by no means fancy. The ambience, service, and food, however, are laudable. This family business, owned and operated by brothers Roy and Boyd Dunn, puts the emphasis on what they call "the 3-Qs: Quality, Quantity & Quick Service."

Our chopped pork sandwich with coleslaw, hushpuppies, and fries was outstanding. We got regular chopped, unlike the diners next to us, who made sure the server understood they wanted theirs chopped "extra fine." That's how they got it, and judging from their body language, the Boyd brothers had once again lived up to their 3-Qs motto.

If the banana pudding is homemade, and it is one of the best we had in North Carolina. That being said, we regret that we couldn't get the exact recipe. Paul came up with one that is sure to please and reminds us of what we had at Speedy's, plus meringue.

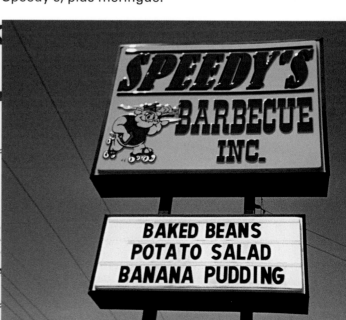

SPEEDY'S BARBECUE, INC

BEST BARBECUE IN LEXINGTON

(336) 248-2410   **(336) 248-2092**

BARBECUE

Barbecue Sandwiches		Barbecue Plates	
hopped	3.15	Chopped	
iced	3.30	Sliced	
oarse Chopped	3.45	Coarse Chopped	
kin 75¢ extra on BBQ Sandwiches)		(Served with slaw, french fries, SA rolls or hushpuppies)	

170

"Quality plus Quantity spells SPEEDY'S BBQ"

LEXINGTON BANANA PUDDING

Serves 8

½ cup plus 6 tablespoons white cane sugar

Pinch of salt

3 tablespoons all-purpose flour

4 large eggs, 3 separated, the whites set aside at room temperature

2 cups whole milk

40 to 50 vanilla wafers

3 to 4 ripe bananas

½ teaspoon cream of tartar

Preheat the oven to 375°F.

Blend ½ cup of the sugar with the salt and flour. Add the whole egg and the 3 yolks and mix. Stir in the milk. Cook in the top of a double boiler over boiling water, stirring, with a wire whisk, until thickened. Remove from the heat and cool.

In a 1½-quart baking dish, arrange a layer of whole vanilla wafers, a layer of sliced bananas, and a layer of custard. Continue, making 3 layers of each.

To make the meringue, put the egg whites and cream of tartar into a stainless-steel or copper bowl. Using a wire whisk, whip to medium-soft peaks. Beat in the 6 tablespoons sugar and continue to beat until the egg whites are glossy and hold a firm peak. Spread the meringue over the banana mixture, being sure to seal it to the edges of the baking dish.

Transfer the baking dish to the oven and bake until the meringue is browned, 10 to 12 minutes. Chill and serve cold.

BARBEFEUDS: JUSTICE AND THE PITS

We like to think that barbecue brings more people together than it pulls apart, but that's not always the case. Barbecue is no stranger to civil and criminal courts—more the former than the latter, thank goodness. Here are a couple of notable civil cases we've heard about:

Bozo the Clown sued Bozo's Hot Pit Bar-B-Q over the name. The court battle lasted for several years, with Thomas Jefferson Williams, nickname "Bozo," of Bozo's Hot Pit Bar-B-Q emerging as the winner. He had the nickname and named his barbecue joint after it in 1923, before Bozo the Clown, a.k.a. Larry Harmon, came along in 1949. The two Bozos were in court again in 1982 in a dispute over whether Bozo's barbecue could trademark its name nationally. The courts said yes.

Smokaroma vs. the United States of America. This company in Boley, Oklahoma, manufactures a barbecue cooker that is part pressure cooker/part smoker. It doesn't comply with the official U.S. government definition of barbecue, and the feds won't budge.

Bananas Foster

Danna's Bar-B-Que & Burger Shop
963 State Highway 165
Branson, MO 65737
417-272-1945

We hesitated when we saw the big bold yellow sign at Danna's that says, "Best Burgers in Branson." Could we trust the barbecue in this place? Short answer: yes! Don't worry about the "burger" in Danna's name or the burgers on the menus of other Branson barbecue joints. In a town that attracts so many tourists, if you don't have America's favorite fast food, you'll lose customers. Burgers were on the menu at every barbecue joint we checked in Branson. Fried burgers, not smoked or charcoal grilled.

Danna's interior decor is what we call Ozark funky. Old-fashioned signs, pig art, old arcade machines, assorted wooden tables and chairs, high ceilings, and the buzz of happy customers give the place a welcome feel.

Saturday is Ardie's traditional day for a lunchtime fried burger. It goes back to his childhood, when his mother fried burgers every Saturday for the family lunch. He ordered a Danna burger as a side dish to ribs, pulled pork, chicken, beans, fries, and slaw. The former Split-T charcoal-grilled burger with onion and mayo in Oklahoma City is still Ardie's all-time favorite, but Danna's served him one of the best fried burgers he's ever eaten, except the ones his mother served, of course.

Danna's spareribs and pulled pork are winners on appearance, tenderness, and taste— easy to chew, not too heavy on the smoke. The chicken was our favorite—smoky, tender, juicy, and flavorful. If you have to turn down the fries, beans, and slaw to save room for dessert, do it. Although the apple dumpling and Kentucky bourbon pecan pie are memorable, treat yourself to bananas Foster first.

One might ask why a dessert as elegant as bananas Foster at a barbecue joint. That's easy to answer. Any recipe using bananas is a great complement to barbecue. Banana pudding is traditionally served at almost every barbecue joint in the Carolinas, including Speedy's (page 170). Then there's the fantastic banana cream pie at Big Bob Gibson in Decatur, Alabama (page 174).

This isn't Danna's secret recipe, but we think you'll like it, and it makes an impressive tableside presentation.

BANANAS FOSTER

Serves 4

4 tablespoons (½ stick) butter

1 cup packed light brown sugar

½ teaspoon ground cinnamon

¼ cup banana liqueur

4 bananas, peeled, cut in half lengthwise, and halved

¼ cup Myers's dark rum

4 scoops vanilla ice cream, homemade (page 179) or store-bought

Combine the butter, brown sugar, and cinnamon in a flambé pan or skillet. Place the pan over low heat either on an alcohol burner or on top of the stove and cook, stirring, until the sugar dissolves.

Stir in the banana liqueur and then place the bananas in the pan. When the banana sections soften and begin to brown, after 3 to 4 minutes, carefully add the rum. Continue to cook the sauce until the rum is hot; then tip the pan slightly to ignite the rum.

When the flames subside, lift the bananas out of the pan and place 4 pieces over each portion of ice cream. Generously spoon the warm sauce over the top of the ice cream and serve immediately.

Banana Cream Pie

Big Bob Gibson Bar-B-Q

2520 Danville Rd., Southwest
Decatur, AL 35603
256-350-0404
http://www.bigbobgibson.com

We've known and admired Don McLemore and Chris Lilly and their families for years. Don, grandson of the late Big Bob Gibson, and Chris, Don's son-in-law, are well known on the barbecue competition circuit as well as in the barbecue restaurant industry. Chris has produced and starred in a series of barbecue instructional videos, as well as co-hosting in a cable TV series. Don, Chris, their spouses, and extended family make you feel like family when you enter their contest cooking area or their restaurants.

continued on page 176

BANANA CREAM PIE

Serves 8

PIECRUST

1¼ cups all-purpose flour

1 teaspoon sea salt

1 tablespoon sugar

3 tablespoons vegetable shortening or lard, chilled

4 tablespoons (½ stick) unsalted butter, cut into ¼-inch pieces

4 to 5 tablespoons ice water

CREAM FILLING

½ cup sugar

¼ cup cornstarch

¼ teaspoon sea salt

5 large egg yolks, lightly beaten (reserve 4 whites for the meringue)

2 cups whole milk

½ cup evaporated milk

1 to 2 teaspoons vanilla extract

2 tablespoons unsalted butter

2 medium firm-ripe bananas, sliced into ¼-inch- to ½-inch-thick rounds

MERINGUE TOPPING

1 tablespoon cornstarch

¼ teaspoon cream of tartar

½ cup superfine sugar

4 egg whites, at room temperature

½ teaspoon vanilla extract

To make the crust, process the flour, salt, and sugar in a food processor until combined. Add the shortening and process until the mixture has the texture of coarse sand, 10 to 12 seconds. Scatter the butter pieces into the flour and process until the mixture is pale yellow and has the texture of coarse crumbs, with butter pieces no larger than a small pea, ten to twelve 1-second pulses. Turn the mixture into a medium bowl.

Sprinkle ¼ cup of the ice water over the mixture. Using a rubber spatula, fold the mixture a few times. Press down on the dough with the spatula to see if the dough sticks together. Add 1 more tablespoon of ice water if needed and then fold and test again. When the dough holds together, flatten the dough into a 4-inch disk. Wrap in waxed paper or plastic wrap and refrigerate for at least 1 hour or overnight.

Remove the dough from the refrigerator and let it come to room temperature. Roll the dough on a lightly floured surface or between sheets of plastic wrap or parchment paper to a 12-inch circle. Roll the dough over the top of your rolling pin and transfer it to a 9-inch pie plate. Work the dough down the sides to the middle of the plate, gently pressing it into the bottom of the pan. Trim the edges to extend about ½ inch beyond the edge of the pan. Fold that excess ½ inch of dough under itself; pinch the dough to flute it or use the tines of a fork to flatten the dough against the rim of the pie plate. Refrigerate for about an hour to firm up the dough.

Preheat the oven to 375°F and place a rack in the center. Remove the pie plate from the refrigerator. Place a doubled 12-inch square of aluminum foil over the dough and press down.

Fill the foil with 2 cups dried beans or ceramic or metal pie weights. Bake for 25 to 30 minutes, or until the crust is a light golden color under the foil. Carefully remove the weights and foil and continue baking until the dough is light brown, 7 to 8 minutes. Remove from the oven and cool on a wire rack.

To make the filling, whisk the sugar, cornstarch, and salt together in a medium saucepan. Add the egg yolks, then immediately but gradually whisk in the milk and evaporated milk. Cook over medium heat, stirring constantly, until the mixture thickens and begins to simmer, 8 to 10 minutes. Cook for another minute, stirring constantly. Remove the pan from the heat and whisk in the vanilla and butter.

Pour the filling into a heatproof bowl and press a sheet of plastic wrap against the top of the filling to prevent a skin from forming; cool for 20 to 30 minutes. Pour half of the filling into the cooled baked piecrust. Top with the banana slices and then the remaining filling. Place another piece of plastic wrap directly on the filling. Refrigerate for at least 3 to 4 hours, until completely chilled.

Preheat the oven to 350°F.

To make the meringue, mix the cornstarch with ⅓ cup water in a small saucepan; bring to a boil, whisking as it comes to a boil. Continue whisking until the mixture becomes translucent, then remove from the heat. In a small bowl, mix the cream of tartar and sugar together. Place the egg whites and vanilla in a medium stainless-steel or copper bowl and beat them until frothy. Beat in the sugar mixture, 1 tablespoon at a time, until all of the sugar mixture is incorporated and the whole mixture forms soft peaks. Beat in the cornstarch mixture 1 tablespoon at a time and continue beating until it's incorporated and stiff peaks form.

Remove the pie from the refrigerator and remove the plastic wrap. Top with the meringue, forming peaks. Place the pie in the oven and bake for 12 to 14 minutes, until the meringue is set and the meringue begins to turn golden brown. Cool before serving.

Big Bob Gibson's Alabama white barbecue sauce has been famous since 1925. In recent years Don and Chris have added some award-winning tomato-based sauces to the Big Bob Gibson lineup. Their impressive wins at Memphis in May, the American Royal, and other major contests give them bragging rights that are second to none—but their humility and southern hospitality trump any bravado.

You can get the recipe for Big Bob Gibson's grilled chicken breast with white sauce from its Web site, and the white sauce recipe is posted on the Food Network site, but we recommend the real sauce from the restaurant. You can get it by calling or ordering online.

Big Bob Gibson's has a reputation for great barbecue and great pies. Whenever we go to a barbecue contest and we know that Big Bob Gibson is entered, after all the pleasantries have been exchanged and the right opportunity presents itself, we ask Carolyn and Don McLemore, "Did you bring pies?" And most of the time Carolyn will say with a smile, "Why, yes we did, and we will be serving some about seven o'clock. Please stop by."

Big Bob Gibson presents a real dilemma when you go to one of the restaurants. Do you save room for dessert and order less barbecue, or order the usual amount of barbecue and hope to have room for a slice of the fabulous pie? Believe us, this is a real problem. Rather than repeat the chicken and sauce recipes, we wanted to treat you with a famous Big Bob Gibson signature pie, but that's a trade secret to be kept within the family. When you can't enjoy pie at a Big Bob Gibson restaurant or cooking contest, we know you'll like this one.

Deep-Fried Oreos

RUB (Righteous Urban Barbeque)

208 W. 23rd St.
New York, NY 10011
212-524-4300
http://www.rubbbq.net

There are times when you want and deserve pure decadence. What better way to indulge yourself than Deep-Fried Oreos at RUB? Paul first experienced the decadence of this chocolate delight at a barbecue contest in New Holland, Pennsylvania, while filming a pilot episode at the opening of RUB Barbecue for Canadian Food TV. At the time, Paul had no desserts planned for RUB's menu, and this was a real winner, so he just had to try to make them. They are delicious!

This isn't just our opinion. RUB has received some notoriety for its Deep-Fried Oreos; according to *Star* magazine, they were reportedly a favorite of supermodel Giselle Bundchen. When you aren't in New York and the urge hits you, this home version will come to the rescue. You can substitute your favorite dry pancake mix for the Bisquick. They are best when eaten warm. If you want to try a lighter version, use low-fat milk, canola oil, and reduced-fat Oreos.

DEEP-FRIED OREOS

Makes about 45 cookies

2 cups white cake mix or Bisquick

2 large eggs

1½ cups milk

1 tablespoon oil

Canola oil or lard, for deep-frying

1 (18-ounce) package Oreo cookies

Confectioners' sugar, for garnish

In a medium bowl, blend the cake mix or Bisquick, eggs, milk, and oil until it forms a smooth batter.

Preheat your deep-fryer to about 375°F. You can also use a deep skillet filled with enough oil to allow the cookies to float. Just make sure the temperature is 375°F on a deep-frying thermometer.

Dip the cookies in the batter until totally coated and then place in the hot oil. The cookies will float. Fry the cookies until the bottom sides are brown. Keep a close watch, because it takes only a short time to brown them. Turn the cookies over and brown the other side. Remove the cookies, drain on a paper towel–lined plate, sprinkle with confectioners' sugar, and serve warm.

BAR-B-Q
PUTNEY VERMONT
THE 9TH WONDER OF THE WORLD
CHICKEN

177

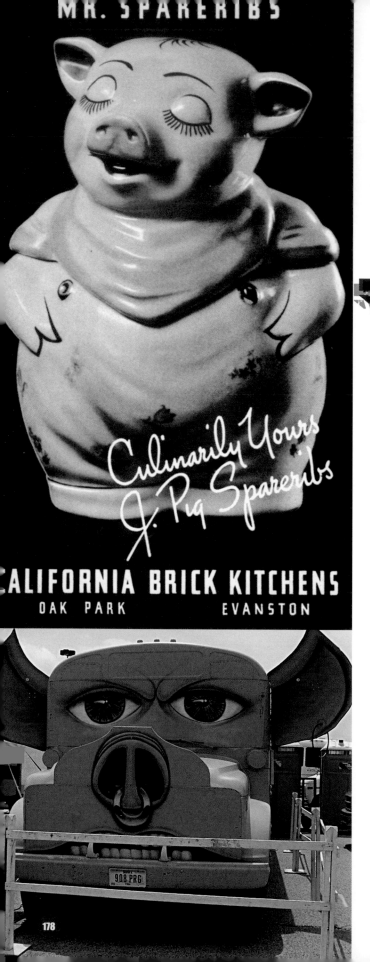

MR. SPARERIBS

*Culinarily Yours
J. Pig Spareribs*

CALIFORNIA BRICK KITCHENS
OAK PARK   EVANSTON

178

Ice Cream

Stamey's

2206 High Point Rd.
Greensboro, NC
336-299-9888
http://www.stameys.com

We've heard so much good talk about Stamey's Barbecue that we had to try it. And why not try it with friends in Greensboro who are barbecue experts and have eaten at Stamey's for years? David Bailey, editor for Delta's *Sky* magazine and one of the most refreshing, entertaining, and informative barbecue bloggers of all (put TrueCue in your search engine), said, "Let's meet at the Stamey's across from the Coliseum." We met him there, with his wife, Anne, for a memorable feast of chopped pork, slaw, beans, fries, Brunswick stew, iced tea, and peach cobbler topped with homemade ice cream.

It's no wonder the pit crew at Stamey's has mastered the art of hickory-smoked pork shoulder barbecue. The Stamey legacy goes back to when founder C. Warner Stamey lived in Lexington and learned barbecue from local experts Sid Weaver and Jess Swicegood when he was in high school. By 1930 Warner was out of high school, had returned to his hometown of Shelby, and started selling barbecue there. Greensboro became his chosen city in 1953, and Stamey's has been a community fixture ever since, now with two locations.

David Bailey has a genuine gift with words. We asked him for a quote about Stamey's. Here's what he gave us:

ICE CREAM

Makes about 6 cups

4 large eggs

2 cups sugar

1 (14-ounce) can sweetened condensed milk

1 (10½-ounce) can evaporated milk

¼ teaspoon salt

2 tablespoons vanilla extract

Milk, 2% or whole, if desired

Beat the eggs well in a large bowl. Add the sugar, condensed milk, evaporated milk, salt, and vanilla, beating well. Pour the mixture into an ice-cream freezer. You can add a little milk if desired until the mixture is 2 to 4 inches from the top of the freezer can. If you add the milk, mix thoroughly. Follow your ice-cream freezer manufacturer's instructions for freezing the ice cream.

Hint: If the freezer stops or hangs up, add about ½ cup or so of water to the ice-cream mixture to aid in thawing, enough so it begins to turn freely.

Variation: You can mix about 4 cups of sweetened fresh fruit (your choice) into the mixture just before you transfer it to the ice-cream freezer.

"I've been eating Stamey's since my daddy first took me to the big city of Greensboro and my momma gave me a spit bath after I'd made a mess of myself and my Sunday-go-to-meeting clothes. It's every bit as good today as it was way back then—consistent, clean, classic, with a sauce that demonstrates that a little bit of ketchup's not a bad thing. If you don't think they use hickory, just sniff the air, look at the wood-pile out back, and get your taste buds checked by your doctor."

We couldn't get an original Stamey's recipe, but this recipe has served us well, and you'll know why when you try it.

Pop's Salt Lick Sundae

The Salt Lick Bar-B-Q

18001 FM 1826

Driftwood, TX 78619

512-858-4959

http://www.saltlickbbq.com

riving along the rural road between Dripping Springs and Austin, Texas, most people would not expect to happen upon a world-class barbecue joint standing by itself in a cattle pasture sprinkled with post oak and large Texas-size shade trees. But there it is, made of limestone and timber, fitting perfectly into the landscape. Out back the gravel parking lot covering several acres of former pasture hints at how popular this joint is. The picnic shelter waiting area outside the restaurant entrance also tells you that this joint is no stranger to crowds.

The Salt Lick Bar-B-Q is a destination. Few customers just happen upon it. The huge parking lot fills up with busloads of tourists and carloads of locals from nearby Dripping Springs and Austin 7 days a week. You may have to wait, but you'll get a table.

Imagine a bunch of wood-beamed picnic shelters stuck together, but with walls and screens instead of open air. Add a round stone holding pit inside the entrance, loaded with barbecue meats that look so good you want to grab a bite right now. Add a reception desk with cash register, shelves of sauce, shirts, and gimme hats for sale, busy servers taking orders and delivering orders, picnic tables filled with people enjoying the barbecue and filling the air with laughter, animated gestures, and gustatory exclamations, and you've found the Salt Lick. It is living proof that barbecue attracts people the way salt licks—blocks of solid salt placed in pastures and woods—attract deer, cattle, and other furry critters.

In hunting season a salt lick can prove dangerous for deer. People attracted to the Salt Lick Bar-B-Q get a much better deal. They feast on tender, lean, juicy mesquite-smoked barbecued beef brisket, pork ribs, chicken, sausage, and/or turkey, with sides of potato salad, coleslaw, beans, bread, pickles, and onions. You get full, satisfied, with reasonable hopes to live another day, and your wallet doesn't take a beating. Be sure to bring cash. The Salt Lick doesn't take credit cards. Excellent Texas barbecue at reasonable prices. Fast, friendly service. Ambience galore.

Hold it! We should have warned you up front to save room for dessert. The homemade pecan pie and the peach cobbler à la mode are not to be missed. If you're adventuresome, however, try a dessert that is not on the menu that you can make for yourself at your table. Mind you, this is not an official Salt Lick menu item. It is the invention of Ken Wilson, jewelry maker and postcard collector/dealer, in Dripping Springs. Ken's grandchildren call him "Pops." Ardie and his wife, Gretchen, have enjoyed several delightful feasts at the Salt Lick with Ken, his wife, Debbie Little-Wilson, artist/print maker with a special interest in women's suffrage and cowgirl themes, and Mary Fischer, ceramics artist who is famous for her ceramic houses. Each time, Ken finishes his meal with a scoop of Blue Bunny Ice Cream,

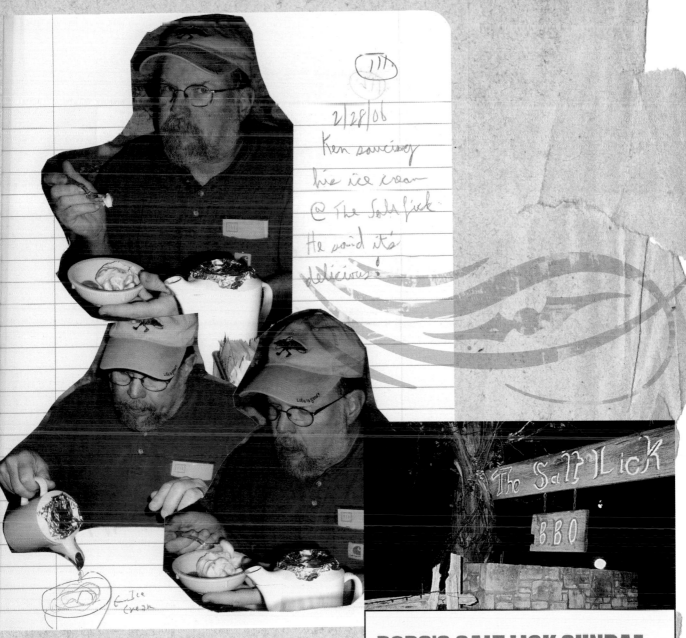

2/28/06
Ken saucing
his ice cream
@ The Salt Lick
He said it's
delicious.

Ice Cream

POPS'S SALT LICK SUNDAE

Serves 1

2 scoops vanilla ice cream

**¼ cup Salt Lick original Bar-B-Q sauce—
no substitutions**

Put the ice cream in a sundae vessel or bowl, top with barbecue sauce, and enjoy.

topped with some original Salt Lick Bar-B-Q Sauce. We call it Pops's Salt Lick Sundae. Debbie has tried it and likes it. Gretchen, Mary, and Ardie haven't yet, but maybe on another visit! Since up to now Ardie's favorite unusual barbecue sauce combo has been McClard's barbecue sauce on fresh cantaloupe, Salt Lick sauce on ice cream oughta be no problem. Make sure you use Salt Lick sauce. You can get it at the restaurant, on-line, and at gourmet stores and supermarkets.

Turtle Cheesecake

Dead Mike's BBQ

4020 Pontoon Rd.
Pontoon Beach, IL 62040
618-797-7910
http://www.granitecitygossip.com/
DeadMikesBBQ.html

 Don't let the dead theme at Dead Mike's dissuade you or limit your visits to Halloween. It's a fun place you'll want to frequent on a regular basis. Menu items are embellished with names evoking grave connotations, but you'll find the all-time regular barbecue favorites—pulled pork, brisket, ribs, and chicken—plus the mandatory metro Saint Louis grilled pork steak. If you're truly not in the mood for barbecue, order the fried catfish with malted vinegar. Or, if fish isn't appealing, get the grilled Italian sausage with caramelized onions.

Surprisingly there is no "death by chocolate" dessert here—but a tempting selection of bourbon pecan pie, caramel granny apple pie, or turtle cheesecake makes amends. We couldn't get a recipe out of Dead Mike, so here's our version of the turtle cheesecake.

TURTLE CHEESECAKE

Makes one 9-inch cheesecake

CRUST

2 cups vanilla wafer cookie crumbs

6 tablespoons butter, melted

FILLING

About 35 Kraft caramels

1 teaspoon butter

¼ cup evaporated milk

1 cup chopped pecans

1 cup chopped good-quality milk chocolate

2 (8-ounce) packages cream cheese, at room temperature

½ cup sugar

1 teaspoon vanilla extract

2 large eggs

CHOCOLATE TOPPING

4 (1-ounce) squares semisweet chocolate

1 teaspoon butter

3 tablespoons whipping cream

GARNISH

12 pecan halves

Best Bar-b-que you'll ever eat in a bu that hasn't already been condemn

The All Girls Cooking Team

Preheat the oven to 350°F. To prepare the crust, mix the cookie crumbs and melted butter until the crumbs are thoroughly moistened. Press them in the bottom and up the sides of a 9-inch springform pan. Bake for 10 minutes. Remove from the oven and allow to cool. Leave the oven on.

For the filling, melt the caramel, butter, and evaporated milk in a saucepan over very low heat. Add the chopped pecans and stir for a while to cool a bit. Pour into the cooled crust and allow to cool for 30 minutes before sprinkling about ½ cup of the chocolate pieces over the caramel mixture.

While the caramel mixture is cooling, you can make the rest of the filling. Beat the cream cheese with the sugar and vanilla until fluffy. Add the eggs one at a time and continue beating. Fold the remaining chocolate pieces into the cheese mixture. Spoon the cheese mixture over the caramel and bake for 40 minutes. To prepare the chocolate topping, combine the chocolate, butter, and whipping cream in a small saucepan and stir over low heat until smooth. Drizzle it over the cheesecake. Refrigerate the cheesecake to cool it completely, then sprinkle with pecans just before serving.

Kaiser Aluminum sponsored two Kaiser Cookouts in 1959 and 1960. The coveted prize was to be named "America's Cookout Champion of the Year." Women were not eligible to enter. Imagine trying to get by with a "for men only" barbecue contest today!

So many women are actively involved in the sport, art, or business of barbecue today that a complete listing of names would fill a directory the size of a small city. Women compete in and win barbecue contests. Women own and run successful barbecue businesses. Women write about barbecue and pen best-selling barbecue cookbooks.

When Ardie wrote an article about women and barbecue for the National Barbecue News and the Kansas City Barbeque Society's the *Kansas City Bullsheet*, he gave a few examples of women who are active in various barbecue venues. Several readers asked, "Why didn't you mention so-and-so?" With that in mind, we won't mention names here. Trust us, however, women are very involved in barbecue today! Today we are seeing the crumbling of the gender walls in barbecue, and that's good.

WOMEN IN BARBECUE

ding
ed"

Bread Pudding with Whiskey Sauce

The County Line Bar-B-Q

6500 Bee Cave Road
Austin, TX 78746
512-327-1742
http://www.countyline.com/

e've never been disappointed at any of the County Line locations, although we're partial to the original. The view of metropolitan Austin, the roadhouse history, and the rustic woodsy Texas Cowboy Country Club ambiance feel right to us.

Before you sate your appetite on those gargantuan barbecued beef ribs the County Line is famous for, stop yourself. You have to save room for dessert—especially the bread pudding with whiskey sauce. Portions are big enough for two or more, so go easy or plan to take some home.

Legend has it that this former roadhouse is haunted by the ghost of a young woman who lost her life there years ago. We think we saw her about five minutes after we cleaned the last remnants of our whiskey sauce from the plate!

The County Line has their "Mom's Bread Pudding Recipe" online. Here's our version, which is similar and slightly easier to make. Our whiskey sauce is adapted from the County Line's recipe.

BREAD PUDDING WITH WHISKEY SAUCE

Serves 6 to 8

2 cups cream, half-and-half, or whole milk

4 tablespoons (½ stick) unsalted butter

¾ cup granulated sugar

3 large eggs

1 tablespoon ground cinnamon

½ teaspoon ground nutmeg

1 teaspoon vanilla extract

3 cups bread, torn into small pieces (French bread works best)

½ cup raisins or berries (optional)

TENNESSEE WHISKEY SAUCE

1 pound (4 sticks) Grade A butter

2¼ cups packed light brown sugar, no clumps

1 cup heavy whipping cream

¼ cup Jack Daniel's Tennessee Whiskey (your choice of Black Label, Green Label, Single Barrel, or Gentleman Jack) (no substitutes)

Preheat your oven to 350°F and place a rack in the center. In a medium saucepan, over medium heat, heat the cream just until a film forms over the top. Add the butter to the cream, stirring until the butter is melted. Cool to lukewarm.

In a mixing bowl, combine the sugar, eggs, cinnamon, nutmeg, and vanilla. Beat with an electric mixer at medium speed for 1 minute. Slowly add the cream mixture to the sugar mixture.

Place the bread in a lightly greased 1 ½-quart casserole dish. Sprinkle with raisins or berries if desired. Pour the batter on top of bread. Bake for 45 to 50 minutes or until set.

While the bread pudding is baking, make the whiskey sauce. Melt the butter in a clean, heavy stainless steel pan over medium heat. Be careful not to burn the butter. Slowly add the brown sugar, stirring constantly with a wooden spoon until the sugar is dissolved and the mixture is smooth and hot, but not simmering. Simmering or boiling will make the sauce too thick, so avoid too much heat. Slowly add the heavy whipping cream, stirring as you add it. Blend well and remove from heat. Add Jack Daniels Whiskey and whip it into the sauce, mixing well. Pour a generous portion atop the finished bread pudding and lick the pan clean!

OUR FAVORITE BARBECUE RESTAURANTS

ARDIE'S TOP 10

1. Cooper's Old Time Pit Bar-B-Que (Llano, TX)

2. Arthur Bryant's Barbeque (Kansas City, MO)

3. Oklahoma Joe's Barbecue and Catering (Kansas City, KS)

4. Johnny Harris Restaurant & Barbecue Sauce Company (Savannah, GA)

5. Allen & Son (Chapel Hill, NC)

6. Louie Mueller Barbecue (Taylor, TX)

7. A & R Bar-B-Que (Memphis, TN)

8. The Bar-B-Q Shop (Memphis, TN)

9. Head Country Barbecue (Ponca City, OK)

10. RUB (New York City, NY)

PAUL'S TOP 10

1. The Dixie Pig (Blytheville, AR)

2. Oklahoma Joe's Barbecue and Catering (Kansas City, KS)

3. Cooper's Bar-B-Q & Grill (Junction, TX)

4. Cooper's Old Time Pit Bar-B-Que (Llano, TX)

5. RUB (New York City, NY, and Las Vegas, NV)

6. Danny's Place (Carlsbad, NM)

7. Leonard's Pit Barbecue (Memphis, TN)

8. Ironhorse Barbeque Company (Paragould, AR)

9. Head Country Barbecue (Ponca City, OK)

10. Arthur Bryant's Barbeque (Kansas City, MO)

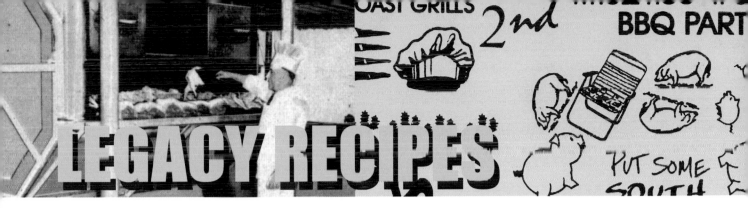

Red's Barbecued 'Coon

Ira Ray "Red" Gill
**Razorback Cookers Catering,
Blytheville, AR**

Ira Ray "Red" Gill was born in the very small town of Dell, Arkansas, in 1928. He used to say that the only way the population ever went up was when someone was born and the only way it went down was when someone died. Ray died on June 3, 2003, in Blytheville, Arkansas, at age 75.

Ray was one of the most colorful characters we have ever met on the barbecue trail, and it had nothing to do with his red hair. He was short in stature and a teller of tall tales, a rodeo clown, a Brahma Bull rider, a jack of all trades, and one hell of a good barbecuer. Besides being a legend on the barbecue circuit, he was asked to cater President Clinton's first inaugural party.

Ray was a World War II and Korean War veteran, serving in both the U.S. Army and the U.S. Air Force. After his military career, Ray settled in Blytheville, Arkansas, with his wife, Eva Lannum Gill. He loved barbecue and had been doing it all his life, so naturally he established a barbecue catering business, Razorback Cookers Catering. By age 37 Ray had been honored by the Jaycees as one of the Outstanding Young Men of America.

In 1986, at the age of 58, Ray formed the River City Spice Company. Inspired by great-grandfather William Thomas Gill, Ray adapted some secret family recipes into a line of barbecue seasonings and sauces (which you can order at http://www.rivercityspice.com). River City Barbecue Products was born, branded as Razorback Bar-B-Q. Razorback products and the Razorback cooking team established a winning reputation in the worldwide barbecue contest network.

Ireland, Scotland, Wales, and twenty-six states in the United States have awarded Red and his son, Ray Alan, and the Razorback Cookers championships, including World's Best Barbecue Sauce, World's Best Baby Back Ribs, Best Ribs in the World, Virginia Invitational World Barbecue contest, Best in the West . . . the list goes on. The Memphis in May World Championship Barbecue Cooking Contest committee awarded Ray a plaque that reads: "To Red Gill and his Razorback Cookers, A great showman and the World's Best Barbecue and Pork promoter."

Ray will be remembered for his clever way with words. Here are some of his great sayings:

**"Good Food Ain't Cheap.
Cheap Food Ain't Good!"**

**"Serve no swine before its time;
serve no beef at any time."**

"You gotta start with good meat and you gotta have slow cooking. You gotta cook it low and cook it slow."

—Ray "Red" Gill, DP, UHOH (Doctor of Porkology, University of High on the Hog)

Everything now is run by a new legend in the making, Ray and Eva's son, Ray Alan, along with his wife, Glenda, and the help and direction of Eva Gill.

Before his death, Ray posted several recipes on his Web pages for posterity. The barbecued raccoon recipe stands out as the most unusual. We can easily imagine Ray embellishing the recipe with stories and cooking tips. May he rest in peace.

RED'S BARBECUED 'COON

Serves 10 to 12

1 (8- to 10-pound) raccoon, dressed

2 medium onions, chopped

3 to 5 dried red peppers

Salt and black pepper

Razorback Brand Barbeque Sauce, hot or mild

Wash the raccoon and cut it into 10 to 12 serving-size pieces. Cover with cold water in a Dutch oven. Bring to a boil for 15 minutes. Pour off the water and add fresh water along with the onions, dried peppers, and salt and black pepper to taste. Boil for 1 to 2 hours, or until tender. Remove and dry on paper towels. Dip the meat in barbecue sauce and place on a hot grill for 45 minutes, basting frequently. Remove from the grill and place in shallow pan. Pour the sauce over the meat and bake at 350°F for 1 hour.

Grilled Rattlesnake

Jim Quessenberry
Arkansas Trav'ler

Jim Quessenberry was one of those larger-than-life characters in the barbecue network who will never be forgotten. He was a big man with big dreams and a big appetite for excellent barbecue and fun. Jim was a great storyteller and practical joker.

Anytime you visited Jim in his cooking area at a contest he'd treat you like family. He would offer you a drink, invite you to sit down and rest your feet, and then ask, "Did you hear about what kind of mess old so-and-so got himself into?" That, or a similar question, was the platform for a tall tale or a joke. Anyone was fair game for Jim's practical jokes; ladies had to be especially on guard. We remember the year Jim brought a big bullfrog to the Memphis in May World Championship Barbecue Cooking Contest. He rigged up an inconspicuous trapdoor at the back of his porta-potty. Since access to a private facility has always been a premium at the contest, Jim was quick to oblige when friends were in need. The Year of the Bullfrog was one of his finest moments. After giving a female guest sufficient time to be seated inside, Jim would quietly slip the bullfrog through the trapdoor. Soon there would be a scream and the door would burst open. We'll leave it at that, except to note that one time the joke didn't work. A lady who could be described as a "country girl" not given to fear of critters didn't—to Jim's surprise—come bursting out the door, nor did she scream. "The funniest darn thing happened in there," she told Jim. "I looked down and saw a big bullfrog sitting next to me. Poor thing took a hop to his demise when I stood up." Jim decided against rescuing the unfortunate critter.

We're baffled as to why Jim never took the grand championship at Memphis in May with his whole hog. He barbecued some of the best hogs we've ever tasted, right up there with what Ed Mitchell turns out in Raleigh, North Carolina (see page 86). As far as we know, Jim and Ed never met, but they would have been instant buddies and an unbeatable whole-hog cooking team. Jim did, however, win the Irish International Barbecue Cooking Contest in Lisdoonvarna in 1985 and 1987, plus many other contests in the United States.

Jim wasn't the first or last Arkansan to call himself the Arkansas Trav'ler. It was a term he used mostly for branding his team and his products—Sauce Beautiful and Spice Beautiful. To the many barbecuers who knew him and loved him, he was "Ques" (pronounced "Kwez"). Fortunately, Jim's hot and mild Sauce Beautiful and his Spice Beautiful did not pass away with him like a dream. That would have been sad poetic justice, since Jim swore with a straight face that the recipes came to him in a dream. Wherever the source, they were tasty and beautiful, and Jim was wise enough to pass along the recipes to his sons, Lee and Michael. You can visit the product site and order at www.bbqberry.com.

We never asked Jim exactly how he cooked his Hogs Beautiful. Unless he taught his sons, or his faithful sidekick, Arthur, the recipes and techniques went with Jim to the Great Barbecue in the Sky. We do remember, however, what he told us about how to cook rattlesnake.

ARKANSAS TRAV'LER RATTLESNAKE BEAUTIFUL

Serves 8 to 12 as an appetizer

RATTLER RUB

1½ tablespoons sea salt

1½ tablespoons black pepper

2 teaspoons granulated garlic

2 teaspoons paprika

RATTLESNAKE

1 rattlesnake, about 12 ounces, skinned

2 tablespoons canola oil

¼ cup Rattler Rub or Spice Beautiful

Combine the sea salt, black pepper, granulated garlic, and paprika and mix well.

Using a very thin, sharp fillet knife, start at the middle of the snake's backbone and work around the bone to the belly. Take your time. This is very delicate and expensive meat. Cut into bite-sized fillets.

Coat the fillets with canola oil and lightly sprinkle with the Rattler Rub or Spice Beautiful. Use a grill topper to avoid dropping the meat through the grill grate. Grill over medium heat for about 1 minute per side until done. Overcooked rattlesnake will be rubbery

REFLECTIONS OF AN OMAHA PITMASTER

Our longtime friend Mason Steinberg, proprietor of the former Mason's Old Mill Bar-B-Que in Omaha (page 194), wrote the following piece of personal barbecue history for us to share with you. It's a keeper!

"This Bar-B-Que Should Satisfy All," New Orleans–born restaurant critic for the *Omaha World Herald* Jim Delmont said in his three reviews of Old Mill Bar-B-Que in five years.

I opened Old Mill in 1990 because I couldn't get my style of barbecue in Omaha anymore. I like green hickory–smoked brisket, pork butt, and spareribs, like I got in the early fifties at Omaha's premier barbecue joint, The Silver Pit. I will never forget the first time I walked in the Silver Pit and walked up to the pit boss, Jasper Jones. He asked me what I wanted, and after looking at the menu board I ordered a rib sandwich. Four spareribs, 2 slices of barbecue bread, and sauce on the side. To drink, Whistle Orange out of the 10-cent Coke machine next to the screen-door entrance.

From that moment on, I was addicted and never wanted to go through treatment. My many years traveling all over the world eating barbecue helped feed my addiction.

In 1989, while reminiscing about our high school years, the discussion got around to my favorite food . . . you guessed it: barbecue. Talk then focused around late-night trips to the black community in North Omaha for barbecue. Most that night agreed that the old-style barbecue we had as big-shot high school athletes was no longer available.

Having had too many Jack Daniel's and water, I opened my mouth and said I could open a barbecue restaurant within 6 months and it would taste just like the old days. Barbecue bread and all!

It happened in October 1990 and gave me some of the best years of my life—my customers, friends I met, knowledge I gained about barbecue, traveling, and all the time feeding my addiction. Who could ask for anything more?

I featured triple-deck thin-sliced brisket sandwiches, pulled pork, spareribs, whole smoked chickens cut into two-bone, four-bone, or whole birds, and naturally everything came with barbecue bread and mild, medium, or big-boy hot sauce on the side.

After a couple of years I added brisket burnt ends, smoked catfish, and smoked feather bones. Feather bones (riblets, for the unenlightened) were a Sunday all-you-can-eat special from noon until we sold out. Record: 84 pieces and 3 pitchers of beer.

An all-time favorite is the homemade smoked beans—rich, dark, spicy, on the sweet side, smoky, with large cubes of smoked brisket in a thick sauce, cooked with our special blend of bean seasoning, all smoked in our hickory pit.

Barbecued Pork Shoulder

Gary Wells

**Founder and Former President,
Kansas City Barbeque Society**

The people of barbecue are not just friends, they are family.

One well-known barbecuer said it this way, "You can always say that your barbecue is better than his barbecue. What you don't say is anything derogatory, for instance, saying his barbecue tastes like mud or is as tasty as a piece of wood. It's just a common courtesy. You don't tear down your barbecue family."

Gary Wells belongs in the legacy section of this cookbook. Although he owned a restaurant and hotel once, Gary never owned or managed a barbecue restaurant. Gary's involvement in the sport of barbecue, however, has resulted in an explosion of new pitmasters and barbecue restaurateurs.

Gary and his wife, Carolyn, started the Kansas City Barbeque Society (KCBS), the world's largest and foremost barbecue organization. The KCBS can be viewed as a Barbecue Restaurant Farm System. Out of the barbecue contest system and training programs Gary and Carolyn started, many successful barbecue teachers, pitmasters, and restaurateurs have emerged.

When Gary cooked barbecue in competition, he especially liked to cook pork shoulder. Here is one of his treasured recipes.

GARY WELLS'S BARBECUED PORK SHOULDER

Serves 8 to 10

¼ cup onion salt

2 tablespoons celery salt

2 tablespoons seasoned salt

½ cup packed light brown sugar

¼ cup paprika

2 tablespoons black pepper

1 tablespoon cayenne

1 (18- to 20-pound) whole pork shoulder, trimmed, with skin on

2 (24-ounce) bottles Wicker's Original Marinade

Preheat your smoker to 250°F. Combine the onion salt, celery salt, seasoned salt, brown sugar, paprika, pepper, and cayenne, and blend well. Rub all of the exposed meat with the rub, but don't season the skin.

Place the shoulder in the smoker skin side up. Turn and baste the meat side with the Wicker's every 3 hours. Cook until the internal temperature is 185°F for slicing or 195°–205°F for pulling or chopping (see page 212). Serve with your favorite barbecue sauce on the side.

Bistecca alla Fiorentina

Giancarlo Gianelli
Barbecue Baron of Tuscany

The call came when Ardie and his dining companions had finished one of the most memorable meals of their lives: a fantastic multicourse dinner of Tuscan gourmet delights prepared by Chef Giancarlo Gianelli. They were visiting with and praising Giancarlo in the outdoor courtyard of his small restaurant, the Locanda dell 'Oste Poeta, at Tocchi, Monticano, Sienna. "Giancarlo, I just shot a wild boar in my cornfield," his friend, Vittorio, said over the phone. "Will you please come help me butcher it?" Giancarlo asked, somewhat hesitantly, so as not to offend the diners, if they would like to come along. Having just dined on grilled wild boar chops marinated in balsamic vinegar and herbs—plus seven other superb Tuscan dishes, with complementary local table wines—they were ready for adventure.

It was a very dark night as they navigated a narrow dirt road in the Tuscan hills to Vittorio's farm. The darkness was broken occasionally with flickering gravesite candlelights in cemeteries, honoring the dead. Giancarlo hopped out and opened a gate, crafted of sticks and branches from nearby trees, and they proceeded into Vittorio's farm. In the doorway of the barn was a huge dead male wild boar, still warm, resting in a big stainless-steel wheelbarrow below chains on a pulley to hoist him up by the hind legs for butchering. Tools and artwork adorned the walls. It was like walking into a Fellini movie with the set designed by Salvador Dali—but it was real.

Giancarlo went to work on the boar—hoisting it upside down by the back legs, slicing through the belly and spilling the contents into the wheelbarrow. Vittorio tossed some of the organs outside to his exuberant, barking hunting dogs. Soon the boar was stripped of its hide and removed to a cooler for further processing later. It was done. Everyone cheered and toasted with a round of Chianti. This is only one of many memories that friends of Giancarlo were left with in the wake of his untimely death from a respiratory illness at age 57. His dear wife, Adriana, preceded him in death by two years—two years of grief and deep sorrow for Giancarlo.

When Ardie first met Giancarlo in 1995, he and Adriana ran a restaurant in leased space in the small village of Stegliano. Robust and bearded, he was grilling a spatchcock chicken, covered with a brick, on his Tuscan grill with oak charcoal. Ardie's rudimentary Italian and Giancarlo's rudimentary English didn't make for a smooth conversation, but with gestures and words their rapport was instant—especially when a mutual passion for barbecue and Jack Daniel's became apparent. Ardie dubbed Giancarlo the "Barbecue Baron of Tuscany," and asked that he please have wild boar on his menu the next time Ardie came to Italy, despite the Tuscan custom of only serving wild boar—except in the form of cured sausage—in the winter months.

Two years later Ardie returned to Tuscany, bringing some barbecue and Jack Daniel's memorabilia and encouraging Giancarlo to compete in the Jack Daniel's World Championship Invitational Barbecue. Lo and behold, he eventually found a sponsor and made the trip. He, Adriana,

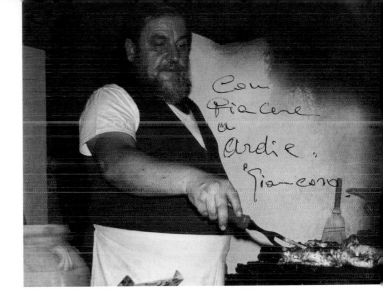

and their friends Susan Pennington from Montestigliano and Ellen and Peter Brown from Minneapolis, formed team Allegri Cinghiali. Thanks to Cliff and Donny Weddington of Oink, Cackle & Moo, team Allegri Cinghiali had a pit and some excellent mentoring. Billy Bones also stopped by to welcome them and share a few tips for success. To Giancarlo's regret, the grand championship eluded him, but he and Adriana were thrilled to take home the First Place trophy for "Home Cooking from the Homeland." Giancarlo was truly a Renaissance Man—chef, poet, artist, expert on Etruscan dietary habits, teacher, father, husband, friend, and founder of a movement dedicated to contemporary interpretations of Tuscan cuisine, the "Blue Kerchiefs."

What follows is a recipe adapted from Giancarlo's self-published book, *The Taste of Memories*. Giancarlo was a native of Florence, where he learned the Florentine manner of cooking. His many Florentine dishes were second to none, including this classic Florentine Steak.

BISTECCA ALLA FIORENTINA
(STEAK IN THE FLORENTINE MANNER)

Fillets of beef, cut to a thickness of three fingers (T-bone cut suggested)

Salt

Freshly ground black pepper

Extra-virgin olive oil

Remove the steaks from the refrigerator at least 3 hours before they are to be cooked so that the middle of the finished steaks will not be cold. Giancarlo would suggest that at the same time you open a bottle of good Chianti that has been aged for at least three years. Place a large amount of charcoal under the grill, set the grate above it (preferably at least the width of four fingers above the coals), and preheat it until it is glowing but with no flame.

Place the steaks on the grill. Let them cook on one side, without adding salt and under no circumstances prodding them with a fork. When they have formed a crust (after seven to eight minutes), turn them over with a spatula, sprinkle the cooked side with salt, and grill them on the other side for seven to eight minutes. Turn over again and salt the other side. At the end they should still be rare in the middle and well cooked on the outside. Before serving, season each steak with a little freshly ground black pepper and a couple of drops of extra-virgin olive oil. This and only this is the real fiorentina—a T-bone cut of sirloin steak, no lemon, never well-done, and only grilled over charcoal.

Note: One day the man who taught Giancarlo to cook suggested packing the steaks in some dry hay and putting them in the refrigerator for 5 or 6 hours so that the meat absorbs the most intense of the flavors on which the animal feeds. Giancarlo sometimes did that, and he would also burn the same hay next to them as they cooked. He thought it might be a rather sacrilegious thing to do, but a little bit of blasphemy every now and then is certainly not going to get us sent to Hell.

3 for the Money Barbecued Ribs

Mason Steinberg

Old Mill Bar-B-Que, Omaha, NE

Mason Steinberg was the creator and facilitator of Old Mill Bar-B-Que, which is closed now but may be reopened in the Omaha area soon by his son Jason.

We would venture to say that Old Mill Bar-B-Que was one of the best barbecue restaurants in the Midwest, with good food, ambience, and great barbecue. Mason, being a very frugal person and good businessman, would buy natural-fall ribs (full slab, untrimmed), 3 and down spare ribs, which means the slabs weighed 3 pounds or less. Mason cut the slabs into St. Louis–style ribs, which means he squared up the slabs and cut the breastbone and the gristle from the top of the slab. These are called rib tips. When you do this, you also take the skirt (a flap that is attached to the diaphragm) off the inside of the slab. It's all clear as mud, right?

---

3 FOR THE MONEY BARBECUED RIBS

Ribs serve 4 to 6; rib tips serve 2; skirts serve 1

2 slabs St. Louis spareribs

2 rib tips

2 skirts

1 cup barbecue rub of your choice

Remove the membrane from the back of the ribs and trim any excess fat. Season the ribs all over with your favorite barbecue rub. Cook the ribs and rib tips using the indirect method at 230°–270°F for 5 to 6 hours, or until the ribs tear easily. Rib tips take 4 to 5 hours. Grill the skirts at 400°–500°F using the direct or indirect method, which will take 1 to 3 hours.

Mason barbecued ribs every day for his business, and he saved the rib tips to run a Saturday night special. For Sunday afternoon, he ran a barbecued skirt special. That's why we dedicate this 3 for the Money Barbecued Ribs recipe to Mason.

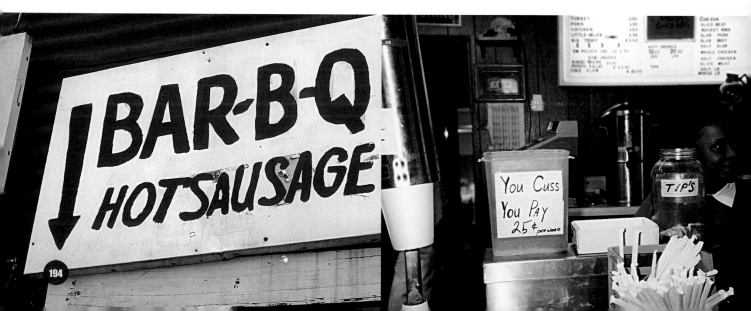

MASON'S BARBECUED FEATHER BONES

Serves 6 to 8

1 tablespoon garlic powder

1 tablespoon onion powder

1 tablespoon salt

1 teaspoon allspice

1 teaspoon chili powder

1 teaspoon black pepper

½ teaspoon ground nutmeg

½ teaspoon cayenne

¼ teaspoon ground cinnamon

2 pounds feather bones (1 ½ by 3½-inch bones cut from a hog's backbone)

In an airtight container, combine the garlic powder, onion powder, salt, allspice, chili powder, black pepper, nutmeg, cayenne, and cinnamon. Mix well, seal, and store in a cool, dry place until ready to use, up to 6 months.

Preheat your offset smoker to 225°–250°F. You can also use your grill for smoking (page 201). Season the feather bones fairly heavily with the spice rub. Then let the meat sit at room temperature for about 1 hour. Place the meat bone side down on a screen or cookie sheet in your smoker and smoke for about 30 minutes. Turn the meat so that you'll have marks on both sides; then smoke for another 30 minutes. The internal temperature of the meat should be about 160°F when it is finished. Make sure there is plenty of smoke in the smoker throughout the cooking time and do not sauce the featherbones while cooking, as the heat and smoke should give them a nice mahogany color with a wonderful flavor. If you do serve sauce, do so as a light dipping sauce with plenty of BBQ bread (page 67) for mopping up the juices and maybe some sauce.

Note: You can cook the feather bones the day before you plan to serve them. Cook until they reach an internal temperature of 140°F on an instant-read thermometer, let them cool, and refrigerate overnight. Let sit at room temperature for 1 hour before placing them in your smoker at 225°–250°F for about 30 minutes, until the internal temperature reaches 160°F.

Barbecued Baby Back Ribs

John Willingham

World Champion Barbecuer, Cookbook Author, and Teller of Tall Tales Memphis, TN www.willinghamsbbq.com/

John Willingham is a barbecue legend, icon, entrepreneur, and public servant who is second to none in the barbecue network. His barbecue contest awards—including two grand championships at Memphis in May and the American Royal—could fill an entire room in a barbecue hall of fame. Not one to rest on his laurels, John is fully engaged each day in the pursuit of barbecue excellence. Although we consider John's barbecue work to be a public service, he also provides a public service in the traditional sense. He is a former Shelby County commissioner as well as an active member of Ascension Lutheran Church with his wife, Marge. Marge and John are the proud parents of three daughters and seven grandchildren. John's popular cookbook, *John Willingham's World Champion Bar-B-Q*, spells out some of his many secrets to barbecue success.

John's search for the best way to cook barbecue prompted his invention of the famous W'ham Turbo Cooker, for which he holds a U.S. patent. He also developed an award-winning line of W'ham seasonings, both dry and wet. John was also one of the first barbecuers to use Worcestershire powder and powdered vinegar.

John has been our friend and barbecue buddy since the mid-1980s, when we met him at Memphis in May. He is Paul's Memphis counterpart in several respects. Both John and Paul designed and built their own pits; both hang their barbecue, Chinese style; and both have been cooking competition barbecue since the early 1980s. In addition, both have won the American Royal Grand Championship—the Open and the Invitational—and both have been Grand Champion of the Jack Daniel's World Championship Invitational Barbecue. Both of their cooking teams have won Team of the Year for Memphis in May and the Kansas City Barbecue Society, respectively. Both have a background and an association with Trader Vic, a world-renowned restaurateur known for his Asian cuisine, which might explain their love for Asian foods, flavorings, and sauces. And last but not least, John and Paul are considered barbecue mentors and gurus, among other things.

John's world championship cooking team is called the River City Rooters. John has owned three barbecue restaurants in his long tenure as "the man of Memphis barbecue," but he is now out of all of them. He concentrates on selling his W'ham products and is involved in Memphis politics.

John is known for his great championship ribs. Here is a recipe he gave to Paul, saying, "It's simple. Just use my W'ham seasonings and you can't go wrong."

BARBECUED BABY BACK RIBS

Serves 4 to 6

2 slabs baby back ribs

½ cup W'ham seasoning of your choice (or use the recipe that follows)

Apple juice, for basting

Set up your smoker to cook indirectly at 250°–275°F. This temperature is a little higher than usual, but John believes that ribs should be cooked hotter than most barbecue. To prepare the ribs, trim them of excess fat. Do not remove the membrane from the back of the ribs before you cook them. John, like many other Memphis pitmasters we've met, says that leaving the membrane on keeps the meat juices in. Paul and John have a friendly disagreement on this technique. Sprinkle the ribs all over with the W'ham seasoning. Place the ribs in the smoker. If you hang the ribs like John and Paul do, you don't have to turn them. Just baste them with apple juice after 1½ hours. If you cook the ribs on a grate or in a rib rack, turn them after 1½ hours and baste with apple juice. Cook the ribs 3 to 4 hours or until you can take two ribs side by side and easily tear them apart. When the ribs are finished cooking, remove the membrane and serve.

W'HAM-STYLE SEASONING

Makes about 2¾ cups

½ cup cane sugar

½ cup onion salt

½ cup garlic salt

2 tablespoons chili powder

2 tablespoons Worcestershire powder

1 tablespoon lemon pepper

1 tablespoon black pepper

1 tablespoon vinegar powder

1 teaspoon cayenne

1 teaspoon rubbed sage

1 teaspoon dried basil

½ teaspoon ground rosemary

Combine all of the ingredients and blend well. Store in sealed jar in a cool, dark place until ready to use, up to 6 months.

BBQ Mutton

Otis Boyd

**Boyd 'n' Son Bar-B-Q,
Kansas City, MO**

Otis Boyd was a pitmaster's pitmaster and a Kansas City barbecue icon. He has gone on to his heavenly reward, and it is only appropriate that where his barbecue restaurant stood at 5510 Prospect Avenue is now a church. Thank you, Otis, for your wonderful barbecue and for being a true gentleman.

Over the course of a 6-hour visit several years ago, Mr. Boyd shared his recipe for barbecued mutton. His was one of the few places in town that sold mutton. It was smoked to tender perfection and sauced with Mr. Boyd's tomato-based barbecue sauce for a perfect complement.

BBQ MUTTON

Serves 6 to 8

3 slabs mutton breast (ribs)

2 quarts buttermilk

BARBECUE RUB

½ cup sea salt

½ cup packed dark brown sugar

1 tablespoon ground allspice

1 tablespoon finely ground black pepper

2 teaspoons ground coriander

2 teaspoons ground juniper berries

1 teaspoon ground rosemary

1 teaspoon ground thyme

½ teaspoon ground nutmeg

MUSTARD SLATHER

2 large cloves garlic, peeled

½ teaspoon sea salt

½ cup Dijon mustard

1 tablespoon soy sauce

1½ teaspoons ground rosemary, thyme, or oregano

2 tablespoons fresh lemon juice

¼ cup olive or peanut oil

Heat your grill or smoker to 230°–250°F. Trim any excess fat from the ribs and place the ribs in a large plastic bag. Pour the buttermilk over the ribs, press the air from the bag, seal the bag, and place it in the refrigerator to marinate for 8 hours or overnight.

Combine the rub ingredients in a small bowl and blend well. To make the mustard slather, mash the garlic with the salt in a small bowl. Whisk in the mustard, soy sauce, herb, lemon juice, and then the oil, to make a mayonnaise-like cream.

Remove the ribs from the marinade, shake off any excess marinade, and blot with paper towels. With a pastry brush, lightly brush the mustard slather on the bone side of the ribs; then season that side with the rub. Repeat with the meat side. Place the ribs in your cooker and cook for about 6 hours, or until the ribs pull apart easily.

BARBECUE BASICS

WHAT IS BARBECUE?

There is no easy answer. Barbecue is a method of cooking. Barbecued meat is also barbecue. A gathering of people to eat barbecue is a barbecue, too.

The barbecue method of cooking involves cooking meat at low temperatures (225° to 275°F) for several hours—from 4 to 24, or more. The result is meat that is tender and smoky, with about 25 percent of the original bulk lost through rendering of fat and juices. When barbecue is called "smoking," the reference is to "hot smoking" in a barbecue pit, as opposed to "cold smoking," which involves cooking brined meats at a low temperature, usually for several days. Traditionally that is done in a smokehouse. Both methods impart smoke flavor in the meat.

The word *barbecue* is sometimes used interchangeably with *grilling*. Grilling is a method of cooking foods directly or indirectly over hot coals or flames for short periods of time, from a few seconds to more than an hour. Thus, grilling is hot and fast; barbecue is slow and low.

Purists insist that grilling is not barbecue. While technically that is true, we have no argument with backyard cooks who invite friends and family to a "barbecue" featuring grilled hot dogs, sausages, steaks, or burgers.

DIRECT VS. INDIRECT GRILLING

Direct grilling is a method of quickly cooking food by placing it on a grill rack directly over the heat source. Direct grilling works best with smaller portions of food and foods that require short cooking times, such as burgers and/or foods with a low fat content, such as well-trimmed steaks and chops. It is faster than indirect cooking because more intense heat is provided and allows for browning on the outside of foods. Food is often cooked uncovered on a charcoal grill but covered on a gas grill.

Indirect grilling is a method of grilling slowly, to one side of the heat source, over a drip pan in a covered grill. Hot air circulates around the food, much like in a convection oven, and it cooks more slowly because less heat is provided. Indirect grilling is ideal for larger cuts of meat that require longer cooking times.

BARBECUING EQUIPMENT

Barbecue joints use a variety of cooking equipment, from custom-made to commercially manufactured. Fifty-five-gallon drums made into cookers, cinder block pits—above or below ground—with grates and steel plates for lids, brick pits with carousel grates, "aquarium" pits with glass walls, stainless-steel pits fueled with gas, wood, electricity, or wood pellets, and large steel custom-made pits are what we've seen most often at barbecue joints.

Home barbecue equipment can range from low-tech and inexpensive to high-tech and very expensive. If you don't already have a grill, we recommend starting with the low-tech and

FOIL DRIP PAN FOR INDIRECT GRILLING

A drip pan is a helpful accessory for indirect grilling. Make a foil drip pan by tearing off a sheet of heavy-duty foil about 2½ times as large as the food you will be cooking. Fold the foil in half; then fold up the edges to make 2-inch-high sides. Crease the corners to seal.

inexpensive icon of backyard cooking, the kettle grill. In either case, begin with studying the owner's manual for basic guidance and tips.

GRILLS: GAS OR CHARCOAL?

Both gas grills and charcoal grills have their proponents. When we barbecue, we prefer charcoal and wood, but not everyone feels that way. Paul has done two blind taste tests using gas vs. charcoal, and gas won both times.

The recipes in this book are from barbecue restaurants and professionals, where they almost always use charcoal, but you can use what you have and what you're comfortable with. The results may not be exactly the same, but you'll still end up with some great barbecue.

Here's a quick summary of gas and charcoal grill features.

GAS GRILLS

Gas grills come in all shapes and sizes. They use propane tanks or a natural gas hookup. They are essentially a metal box lined with tube-shaped liquid propane burners on the bottom. The burners are topped by a heating surface of metal bars, lava rocks, which are natural rock resulting from volcanic lava, or ceramic briquettes, which are radiant materials compacted into a brick shape. Ceramic briquettes don't burn completely as charcoal does. Lava rocks and metal plates are more similar alternatives to charcoal. Lava rocks can be used many times, but eventually need to be replaced.

Benefits of Gas Grills

Gas grills are quick to preheat—10 to 15 minutes. Multiple burners allow you to control the heat better than a charcoal grill. Gas grills are also less messy—no charcoal or fire starters—and they burn longer than charcoal. One 20-pound tank lasts for 12 to 14 hours. It's easier to maintain higher temperatures on a gas grill than on a charcoal grill, but if you're cooking for long periods of time, you'll use a lot of gas.

What to Look For

When selecting a gas grill, look for one made from materials such as cast aluminum, stainless steel, or porcelain-coated steel. Stainless-steel or porcelain enamel–coated grill racks are easy to clean. Push-button ignition allows easy, safe lighting

You'll want a minimum of three burners that work independently for greater grilling flexibility and heat control. A gas gauge to monitor fuel levels is especially helpful for barbecuing, when you're cooking for long periods of time. Also look for a built-in thermometer to monitor grill temperature.

Other options you'll find are removable secondary grill racks, side burners for cooking other foods while you're grilling, extra outside shelving for storage, extra outside workspace for food prep, and rotisserie fittings.

An offset smoker is nice to have if you do a lot of smoking, but if you only occasionally smoke food, you can use your grill. You can purchase an accessory metal smoker box, a small perforated metal container placed on a gas grill's lava rocks or ceramic briquettes to hold wood chips and provide smoke. It can also be used on the grill rack of a charcoal grill. If you don't want to purchase a smoker box, you can put soaked wood chips in heavy-duty foil, seal and poke holes in the top, and place on the hot briquettes, rocks, or coals.

Maintenance
Simple maintenance adds years to the life of a gas grill. Check the gas fitting for leaks each time you connect and disconnect by using a mixture of soap and water. Bubbles indicate a leak. You'll also want to periodically check the tubes connecting the propane tank to the grill to ensure there are no cracks or holes. Regularly empty the grease catch pan to prevent flare-ups and fires. Store the tank outdoors, not in an enclosed space, and detached from the grill.

After every use, turn your grill on high for 10 to 15 minutes with the lid closed. Turn off the grill and let it cool slightly. Loosen the residue from the grill rack with a brass-bristle brush. This not only prevents sticking but also helps to prevent flare-ups. When the grill is completely cool, wipe the inside and outside surfaces of the grill with a soft cloth and warm, soapy water. Rinse with clean water and wipe dry.

CHARCOAL GRILLS
Charcoal grills have either a round or square box construction. A kettle grill is a popular round one with a heavy cover that can be used for either direct or indirect grilling. A charcoal grate holds coals on the bottom, and a grill rack above the coals holds the food. Vents on the bottom and in the lid help control temperature (on most models).

Benefits of Charcoal Grills
Charcoal grills are more affordable than gas grills, and they can reach higher temperatures.

BARBECUE TERMINOLOGY

Stick burner—Barbecue contestants' jargon for cooks who use hardwood as their primary fuel instead of charcoal, charcoal briquettes, or wood pellets.

Pellethead—Barbecue contestants' jargon for cooks who use pellet-burning barbecue pits.

WSM—Acronym for Weber Smokey Mountain Cooker Smoker. Due to its shape, it is also called the Weber Bullet. It is built for the slow and low barbecue method of cooking. Hot briquettes are placed in the bottom; a water pan and two racks for meat fill the remainder of the bullet. More information on the WSM is on the Weber Web pages.

What to Look For

Vents on both the top and bottom allow greater temperature control. Use stainless-steel or nickel-plated cooking and charcoal grates (sometimes referred to as a grill grates or grids). The grill should have a heavy-gauge bowl, a tight-fitting lid, a porcelain-coated finish, sturdy legs and construction, and heatproof handles. Look for preassembled or welded parts, which are more stable and less likely to rust.

Some charcoal grills include a built-in thermometer, which helps you maintain the right temperature for the foods you're cooking. A hinged grill rack will give you easier access to replenish coals, which is especially helpful when you're barbecuing. An ash catcher underneath the grill makes cleaning more convenient, and you can buy fire retardant mats to place under your grill to protect the ground beneath it.

Maintenance

Charcoal grills are pretty easy to maintain. Keep the grill rack clean, and after the grill cools, remove the ashes to ensure proper air flow the next time you grill. When the grill is completely cool, wipe the inside and outside surfaces of the grill with a soft cloth and warm, soapy water. Rinse with clean water and wipe dry. To help protect the body from the weather and minimize white spots and oxidation, use a paper towel to apply a light coating of vegetable oil to the outside of the grill while it's cool. You can also buy a water-resistant cover to protect your grill when not in use.

HANDY UTENSILS AND EQUIPMENT

Long-handled tongs, basting brushes, spatulas, and heavy-duty oven mitts are useful for tending foods while cooking. It's also a good idea to keep an ABC fire extinguisher handy, just in case.

CLEANING YOUR GRILL GRATES

It's easiest to clean your grill grates when they're warm. After each use, scrub the grates with wire brushes and scrubbers so that they're clean and ready to go next time you grill. Use brass-wire brushes on stainless-steel grates and stainless-steel brushes on cast-iron grates. You can also use crumpled pieces of foil to remove buildup. Another way to clean them is to turn up your gas grill to high or build a hot fire in a charcoal grill and cover the entire grate with heavy-duty foil, weigh it down with bricks or rocks, cover the grill, and let it burn for about 10 minutes. Remove the foil with tongs and dispose of it. Hit the grate with a long-handled brush, and the charred bits will turn to powder that will fall off into the fire.

COOKING WITH CHARCOAL

You can buy two different kinds of charcoal. Charcoal briquettes made of compacted ground charcoal, coal dust, and starch are most common. They come in standard and easy-lighting. Easy-lighting briquettes are pretreated with a lighting solution for a quick start and need to burn for only 10 minutes before they are ready for grilling. They can be a real time-saver, but we don't recommend them because they can lend a petrochemical flavor to whatever you are grilling or barbecuing. You can also use lump charcoal, the carbon residue of wood that has been charred, usually in the form of lumps.

Try one of the following setups for direct or indirect grilling.

For direct grilling: Use long-handled tongs to spread the coals evenly in a single layer. Extend them about 1 inch beyond the area of the food.

For indirect grilling: You need a disposable drip pan large enough to cover the surface below the food. Use a purchased disposable foil pan or make your own (see page 200). Place the drip pan in the center of the firebox. Use long-handled tongs to arrange the coals around the pan.

LIGHTING A CHARCOAL GRILL

Charcoal grills are easy to start if you know the tricks of the trade. Remove the top grill grate and set it aside. Leave the lower charcoal grate in the grill, as you'll need to put the charcoal on top of that, not directly on the bottom of the bowl.

There are several ways to light the charcoal. The best and easiest way for home grilling is to use a chimney starter. You can stuff the bottom of the chimney starter with paper, turn the chimney over, put it on the fire grate, fill it with briquettes (around 92 in a standard chimney), and set the paper on fire. The fire will then move to the coals. Once the coals are ash gray (20 to 30 minutes), use a fireproof glove or mitt to grasp the chimney handle and dump the hot coals on one end of the fire grate.

The way Paul likes to light his fires is to use a small propane torch, available at most major hardware stores; it's also known as a weed burner. Mound the coals in the center of the grill, follow the torch manufacturer's instructions for lighting the torch, and hold it on the coals until they ignite. Once the coals have preheated, use long handled tongs to distribute the coals how you want them. Or you can use an electric starter to light coals. To do this, place the starter in the coals and heat for the manufacturer's suggested time. Unplug the starter, remove it from the coals, and place it on a heatproof surface away from children and pets to avoid accidental burns. Distribute the coals when you're ready to cook.

Using lighter fluid is a very popular way to light your fire, and that's the only reason we mention it. It's the very last way we would light a barbecue fire because it usually leaves a petrochemical taste on all cooked products. To light the coals using fluid, arrange them in a mound in the center of the firebox. Add lighter fluid according to the manufacturer's directions. Let stand for about 1 minute and then ignite with a match. Never add more lighter fluid after the fire has started. Once the coals are ready, use long-handled tongs to distribute them for cooking. You can also light your charcoal fire or chimney with gelled alcohol starter, such as Sterno, or just crumpled newspaper. If using a chemical fire starter, make sure all chemical residue has burned off before putting the meat in the kettle.

Once the coals are lit, allow them to heat for 20 to 30 minutes (10 minutes for easy-lighting) or until they turn ash gray in daylight or glowing red at night. When the coals are ready, use an oven mitt to close any two of the three vent holes in the bottom of the kettle. This lets oxygen in, which fuels the flame. Rub vegetable oil on the grill grate (or spray it with nonstick cooking spray) and put it in the kettle. Place the meat opposite the hot coals. If using wood chips, drain the water from them and dump them atop the hot coals. Put the lid securely on the kettle with lid vents open.

You can monitor temperature with a thermometer in the lid vent hole, and you can maintain your desired temperature by controlling oxygen intake to coals by adjusting bottom vent holes. More air means faster, hotter cooking. Less air allows for slower cooking. If you're direct grilling with an uncovered grill, charcoal briquettes will burn for 40 to 45 minutes, as a general rule. If you leave the lid on, most kettle grills will hold a steady temperature of 225° to 275°F for at least six hours. Avoid lifting the lid to check the meat, as this will prolong the cooking time. Turn items only once (halfway through cooking time). When you must lift the grill cover, lift it to the side rather than straight up—suction may otherwise draw ash onto the food.

To keep the grill going for several hours, you'll probably need to add more charcoal. It's best to maintain a constant temperature while barbecuing, and you can do that by adding hot coals instead of fresh briquettes when you need to refuel. Just before you put the grill grate over your first batch of coals, remove two and place them in the bottom of a chimney starter. Then fill the chimney starter with fresh briquettes and set it aside on a heatproof surface, such as concrete or bricks (not asphalt), so that it can preheat while you put your meat on the grill. By the time you need to add more coals to your fire, the coals in the chimney should be preheated and ready to go.

Cooking times will vary depending up type and weight of meat. Don't leave your grill unattended while it's lit. When the meat is done, remove it from the grill and let it rest for 5 to 15 minutes before slicing, chopping, or pulling.

COOKING WITH GAS

You will want to refer to your owner's manual for specific directions for direct and indirect cooking on a gas grill.

In general, for indirect cooking on a two-burner gas grill, after preheating with both burners, you will turn off one burner and place the food over the unlit side, away from the heat source. For three-burner gas grills, you will turn off the middle burner after preheating and place the food in the center of the grill. Drip pans are required for foods that have juices, such as roasts and ribs. The food is placed on a rack in a roasting pan, and the roasting pan is set on the grill rack. The lid of the gas grill is then closed for grilling.

LIGHTING A GAS GRILL

As with a charcoal grill, it's a good idea to lightly coat your clean grill grates with a little bit of vegetable oil or nonstick cooking spray. Be sure to follow your owner's manual when lighting a gas grill. Before starting your gas grill, open the lid and turn all the burner control knobs to off. Turn the gas on at the source. From this point you should refer to your owner's manual for specific lighting instructions. After

GRILL THERMOMETERS

A grill thermometer is a handy tool when barbecuing. An easy way to modify your grill is to take a wine cork and drill a hole the diameter of your thermometer through the middle of the cork from top to bottom. Fit the cork into one of the top grill vents, and push the thermometer through the hole in the cork. That way you can constantly monitor the internal temperature and your thermometer won't touch the metal of the grill, which could give you an inaccurate reading.

lighting your grill, close the lid and preheat the grill on high for 10 to 15 minutes. Again, you will want to refer to your owner's manual for the recommended preheating time and instructions for adjusting the heat while you're cooking. Avoid lifting the lid while you're grilling, as that will prolong the cooking time. When the meat is done, remove it from the grill and let it rest for five to fifteen minutes before slicing, chopping, or pulling.

TIP

YOU CAN HELP KEEP YOUR MEAT MOIST WHILE COOKING BY SPRITZING IT WITH APPLE JUICE, WHICH WON'T CHANGE THE FLAVOR OF THE FINISHED MEAT.

AVOIDING FLARE-UPS

Sometimes meat juices drip into the coals, briquettes, or rocks, causing flare-ups that can burn your meat. Flare-ups can, in fact, wreck a great meal in seconds.

To avoid flare-ups when barbecuing, place the meat opposite the hot coals, briquettes, or rocks. This creates a cool zone so that you can move meat back and forth from flames to cool zone as necessary. Trimming excess fat from the meat also helps prevent flare-ups. You can also try lowering the heat by raising the grill rack and spreading the coals so there is more space

WOODS

Natural wood chips and chunks can be added to a fire to impart a smoky flavor to food as it cooks. Alder, apple, cherry, hickory, maple, mesquite, oak, and pecan are commonly used. The chips are soaked in water, drained well, and added to a fire just before putting food on the grill. In kettle grills or gas grills, water-soaked wood chips or dry smoke pellets work best. Large cookers with a firebox on the side take well to wood logs or chunks.

We encourage the use of the hardwoods available locally. In the Pacific Northwest, that would be alder. In the Midwest and South, hickory, pecan, and oak. In the Southwest, mesquite. In the Northeast, maple. Also check for availability in your area of fruit woods such as apple, peach, cherry, and pear. If you're partial to a certain wood that isn't local—say, you're a Texan living in Maine—no problem. Barbecue woods of any variety can be shipped worldwide from a variety of suppliers. Call your local barbecue supply store or search online.

between them. Or you can remove some of the coals or cover the grill.

For excessive flare-ups in a charcoal grill, you may need to remove the meat from the grill and mist the flames with a water-spray bottle. Once the flames die down, you can return the food to the grill and resume grilling. Do not mist flare-ups on a gas grill. Simply close the lid and wait for the flare-up to die down. Some lava rock systems can collect grease that may result in flare-ups, so be especially watchful when using them, and change them once a season if you use your grill a lot. When you open your propane tank valve, it might help to turn it only one turn so that you can turn it off in a hurry in the event of a flare-up.

TESTING GRILL TEMPERATURE

Most grills have thermometers, and if yours didn't come with one, you can purchase one. If you plan to do a lot of barbecuing, it's a good investment. If you don't have a grill thermometer, you need to be able to judge how hot the heat is coming from your grill, because not all foods are cooked at the same temperature. Hold your hand, palm side down, where your food will cook and at the same height as the food that will be grilled. Count by saying, "one thousand-one, one thousand-two" for each second you can hold your hand there.

**1 second (or less) =
Very Hot Fire—600°F or higher**

2 seconds = Hot Fire—550°–599°F

3 seconds = Medium-Hot Fire—500°–549°F

4 seconds = Medium Fire—400°–499°F

5 seconds = Low-Medium Fire—301°–399°F

**6 seconds (or more) =
Low Fire—300°F or less**

These are rough estimates and can vary depending on where you place your hand. For example, there may be more heat in one location than another.

TESTING FOR DONENESS

A meat thermometer guarantees perfectly cooked meat every time. Insert the meat thermometer into the center of the thickest part of the uncooked meat. The thermometer should not touch any fat, bone, or the grill. The chart on page 211 gives suggested doneness temperatures for a variety of meats. When the meat reaches the desired doneness, remove it from the grill. Let it stand for about 15 minutes before slicing. This will make the meat easier to slice.

If you don't have a meat thermometer, the following are general cues for meat doneness:

Rare doneness: The center should be bright red, raw, and room temperature. This is generally not considered to be safe, as the meat does not get hot enough to kill any germs or bacteria that may be in it.

Medium-rare doneness: The center of the meat should have a bright red color and be slightly springy when pressed. This is not recommended for veal, pork, or ground meats.

Medium doneness: For this doneness, the center of the meat should have a slightly pink to red color. The meat will be slightly firm and springy when pressed.

Medium-well doneness: The center of the meat should have very little pink color and be firm and springy when pressed.

Well doneness: The center of the meat should have no pink color and be firm when pressed.

BARBECUE TERMINOLOGY

Rub—A dry spice or a combination of dry spices, from salt and pepper, to any concoction you can dream up to season whatever you are going to barbecue or grill. It is also known as a dry marinade. Always season the food with dry rubs before cooking, not during or after.

Sauce—A seasoned liquid barbecue condiment. Popular bases are tomato, vinegar, and mustard; soy sauce, mayonnaise, and pureed fruit are also used.

Marinade—A marinade is a liquid solution that you soak foods, particularly meats, in before cooking. A marinade adds flavor to foods and makes them somewhat tender by beginning the breakdown process of cooking. The seasonings you add to a marinade are carried into the food by use of an acidic ingredient in the marinade such as vinegars or fruit juices. It is important to have this acidic base not only to do these things but because it protects the food from the formation of harmful substances of the surface while cooking. Marinades are particularly important and useful in grilling because of the high, intense heats produced by grills. Always marinate foods in the refrigerator to prevent bacteria from forming. Do not baste the meat with used marinade. Discard it to avoid bacterial contamination.

Sops, Mops, and Bastes—Sops, mops, and bastes are really all the same thing. They are liquid agents to keep your barbecued meat moist. They all got their name by their delivery systems. In the early days of barbecuing, the meat was drying out and there was a need to get some moisture on the meat. So they concocted a liquid they thought would not only keep the meat moist but would also flavor it. They got Grandma's clean rags and dipped them into the concoction and sopped the meat to keep it moist. Then came the little dish mop, so they used a clean one and mopped the liquid on. Then it became a baste, and now most barbecuers use a spray bottle to deliver the moisture.

Brine—A solution of fresh water, salt, and sugar. Meat is soaked in brine in the refrigerator for varying lengths of time, based on the size of meat cuts. Some brine recipes add sugar and other spices to the salt. Individual recipes vary. It is believed that brined meat is more moist and flavorful than meat that has not been brined.

BASIC DIRECTIONS FOR BARBECUED MEAT

Some of the recipes in this book call for barbecue in a salad, baked potato, or other dishes. Here's some basic guidance for readers who don't have a favorite barbecue joint nearby, or who want to cook barbecue at home. Follow the step-by-step procedures below, varying cooking times as follows:

Pork Shoulder: 8 or more hours until tender.

Beef Brisket: 12 or more hours until tender.

Whole Chicken: 1½ to 2 or more hours until done.

Sausages: 45 minutes to 1 hour until done.

Prepare meats as follows:

If you like to season meat before cooking, use your favorite rub or this all-purpose rub:

ALL-PURPOSE RUB

2 parts ground black pepper

1 part kosher salt

1 part granulated garlic

Stir the ingredients together. Sprinkle the rub on the meat lightly, the evening before or prior to putting meat in the grill.

PORK SHOULDER

Sold as the leg portion (arm shoulder) or upper, blade shoulder (Boston butt). The latter is popular with barbecuers.

To prepare pork shoulder, little if any trimming is needed. Sprinkle the meat with rub. Cook fat side up at 225° to 250°F for 2 hours per pound until tender. Cooks take pride in cooking a butt so tender that the shoulder blade can be pulled out with ease.

BEEF BRISKET

For best results get a whole (7- to 10-pound) brisket in Cryovac. Do minimal trimming of fat. Sprinkle all surfaces lightly with rub. Cook fat side up at 250° to 275°F for 10 to 12 hours or more, until tender. Remove from the grill and let sit for 30 minutes before slicing against the grain.

WHOLE CHICKEN

Decide if you want to barbecue the chicken whole intact or flat, spatchcock. The latter will take less time. For spatchcock preparation, refer to the B's Barbecue recipe on page 110. For whole chicken, lightly sprinkle it with rub, and place it upright in the grill, opposite the hot coals. Cover the grill and cook at 125° to 150°F for 1½ to 2 hours until done.

SAUSAGE

Cooking times will vary by type of meat in the sausage, size, and whether the sausage is raw or smoked. If it's smoked, it's enough to simply heat it in a microwave, conventional oven, or skillet.

If it's not already smoked, you'll need to cook it longer, and a grill or pit is a great way to do it. To prevent sausages from burning on the grill, precook or poach the sausages in water before barbecuing. To do this, put them in barely simmering water and poach for 20 to 30 minutes. Be careful not to cook them too fast or the skins

continued on page 210

SO YOU WANT TO START A BARBECUE BUSINESS?

Many backyard pitmasters and championship barbecue contest winners have taken the leap to make barbecue their full-time business. Some have succeeded. Many have not.

Beyond taking a reality course in small business development from your local Service Corps of Retired Executives (SCORE) and reading the self-help books that tell you how to develop a vision statement and business plan, we strongly advise would-be barbecue entrepreneurs to talk with others who are or have been successful in the business. We asked some, and here, with some advice of our own, is what we heard:

- "Go see a very, very good psychiatrist," says Paul.

- Have enough money to live on for at least two years.

- You have to know that it is a very competitive business—much more so than in the past. These days it's hard to crack a new restaurant.

- Think twice and a third time after that.

- Don't go the family route when hiring help. Sometimes it works out for the better, but often it doesn't. Good-quality people are hard to find.

- If you don't have two of you, don't do it. "If I could find another me, I'd hire him," says Johnny White.

- The right amount of start-up capital is important. Today you need a bare-bones minimum investment of $300,000.

- Planning and learning from mistakes is important. Paul says, "This is not only important; it is paramount."

- You need business savvy and need to know how to keep up with taxes and local, state, and federal rules.

- It's a labor of love. "I like it," says Johnny White. "That's why I'm still here. If you don't like it, don't do it."

- If you're married, remember to put family first. If you marry the job, you can lose your family. Learn how to train and delegate.

We're not saying don't do it. Just do the important self-examination and resource development before you take the leap!

will burst. Grill the precooked sausage for 5 to 10 minutes over medium-hot heat (see page 206). This will heat the sausages through, giving them color and a smoky flavor.

Remember these golden rules when cooking sausages:

- Cook sausages slowly to ensure that the skin doesn't burst.

- Never prick a good-quality sausage, as the casing helps to retain moisture.

- Cut the links between the sausages cleanly with a sharp knife. When cooked, a sausage should be cooked right through but still juicy and succulent and not charred.

For more information on grilling sausages, you can also refer to the Meyer's Elgin Smokehouse recipe on page 82 or the Black's Barbecue cooking procedure on page 38.

THE BASICS OF MEAT FOR BARBECUE

PORK RIB BASICS
Baby backs: Loin back ribs. The term is often applied to any size slab of loin back ribs, but a true baby back rib slab is 1¾ pounds or less.

Spareribs: The intact rib section removed from the belly; may include costal cartilages with or without the brisket bone (breastbone) removed and diaphragm trimmed. A slab of spareribs should have at least eleven ribs.

St. Louis–style ribs: Spareribs prepared by removing the brisket bone parallel to the rib side, exposing cartilage on the brisket bone side. Skirt

meat is usually removed. If left on, the outside edge of the skirt should be trimmed.

Skinned: The membrane on the back, or bone side, of the rib slab has been removed.

Long end: The first six ribs from the breastbone end.

Short end: The meatier ribs from number 7 to the end of the slab.

Wet: Ribs served with barbecue sauce on them.

Dry: Ribs served with a dry rub on them.

Shiners: Bones that show through the meat.

PORK BUTT BASICS
Pork butt/shoulder/ham: A pork butt is the top half of a swine's front legs; the bottom half is known as the *picnic*. The two pieces together are known as the *pork shoulder;* both picnic and shoulder have the feet removed. The hams are the back legs of the pig with the feet removed.

Bark: Bark is the crust on the outside of the piece of meat that you are barbecuing, which develops with the long barbecuing process.

Bone in/bone out: Pork shoulders can be purchased boneless or with the bone blade in. It is a matter of pride and accomplishment when a cook's shoulder is so tender that the bone can easily be pulled out when the meat is done.

Brown and white: The outside of a barbecued shoulder is dark, or brown, from cooking. Past the bark the meat is light, or white. You can order brown only, white only, or a mix of brown and white.

Food Doneness and Temperature

FOOD	DONENESS	INTERNAL TEMPERATURE °F
BARBECUED PORK	Sliceable and Chopped	180°F (82.2°C)
SHOULDERS, PICNICS	Sliceable, Pullable, and Chopped	185°F (85° C)
BOSTON BUTTS	Pullable	195° to 205°F (91° to 96°C)
BARBECUED BEEF BRISKET	Sliceable	185°F (85°C)
BEEF STEAKS	Rare	135°F (57°C)
	Medium-Rare	140°F (60°C)
	Medium	145°F (63°C)
	Medium-Well	160°F (71°C)
	Well Done	170°F (77°C)
BEEF ROAST	Rare	130°F (54°C)
	Medium-Rare	140°F (60°C)
	Medium	145°F (63°C)
	Medium-Well	160°F (71°C)
	Well Done	170°F (77°C)
CHICKEN Whole or Pieces	Done	170°F (77°C)
Breast	Done	165°F (74°C)
CORNISH HEN	Done	170°F (77°C)
DUCK	Done	170°F (77°C)
GROUND MEAT	Medium	165°F (74°C)
BEEF, PORK, LAMB	Well Done	170°F (77°C)
HAM Fully Cooked	Well Done	140°F (60°C)
Not Fully Cooked	Well Done	160°F (71°C)
LAMB CHOPS AND RACK	Rare	120°F (49°C)
	Medium-Rare	125°F (52°C)
	Medium	130°F (54°C)
	Medium-Well	140°F (60°C)
LAMB ROAST	Rare	115°F (46°C)
	Medium-Rare	125°F (52°C)
	Medium	130°F (54°C)
	Medium-Well	140°F (60°C)

continued on page 212

FOOD	DONENESS	INTERNAL TEMPERATURE °F
PHEASANT	Well Done	165°F (74°C)
PORK CHOPS	Medium-Rare	130°F (54°C)
	Medium	140°F (60°C)
	Medium-Well	150°F (66°C)
PORK TENDERLOIN	Medium-Rare	135°F (57°C)
	Medium	140°F (60°C)
	Medium-Well	150°F (66°C)
SAUSAGE	Well Done	170°F (77°C)
TURKEY Whole	Done (Check Thigh)	175°F (79°C)
Breast	Done	165°F (74°C)
Dark Meat	Done	175°F (79°C)
VEAL CHOPS & ROAST	Medium-Rare	125°F (52°C)
	Medium	140°F (60°C)
	Medium-Well	150°F (66°C)
VENISON	Medium	160°F (71°C)

Sliced, pulled, or chopped: Refers to pork or any barbecued meat. Sliced meat is cut across the grain of the meat for a tender cut. Pulled meat has been cooked to 195°–205°F and shredded with the grain of the meat. You can use two heavy-duty dinner forks to do this, or you can use your hands, wearing heavy-duty rubber gloves. Some cooks like to use heavy-duty plastic "claws" to pull pork. Chopped meat is cooked to 185°F and chopped across the grain into small pieces.

Carolina style: Barbecued pork shoulder is the meat of choice in western North Carolina, compared to the preference for whole hog in eastern North Carolina. Some places serve pulled pork. Others serve chopped pork. Texture ranges from coarsely chopped to finely chopped. The latter is done by special request.

BRISKET BASICS

Anatomy: A cut of beef taken from the breast section under the first five ribs. Brisket is usually sold without the bone and is divided into two sections. The flat cut has minimal fat and is usually more expensive than the more flavorful point cut, which has more fat. Brisket requires long, slow cooking and is best when barbecued.

Flat/point: The flat cut or first cut is the lean part of the brisket. The point, or deckle, is the fat end and is the tastier part of the brisket.

JOINTS WE LIKE TO VISIT

We've lived almost our whole lives in barbecue, traveling the country to participate in and judge contests, visiting restaurants in far-off places, writing books and articles, and talking to all kinds of people about barbecue. Consequently, it was a real challenge to single out our top 100 places. The following places are places we like to go, and we enjoy them, but for some reason or another they didn't make the list of 100. Maybe they had an off day when we visited, or maybe we couldn't agree on them, but all have their fans, and it would be remiss of us not to mention them.

ANGUS PIT STOP

608 S. Service Rd.
Calera, OK 74730
580-434-7867

You'll find Angus Pit Stop off Highway 69, only ten miles beyond the Red River when you've crossed over from north Texas to southern Oklahoma. You may think you haven't left Texas at the Angus Pit Stop, however. Like the joints in central Texas and elsewhere, you choose your mesquite charcoal smoked meats from a holding pit, and then they're sliced and weighed. Meats include brisket, pork chops, sausage, chicken, spare ribs, tri-tip, and ham. Grote, "The Boss," has been slow smoking barbecue since the late 1970s, and you can tell by the tender smokiness that he has learned a thing or two about barbecue over the years. Make room for a tasty hot cobbler or other dessert prepared by Diane, a certified gourmet cook.

BBQ PETE'S

6621 S. 211th St., Ste. 106
Kent, WA 98032
425-251-0778
http://bbqpetes.com

We're glad BBQ Pete's is back, thanks to Pete's son, Ryan. It was a sad day for us when Pete retired in 1995. Now the BBQ Pete's reincarnation is serving the same great-quality barbecue pork, beef, ribs, chicken, links, and sides that we enjoyed from the 1970s.

COUCH'S CORNER BAR-B-Q

5323 E. Nettleton Ave.
Jonesboro, AR 72401
870-932-0710
http://www.couchsbbq.com

When our travels take us anywhere near Jonesboro, we make sure we stop at Couch's for a chopped pork sandwich. Someday we'll try the Couch Potato, if for no other reason than we like the name.

CORKY'S

5259 Poplar Ave.
Memphis, TN 38119
901-685-9744
http://www.corkysbbq.com

Our favorite Corky's is the original on Poplar Avenue. It is one of the most popular barbecue joints in town, and you'll know why when you dine there. We especially like the wet ribs with beans and fries.

COZY CORNER

745 N. Parkway
Memphis, TN 38105
901-527-9158
http://www.cozycornerbbq.com

We love the Cornish hen, baloney, and rib tips. Although we still really miss the presence of the late Ray Robinson, we know he'd be proud that his wife, Desiree, continues the Cozy Corner legacy.

EARL QUICK'S BAR-B-Q

1007 Merriam Ln.
Kansas City, KS 66103
913-236-7228
http://www.quicksbbqandcatering.com

You can tell that Ron Quick, pitmaster/ proprietor, learned his barbecue lessons well from his dad, Earl Quick, and the late Anthony Rieke of Rosedale Barbeque fame. One hundred percent hickory-smoked barbecue, slab specials on Wednesdays, friendly service. What could be better?

JETHRO'S BBQ

3100 Forest Ave.
Des Moines, IA 50311
515-279-3300
http://www.jethrosdesmoines.com

Ardie's college roommate, The Rev. Ron Osborne, told us about this place, and we're glad he did! Try the baby backs with Carolina sauce and the smoked chicken with Alabama white sauce. If you guessed from the name that the joint and menu are built on a hillbilly theme, you guessed right.

PORKY'S BAR-BQ

1056 Indian Point Rd.
Branson, MO 65616
417-338-9173

Pitmaster Richard Fent learned the art of barbecue in his hometown, Oklahoma City, and the Branson area is the better for it. From this small roadside joint with limited seating inside and out, Mr. Fent serves some top-notch hickory-smoked ribs and pulled pork with sweet potato fries and corn on the cob.

CHARLIE VERGOS' RENDEZVOUS

52 S. Second St.
Memphis, TN 38103
901-523-2746
http://www.hogsfly.com

Charlie Vergos is a Memphis icon. Revenue from the boxcar loads of charcoal-cooked pork sold at Charlie's Rendezvous and through the Web site is better than a license to print money. Charlie's son Nick and his siblings run the restaurant now while Charlie takes a well-deserved rest. The famous Rendezvous baby back ribs are wet or dry. Wet is with liquid sauce. Dry is with what Charlie calls "dry sauce," his special blend of dried herbs and spices. There's also pulled pork sandwiches and lamb ribs, with sides of coleslaw and beans.

Charlie opened the world-famous Rendezvous in 1948 after cleaning out a basement below his diner, where he discovered a coal chute. The coal chute gave him a vent for his considerable talent over a grill and allowed him to expand from ham and cheese sandwiches to ribs. And thus a legend was born.

The restaurant is downtown and easy to find once you find the Peabody Hotel. The Rendezvous is across the street, down the alley, in the basement. The tables are full of diners animated by the great food and friendly service. The walls are covered with enough memorabilia,

implements, and other stuff to stock an entire flea market mall. Down an alley, in a basement, a coal chute for a vent—the last place you'd expect to find a barbecue goldmine. Talk about overcoming the odds!

You can get Charlie's ribs delivered to your door, or buy his dry seasoning and wet sauce, charcoal-grill some baby backs, and apply the seasonings—dry, wet, or both.

RJ'S BOB-BE-QUE SHACK

5835 Lamar Ave.
Mission, KS 66202
913-262-7300
http://www.rjsbbq.com

RJ's has an excellent all-around menu and a friendly atmosphere. Certified Executive Chef Bob Palmgren is French trained. After successful gigs in some of Kansas City's finest restaurants, he caught barbecue fever, and his many fans are glad he did. Paul likes to meet there for the country breakfasts on weekends. Ardie is a fan of the pork butt burgers.

ROSEDALE BARBEQUE

600 Southwest Blvd.
Kansas City, KS 66103
913-262-0343
http://www.rbjb.com/rbjb/restaurants/
rosedale.htm

The oldest continuously operated barbecue joint in Kansas City still offers the most barbecue for your money. Beer is no longer served in buckets like it was in the 1930s, but you can get a quart bottle of beer to enjoy with your feast.

SMOKIN' GUNS

1218 Swift Ave.
North Kansas City, MO 64116
816-221-2535
http://www.smokingunsbbq.com

Phil and Linda Hopkins know their way around the barbecue pit, and they have the awards and satisfied customers to prove it. Most notable among their many awards is the 1999 Grand Championship at the Jack Daniel's World Championship Invitational Barbecue. "The Jack," as it is called in the barbecue network, is the most prestigious barbecue contest in the world. We can't go near North Kansas City without grazing at Smokin' Guns. On your first visit, share a combo platter with baby backs, brisket, pulled pork, and chicken, with beans and onion rings on the side. You won't have room for dessert, but take home some peach crisp to enjoy later.

JOINTS WE'D LIKE TO VISIT

ometimes when we look back on our travels, we think of that Johnny Cash song "I've Been Everywhere." But surprisingly, there are still a few barbecue joints we haven't visited, even though our barbecue buddies have been singing their praises for years. The following are just a few we hope to make it to soon, and who knows, maybe they'll be in a future edition of *America's Best BBQ*.

CIRCLE M

345 Martin Sausage Rd.
Liberty, SC 29657
864-375-9133

Our barbecue buddy Ronny Lark told us about Circle M, and he made it sound so good we wanted to hop on a flying hog jet to Sausage Road immediately. We haven't caught that hog yet, but Circle M is on our bucket list.

CRAIG'S

U.S. 70 West
DeVall's Bluff, AR 72041
870-998-2616

Ardie is a longtime fan of Craig's grainy vinegar-based sauce with a citrus accent, hot or mild. Craig's has a reputation for great barbecue that we're eager to try, along with pie from the Pie Shop across the road. The restaurant still has a wall that provided for segregated dining when Jim Crow was the law.

GRADY'S BARBECUE

3096 Arrington Bridge Rd.
Dudley, NC 28333
919-735-7243

Not to be confused with Grady's in the Texas Hill Country, another place we want to try, this joint is in North Carolina. Pronounced "Graddy's," Stephen and Geraldine Grady's very popular joint is one of the stops on the North Carolina Barbecue Society BBQ Trail. Our barbecue buddy Carl Rothrock told us Grady's is not to be missed, so it's on our must-do list for the next trip to North Carolina. It's a whole hog place with "zing" in the sauce, and everything is made from scratch. The Gradys have been doing barbecue since 1986, so we know they're doing it right.

MOORE'S OLDE TYME BARBEQUE

36711 Dr. M. L. King Jr. Blvd.
New Bern, NC 28562
252-638-3937
http://www.mooresbarbeque.com/

We were in New Bern on a stormy Sunday, the one day of the week Moore's is closed. To our regret, we couldn't return for swine dining at Moore's the next day or later. We were told we missed some of the finest chopped pork with slaw and hushpuppies this side of hog heaven. Tommy Moore's parents, John and Dot, would be proud that Tommy is continuing the Moore legacy that they started back in 1945.

PAYNE'S BAR-B-Q

1762 Lamar Ave.
Memphis, TN 38114
901-272-1523

Although we've been in Memphis many times, we have yet to visit Payne's. We've heard so much praise of it, however, that it's on our "must try" list for the next trip to Hog Heaven on the banks of the Mississippi.

SHEALY'S BAR-B-QUE

340 East Columbia Ave.
Batesburg-Leesville, SC 29070
803-532-8135
http://www.shealysbbq.com/

Shealy's mustard-base barbecue sauce has been one of Ardie's favorites for years. While en route to Shealy's by way of Columbia one fateful Wednesday, he called for directions, only to find that they were closed that day. Another joint that got away but is not forgotten.

SIMS BAR-B-QUE

716 W. 33rd St.
Little Rock, AR 72206
501-372-6868
http://simsbar-b-que.com

Kansas City friends who have eaten at Sims say we have to try it. There are two other locations, both also in Little Rock.

SNOW'S BBQ

516 Main St.
Lexington, TX 78947
979-773-4640 (Saturday only)
979-542-8189
http://www.snowsbbq.com/

How could a barbecue joint that is open only one day a week be suddenly catapulted into worldwide fame? Blame it on some *Texas Monthly* magazine staffers who tried it in 2008, liked it, and dubbed it the best in Texas. We don't know if the brisket, sausage, chicken, pork, ribs, potato salad, coleslaw, and beans that Ms. Tootsie Tomanetz serves up at Snow's are first rate or not, but we want to try them.

WHOLE HOG CAFÉ

2516 Cantrell Rd.
Little Rock, AR 72202
501-664-5025
http://www.wholehogcafe.com

Becky Bryant, Ardie's friend in the Arkansas Department of Labor, highly recommended this place. Inclement weather blocked our two attempts to visit. We'll make it there for a Whole Hog Plate when flooding and tornadoes are not a threat.

PHOTO CREDITS

Most of the images in the book were taken by Ardie or Paul during their adventures in barbecue. Credit is due for the following:

pages ii, viii, 1, 29, 60, 61, 91, 92, 98, 99, 105, 123, 161: Photos by Ross Wuetherich

page iii: Illustration courtesy of Charlie Podrebarac

pages vi, vii: Postcard by Kocher Photo

pages xi, 114, 116, 117: Photos courtesy of Ron, Mary, and Geof Buchholz

page xvi: Welcome Pardner postcard by Curteich Color

page 5: Curtis All American Bar-B-Q postcard by Jeremy Birch; Oklahoma Joe's postcard by MWM

pages 12, 13: Photos courtesy of the Brooks family

page 21: Photo courtesy of Bob and Ben Kantor

page 25: Photo courtesy of Fred Sauceman

page 28: Bison ribs photo courtesy of Linda Ray

page 43: Photos courtesy of Amy Anderson

page 52: Welcome Pardner postcard by Curteich Color; American Royal postcard by Max Bernstein

page 77: American Royal postcard by Gerald Massey; Underwood's postcard by American Industrial Pictures

pages 78, 79: Photos courtesy of the Tuffs

pages 86, 87: Photos courtesy of Sandi Ford and Lynn Ford, Ford Foods

page 88: Photo courtesy of the Perrins

pages 106, 129: Photos courtesy of Jack Fiorella and Case Dorman

pages 108, 109: Photos courtesy of Linda Ray

pages 112, 113: Photos courtesy of Russ Sifers

page 121: Photos courtesy of DennyMike Sherman

pages 122, 132, 133: Photos courtesy of Jev Vandegrift

page 134: Postcard by Colourpicture

page 151: Postcard by MWM

pages 153, 154: Photos courtesy of N. M. Kelby

page 160: Van's Pig Stands photos courtesy of Jev Vandegrift; "Checkpoint Chicky" wings photo courtesy of Rick Schoenberger

page 176: Postcard by the Vernon Co.

page 177: Cornered by a Boar postcard by Fort Mason Artists (photo by Marco Meniketti); Curtis All American Bar-B-Q postcard by Jeremy Birch

ABOUT THE AUTHORS

Ardie A. Davis, also known as Remus Powers, Ph.B., founded the Diddy-Wa-Diddy National Barbecue Sauce Contest in his backyard patio in 1984. Three years later the contest became the American Royal International Barbecue Sauce, Rub & Baste Contest. He also founded the Great American Barbecue Sauce, Baste, and Rub Contest. A charter member of the KCBS and former three-term member of the KCBS Board of Directors, Ardie is now a board member emeritus, a certified master judge, and an inductee in the KCBS Hall of Flame (1992). He is also a certified Memphis in May barbecue judge, and in 2008, he was a featured judge at the 20th Annual Jack Daniel's World Championship Invitational Barbecue in Lynchburg, Tennessee.

Ardie is a founder of Greasehouse University (1984) and serves as president, Diddy-Wa-Diddy Board of Barbecue at the university. He was interviewed and appeared in two History Channel shows: *Modern Marvels* and *America Eats*. He is currently a freelance writer for the *Kansas City Star* newspaper, the *Kansas City Bullsheet*, official newspaper of the Kansas City Barbeque Society (KCBS), and the *National Barbecue News*, which awarded him a Spirit of Barbecue Award in 2003 at the Jack Daniel's World Championship Invitational Barbecue. In 2002, he was presented with a Judges Choice Award at The Jack Daniel's World Championship Invitational Barbecue. Ardie's previous books include *The Great BBQ Sauce Book*, *Kansas City BBQ Pocket Guide*, *Techniques for Grilling*, and *Techniques for Smoking*.

Paul Kirk, a.k.a. Barbecue Guru, Ambassador of Barbecue, Order of the Magic Mop, Certified Master Barbecue Judge, member of the Kansas City Barbecue Society Board of Directors, and inductee into the Kansas City Barbeque Society Hall of Flame, has won over 475 cooking and barbecue awards, among them seven world championships, including the prestigious American Royal Open, the world's largest BBQ contest.

For more than 12 years, Paul has operated the Baron's School of Pit Masters, teaching classes all over the world. He has also trained barbecue restaurant staffs across the United States, and conducted seminars at national conventions for The International Association of Culinary Professionals (IACP). In 1998 and 2000, he was a member of The Julia Child BBQ Team of Ten at the IACP conventions, raising funds for the Julia Child Endowment Foundation.

Paul's previous books include *Paul Kirk's Championship Barbecue Sauces*, *Smokin'*, *The Big Grill*, *Paul Kirk's Championship Barbecue*, and *500 Barbecue Bites*, and he is featured in a whole host of other barbecue cookbooks. He writes monthly columns for *Kansas City Bullsheet*, the *National Barbecue News*, and the *Goat Gap Gazette*. Paul has appeared on the *Today Show*, Discovery Channel, *CBS This Morning*, *Talk Soup*, and Anthony Bourdain's *In Search of the Perfect Meal*. He has been featured in the AARP's *Modern Maturity Magazine*, *Saveur*, and the *Calgary Herald*. He is a partner in Righteous Urban Barbecue (a.k.a. RUB) restaurants in New York City and Las Vegas. For more on Paul, visit www.baron-of-bbq.com.

INDEX

What Did We Miss?

Is there a joint we didn't include that you think deserves to be in the book? Or a place we picked that you disagree with? Visit our Web site at www.americasbestbbqbook.com and tell us about it.